Contents

Part Two: Overcomers in Christ

FREEDOM FROM ADDICTION

BREAKING THE BONDAGE OF ADDICTION AND FINDING FREEDOM IN CHRIST

NEIL T. ANDERSON
AND MIKE & JULIA QUARLES

Regal Books
A Division of Gospel Light
Ventura, California, U.S.A.

Published by Regal Books
A Division of Gospel Light
Ventura, California, U.S.A.
Printed in U.S.A.

Library of Congress Cataloging-in-Publication Data
Anderson, Neil T., 1942-
    Freedom from addiction / Neil T. Anderson, Mike and Julia Quarles.
        p. cm.
    Includes bibliographical references.
    ISBN 0-8307-1865-6 (trade paper)
    1. Alcoholism—Religious aspects—Christianity. 2. Substance abuse—Religious aspects—Christianity. 3. Freedom (Theology) 4. Spiritual life—Christianity. I. Quarles, Mike. II. Quarles, Julia. III. Title.
    BV4596.A48A53   1996   96-16187
    248.8'6—dc20   CIP

1 2 3 4 5 6 7 8 9 10 11 12 13 14 15 16 17 18 / 03 02 01 00 99 98 97 96

Rights for publishing this book in other languages are contracted by Gospel Literature International (GLINT). GLINT also provides technical help for the adaptation, translation and publishing of Bible study resources and books in scores of languages worldwide. For further information, contact GLINT, P.O. Box 4060, Ontario, CA 91761-1003, U.S.A., or the publisher.

PRAISE FOR *Freedom from Addiction*

*Our society has never before offered us so many choices
to fill the emptiness of our lives. Dr. Anderson and the Quarleses have
provided practical steps to keep from being overrun by these uncon-
trollable passions. They remind us through poignant testimony and
practical helps that Christ desires more for us than just sobriety—He
wants us to experience freedom. I highly recommend this
book to both the "addict" and the church!*

John Coulombe, Pastor to Senior Adults
FIRST EVANGELICAL FREE CHURCH, FULLERTON, CALIFORNIA

*Freedom from Addiction brings the help and hope those bound
by addictions fear they will never find. The biblical principles
Dr. Anderson and the Quarleses teach in Freedom from
Addiction are "block buster" truths that go beyond the
Christianity many of us practice.*

Dr. Richard A. Germaine, Senior Pastor
FIRST CONGREGATIONAL CHURCH, HOPKINTON, MASSACHUSETTS

*The authors' approach to exposing and "hitting head-on" the strong-
holds that feed addiction is great. As a program director who deals
with these painful issues every day, I found myself making notes and
rereading passages from the book, as I gleaned powerful truths that
will change the lives of the people I work with.*

Bob Hall, Program Director
HARVEST FARM NEW LIFE PROGRAM, DENVER RESCUE MISSION

*This is not just a book for the addicted, but for their loved ones also.
Freedom from Addiction is a book filled with truth that will
truly set the captives free.*

Mike Harden, Founder/Director
NO LONGER BOUND, INC.

Appendices

Introduction

I was working as the lead systems engineer on an underwater fire control system for an antisubmarine rocket. Our first production unit just rolled off the assembly line, and I was working night and day to get it up to operational level. A production engineer named Max was assigned to work with me during the night shift. The kindest way I can say it is: Max wasn't much help to me. His wife would call in sick for Max at least once a week. I could never count on him. When he was at work, Max drove me up a wall. By the time the night shift came around, I would already be fatigued from working all day. As I labored into the evening, he would sit behind me eating sunflower seeds.

One night out of frustration, I asked Max if he ever went to church. Max said he wasn't attending any church at the time, but he and his wife had often talked about it. I invited him to my church. That next Sunday I met Max, his wife and their three children, and helped them attend the right Sunday School classes. Tuesday morning my pastor called, "I thought you would like to know that I visited the couple you brought to church last Sunday, and I led them to Christ." I was elated. He continued, "Since Max works with you, I thought you needed to know that he is an alcoholic." Then it all made sense. That is why periodically Max missed work, and why he munched sunflower seeds.

It can be frustrating to work with people who struggle with chemical addictions. It is even more exasperating for those who live with them. As difficult as it is for others, it is much more devastating for the addict. "Who has woe? Who has sorrow? Who has contentions? Who has complaining? Who has wounds without cause? Who has redness of eyes? Those who linger long over wine, those who go to taste mixed wine" (Prov. 23:29,30). These addicts are living a mental, emotional and physical nightmare. For some it is a private ordeal. Others make life miserable for everyone and anyone around them. I suspect that the old saying "misery loves company" was coined for addicts.

Why do they do it? Why would people keep pouring alcohol into their bodies? They know alcohol destroys everything that has meaning to them: their families, their careers and their own health. Why would people continue to stick needles into their veins when they know it is a death warrant? Why would people keep snorting drugs with the full knowledge that it will eventually destroy their brains, much less the damage it does to their nasal membranes? These are not rational decisions. People don't initially make decisions about life with the intention of destroying themselves. I can't imagine a teenager saying, "When I grow up, I would like to be an alcoholic." Most people addicted to drugs or alcohol said or thought at one time, "That will never happen to me."

Nobody is born addicted to alcohol or drugs. A newborn child of an addicted mother can have severe problems, including retardation and deformity. People become addicted through a series of choices they make in the process of "growing older." I hesitate to use the phrase "growing up" because addictions will severely inhibit their emotional growth and maturity. In the same way, nobody at birth is offered a career in engineering, medicine, law or ministry. People achieved those prominent positions through a series of choices, hard work and by the grace of God. If they are successful, it is because they assumed responsibility for their own attitudes and actions.

Be careful about rushing to judge people. If you had been subjected to the same harsh treatment many of these people had to endure, you would have been tempted to make the same decisions. If you had the same parents, it is very likely you would be struggling with the same addictions. Most of these people are products of their past, and are very needy. Who are they? The answer may surprise you. One of the biggest myths about alcohol is that the primary abusers are the "rednecks," the uneducated or the blue-collar workers. Not true! I have gathered the following figures from a variety of sources and rounded off the numbers so you will have a rough idea who the substance abusers are:

According to gender:
75 percent are men;
25 percent are women.

According to job:
45 percent are professional and/or managerial;
25 percent are white collar;
30 percent are manual labor.

According to education:
50 percent graduated from or attended college;
37 percent graduated or attended high school;
13 percent other.

The good news is that people can be free from the past and become new creations in Christ. All of their critical needs can be met in Jesus. That is the message of the gospel made possible by a forgiving and loving God. When that is fully understood and appropriated, then people afflicted with addictions can be filled with the Spirit and not carry out the desires of the flesh (see Gal. 5:16). The fruit of the Spirit is love, joy, peace, patience, kindness, goodness, faithfulness, gentleness and self-control (see vv. 22,23); but the fruit of alcoholism is hatred (mostly of self), depression, anxiety, impatience, unfaithfulness and loss of control. The purpose of this book is to show how Christ is the answer, and how truth will set us free. The Bible says, "They overcame him [Satan] because of the blood of the Lamb and because of the word of their testimony" (Rev. 12:11).

In part two of this book, I will share how the truth sets us free. Part one focuses on Mike and Julia Quarles's testimony. They have an incredible story to tell. Mike was a successful but driven stockbroker. He was living the high life, but it finally drove him to drunkenness and despair. Through it all he turned to Christ, only to have his first wife leave him as he began to pursue the ministry. Enter Julia who helped him through seminary and became a devoted pastor's wife.

Mike and Julia's story would read like a fairy tale if that was where it ended. A man with his driven and highly motivated background would surely find success in ministry. Nobody questioned his commitment nor his hard work. The same zeal that made him a top-notch stockbroker would also make him the best minister in his denomination. Right? Wrong! Mike's driven personality and his past caught up with him. Seven years after becoming a pastor, he realized that what he was preaching wasn't even working for him. How could Mike expect it to work for others? So he quit the ministry and returned again to the life of a stockbroker. He tried, but the old fire was no longer in him. The bottle was the easiest way to deal with his sense of failure. The downward cycle of addiction was swift and more devastating than the first time. Mike tried everything available to stop his downward spiral, but nothing worked. Julia stood by him as long as she could. She struggled with the same disappointments, guilt and shame all co-alcoholics suffer. She wanted to believe Mike's promises and grandiose ideas, but after a while, she had no more trust. Finally she told Mike to leave. Then something incredible happened. The truth that can set all of us free broke through the doubts, despair and depression of Mike's mind. He discovered who he was as a child of God, and that he was alive in Christ and dead to sin. For the first time, he understood the battle that was going on for his mind, and how the truth can set you free. Christian maturity would follow in time, but his freedom was already secured in Christ. Now he could be the person Christ created him to be. When Julia heard the news from her sober husband, she couldn't— no, she wouldn't believe him. Why should she? He had broken so many promises. Eventually Julia could not deny the incredible change that had taken place in his life. Mike was not only sober, but he was also free in Christ. Today they are helping others discover this wonderful truth of "Christ in you, the hope of glory" (Col. 1:27). To be alive and free in Christ is the birthright of every child of God. It can happen in your life; then the Lord can use you to help others find freedom in Christ. Here is Mike and Julia's story in their own words

Part One

....

Mike and Julia Quarles's Testimony

Strapped to a Hospital Bed

I drifted into consciousness. Something was drastically wrong. I lay on my back in a bed in a strange place and looked down. Although fully dressed, blood covered my torn shirt. Then I noticed my ripped pants. In a panic, I glanced around the room. Except for one straight, wooden chair, the room was empty. The walls were painted a dirty gray and flecked with peeling paint.

I wondered, *Where am I? What is going on?* I bolted up in the bed, but abruptly my body jerked back. Then I saw the rigid leather straps that held my hands to the bed. Through the doorway, some people were moving around. *What had happened to me?*

"Help! Somebody please help me!" I screamed in a panic. Two women in white uniforms rushed into the room.

"Calm down," a nurse said to me.

"Be quiet," instructed a second nurse.

"Where am I? What's going on?" I insisted.

Then one of the women explained, "You're in Cooper Green Hospital."

Still confused I persisted, "How did I get here?"

"The police brought you," she answered in a calm, even tone of voice. "You were arrested and had a bad cut on your chin. They brought you here for treatment."

I felt like a fool. In Birmingham, Alabama, Cooper Green was the indigent hospital that treated the homeless and the winos. Now wearing my bloody and torn clothes, I was tied to the bed. Although my mind searched for a reason, I couldn't determine why I was restrained.

When I asked the nurse, she said, "You were brought in last night and thrashing violently. We couldn't do anything with you."

Unbelievable. I pleaded with the nurse, "Please take off these straps. I want to go home."

"No", she replied, "you can't leave." Tears began to run down my cheeks. She continued, "The Birmingham police have a hold on you; you are their prisoner in our custody."

What Have I Done?

My brain was still foggy but I racked it trying to recall *anything* about last night. Alcohol. The last thing I remembered was leaving a bar. Then I remembered the pavement and the street light in the parking lot. I was headed for my car. *My God*, I wondered, *what happened next? Had I killed someone with my car? Maybe that's why the police were holding me.* Terror filled my heart, coupled with an icy fear. I pumped the nurses for more information from the police report, but they didn't know anything else.

"Before long," she said, "the police will be taking you to jail." Wait and pray. It was all I could do. Although it was too late to change anything, I begged God for forgiveness if I had killed anyone. Dreading the worst, I felt like the scum of the earth. The side glances from the nurses didn't relieve my guilty feelings.

Again I shook my head and tried to remember. *What was going on?* My memory was blank about the night before. I couldn't explain the cut on my chin or my ripped clothes. If there had been a fight, I hadn't fared well. How did I reach the hospital? Again I had no idea.

Feverishly I thought about the day before. I left my office around five in the afternoon. My first stop was a men's shop where I picked up a couple of new suits. As the manager of the E. F. Hutton stockbrokerage office in Birmingham, Alabama, I was earning more money than ever before in my life. These two suits were the nicest and most expensive ones I had ever purchased.

That summer evening in 1983 was quite pleasant as I drove across town to the men's clothing store. As I cruised along, I gave myself some mental pats on the back for my financial success. I looked forward to trying on those new suits. The owner and manager of this particular store was a brother of a stockbroker in my firm, and went out of his way to give me good service. For me, this kind of sales help was unusual but I liked the treatment—it made me feel like a person of substance and value. In recent years, my self-image had taken a major plunge and I needed the extra attention.

As I lay in that hospital bed, strapped down like a wild animal, my past seemed almost unreal. Only four years before, I had been a pastor—a respected "man of the cloth." The years and events rolled through my troubled mind; as a 24-year-old fresh out of college in 1961, I entered the business field in a brokerage firm. Eight years later, I began my own company. Then after becoming a Christian in 1970, I felt a call to the pastorate—a call I thought would be lifelong. Deep inside, though, I had a small dark spot—a feeling of hopelessness and failure that alcohol always seemed to alleviate. Then my life took a bizarre twist. After failing in the pastorate, I had spent the last four years rebuilding my life—back in the brokerage business.

Now at 46, selling stocks was the one area of my life where I still felt successful. As one of the top producers in my firm, I successfully managed E. F. Hutton's branch office in Birmingham, Alabama. My immediate supervisor and I maintained a good relationship. He respected my abilities and instincts about the marketplace. The broader management team at Hutton praised me and my job performance. As I staffed the office, I hired quality people and each one was performing well. The office was profitable. Because of my Christian commitment, most of the people I hired were Christians. Throughout the brokerage community, everyone agreed our office was a unique environment.

As I lay in the hospital, my mind again thought back to the events beginning the previous afternoon. Summer was drawing to an end. The late September Alabama heat had cooled. I took the top down on my new VW Rabbit convertible to enjoy the breeze blowing in my face. I thought, *So what if I couldn't make it in the pastorate. My business is making it. I'm enjoying some of the finer things in life. Maybe I am called to be in business— after all, the Lord needs committed Christian businessmen.* I continued to rationalize about my leaving my church. *Everyone can't be in the ministry. Besides, someone has to stay at home and make money to support those in ministry. Making money is what I do best.*

As I went through this line of reasoning, it didn't completely drive away my nagging feelings of failure. In my mind, I continued to play the "what if" game. *What if I had not failed in ministry?* The breezy evening and my successful feelings about my job enabled me to briefly push my painful feelings aside.

Only a Beer or Two

After trying on my suits at the men's store, I selected a few ties and shirts to match. As I left the store, I decided that a cold beer would taste great and be the perfect finish to a pleasant afternoon. For an instant, my conscience pricked the bubble of my plan, "Hasn't drinking gotten you into some trouble lately?" Then I quickly dismissed the idea. Besides, I was only going to drink *one* beer—or at the most two. Down the street from the clothing store was a little seafood restaurant. I had eaten there before and knew they served cold beer on draft. I drove straight over and ordered a large draft beer in a plastic container to go. It was still fairly early—not quite six o'clock. I drove and enjoyed the cool, refreshing taste of the beer and the pleasant scenery of the rolling hills of Birmingham.

As the alcohol took effect, I began to feel relaxed. Inside, I knew it would take more than one beer to satisfy my thirst. The beer was quickly gone so I turned my convertible into the parking lot of the Sheraton Inn. *They've got a nice bar,* I thought.

Inside I ordered another beer. After a couple more beers, I was completely relaxed and oblivious to any responsibilities. I had no plans to go home anytime soon. *The good feelings are enjoyable and besides,* I thought, *after a hard day at work, I deserve it. What can it hurt to sit here and enjoy myself for a while?*

I thought about my wife, Julia, waiting for me at home. In an instant, I knew she wouldn't understand my need to kick back and relax over a few beers. We'd discussed my drinking habits before.

To my knowledge, Julia had never done anything really bad in her life. Sometimes she could be a real stick-in-the-mud. Underneath my cautions, I knew Julia loved me and accepted me no matter what. Throughout our difficult years in the pastorate and now selling stocks, she stood by and cheered for me. Julia was committed to my best interests. *But I need this drink. I'm not going to let her rain on my parade,* I decided. *Should I call her about how I wouldn't be home for supper? No, she won't understand; I know how she would respond.* In an upset tone of voice, she would plead with me to come home. I decided to "forget" about calling home.

As I polished off my third beer, the alcohol coursed into my bloodstream and was having the desired effect. Behind my successful facade, failure stared me in the face. A failed pastorate. My failure as a husband and a father of three children. On top of everything else, my marriage was going down the drain at the same time as my financial problems faded into the background.

I liked this bar. The walls didn't have any mirrors. When mirrors adorned the walls of a bar, I was forced to stare at myself. I became consumed with guilt and condemnation. Wherever I looked deep inside, I carried an ever-present sense of my hopeless, helpless failure. *Could I ever change and escape? Never,* I thought.

If you were to walk past me on the street or meet me in a normal setting, you would know that I am not an outgoing person. In a bar, however, the alcohol removed my inhibitions. I joked and laughed with the barmaid and told stories to the other men at the bar. Under normal circumstances, I wouldn't have much in common with these people, but I found alcohol to be the great equalizer. It joined anyone who carried a shopping list of feelings: being misunderstood, inse-

....

Along with hundreds of thousands of others, I was eventually to discover the ultimate cost of such a place of refuge [the bar] is very high and exacting.

....

curity, guilt, unacceptance and failure. Bars offered more than alcohol to medicate the pain of life and alter my mood. They provided a shelter where anyone could be accepted without questions or explanations.

Along with hundreds of thousands of others, I was eventually to discover the ultimate cost of such a place of refuge is very high and exacting.

I Had Lost Control

Before I drained my fourth beer, I had lost control. Holding my liquor was not a problem. I could still talk, walk a straight line, drive my car and make decisions, but I had lost my control to make any responsible or correct decisions. To stop drinking was no longer an option. I couldn't stop drinking, get up from my seat and return home.

I drank my way through several more bars. At some point, I switched from beer to Kahlúa and crème. My decision to increase the alcohol content definitely was not constructive. By the time I left my last bar in the downtown Hilton, I had lost count of the number of drinks. I am certain it was more than a dozen.

About 1:00 A.M., closing time arrived at the Hilton bar. I punched the button on the elevator for the parking deck. Everything seemed OK until I got into my car. Waves of dizziness and disorientation swept over me. *I can handle it*, I thought as I started my car and began to back out of the space. BAMM! My car crunched into the vehicle behind me.

Better try again, I thought. When I pulled back into my parking space, I smashed my bumper again into the other car. *Can't I even back out of a parking space,* I thought. I shook my head and rubbed my eyes and tried to think straight. I felt as though I was losing it. Stumbling out of the car, I thought, *Fresh air. That's what I need. I'll walk around and clear my head.* After my first couple of steps, the pavement popped up and hit me in the face. The fall knocked out my breath, but I had no sense of falling. For a few minutes I lay on the ground with my face against the hard, cold concrete. One more time. I pushed myself into an upright position, but then it happened again. SMASH! *What was happening to me?*

Destroying Everything Important in My Life

Now hours later, I lay in my hospital bed. Falling onto the concrete floor was the last thing I could recall from the night before. I had no recollection of what happened between the hours of one and six in the morning. *When did the police arrest me? Had I actually started my car, driven it and killed someone? Why was I in the custody of the Birmingham police?* My pleasant summer afternoon had turned into a nightmare from hell.

Who is this forlorn person strapped to a bed reserved for drunken bums brought off the street? By this time, I had been a Christian for 13 years. I had graduated from seminary, was an ordained minister, then spent several years in the pastorate. My consuming desire was to make my life count for Christ. For more than a dozen years, I pursued this course with all of my diligence and zeal.

How could things have changed so quickly? Yesterday I was a top stockbroker in Birmingham and known as a committed Christian throughout the evangelical community. My reputation was a facade, however; for many years, my life had gradually changed. The straps on my hands symbolized a debilitating trap that had been well crafted and artfully designed by Satan. This attack was built on a foundation of lies and deceit. Now I held fast to this destructive pattern that was bringing forth a ripe harvest of despair and misery.

The next hour of waiting was the most agonizing of my life. *What happened during the time between going to my car and when the police arrested me?* Endless possibilities floated through my mind. *Had I wrecked my car or run into someone?* I could barely consider the possibility that I had killed someone.

And Julia? What would this drunken binge do to her, my children and friends who love me? Would I spend the rest of my life in prison?

Why Do You Do It?

Finally the police arrived. The policeman looked about 50 years old and stared as I sheepishly crawled into the rear seat of the police car. In a condescending tone, he said, "Mr. Quarles, you're old enough to know better than to be out at night doing things like that."

My chin dug into my chest. I didn't want anyone to recognize me and I mumbled, "I know. I know."

Then the policeman asked me, "Why do you do it?"

"I really don't know," I said. I knew I had no logical explanation—such behavior defied reason.

While I rode to the police station, the officer filled me in on the missing five hours. "You were arrested while sitting on the floor of the parking deck at the Hilton. Your speech was completely incoherent and you didn't even know your name or what you were doing," he said. "If you had driven, the results could have been disastrous."

For some reason, God protected me. Miraculously, no one had been hurt in my drunken state. I had experienced God's protective hand at other times in my life. For example, as a teenager I drove drunk many times while weaving down the streets in a reckless manner. I seemed to be searching for a way to self-destruct. My teenage buddies told many stories about my brushes with death.

Before I became a Christian, I came home very drunk one night. My first wife, Denise (not her real name), had to take our baby-sitter home. Falling into bed, I passed out. Then a noise from downstairs woke me up. I got out of bed, picked up a gun from our closet, then started down the steps to investigate. In my drunken stupor, I slipped and tumbled down the steps from top to bottom. The loaded gun was still in my hand. I could have easily shot myself, but again God had protected me.

As we made the trip to the station, the officer told me I was being charged with public drunkenness. During the night, the police had called my wife and told her about the situation. When we pulled into the station, Julia was waiting at the jail. She paid my $20 fine and the officers released me. The fine seemed minor compared to the potential cost without God's protection. I left the jail overcome with guilt and shame.

....

I had been sucked into the same lie that plagues everyone who is in bondage: the answer to breaking free lies in changing one's behavior.

....

Craig, the assistant pastor at our church, came with Julia to the jail. Early that morning when Julia heard the news, she had been very upset and had called Craig. To make matters worse, he was a close friend.

Craig and I shared an excitement about serving the Lord. About 10 years earlier when I decided to enter the pastorate, Craig and I attended Reformed Theological Seminary at the same time. During our time there, we started a weekly discipleship group. This small group, which included our wives, looked to the Scriptures for God's best in our marriages and ministries. Many times we prayed together and discussed our desire to serve God and make our lives count for Christ.

Now with this same friend, I walked out of jail unshaven and wearing my bloody, torn shirt, ripped pants and badly scuffed shoes. Julia couldn't lift up her head to look at me. Craig, who is 10 years younger than I am, saw my pitiful state and just shook his head in disbelief. He fell silent and offered no words of encouragement or rebuke. Both of them knew I had heard it all. Nothing else could be said. In my entire life, I had never felt so low. It felt like a bad dream.

The bulk of the community in Birmingham was working on this Thursday morning. My company expected me in the office, but I could barely hold up my head. I couldn't face anyone. When we reached home, I phoned my office. "I'm sick and I probably won't be in today or tomorrow," I told them.

Redoubling My Efforts

After I threw some clothes into a suitcase, I drove to Jack and June's house, close friends who lived about 150 miles away in Atlanta. I had to get away for a few days; I couldn't bear to look at my wife. I hated myself and what I was doing to Julia, but I had no idea how to stop my insane behavior.

What next? My only recourse was to try harder. Maybe my problem was focus. All I needed was to give the problem more attention, then I could quit drinking. As a Christian, I knew God didn't want me to be an alcoholic. I believed the Lord had an answer for me. Driving to Atlanta, I honestly faced the question of how to change, but I had no idea where to find the answer. I had been sucked into the same lie that plagues everyone who is in bondage: the answer to breaking free lies in changing one's behavior. But somehow I just couldn't do it.

At this time in 1983, I didn't understand that a person always acts in accordance with personal beliefs. If I was ever going to change, I needed to examine my misbeliefs (or lies) that gave me permission to continue drinking. Instead, I redoubled my efforts to focus on my behavior and change it.

During those few days in Atlanta, I followed an intense schedule of prayer and Bible reading. I vowed to God never to drink again and pleaded in prayer for Him to help me. Then I made a list of benchmarks to ensure my commitment. I continued to try to change by using my own resources, but I was setting myself up for another fall.

The following Monday morning I returned to work. The Christians at our office gathered on the first day of the work week for a Bible study. To lead a Bible study on this particular morning was the last thing on my agenda. It seemed easier to

....

Bondage doesn't respond to common sense, logic or clear thinking. Alcoholics Anonymous calls such actions "insanity," which they define as "continuing to do the same thing and expecting different results."

....

face an arena of lions. Although no one could see it, I felt as though I wore a striped jail outfit and everyone in Birmingham knew about my night in the local hospital. I felt as though they could read it in my face.

I put on my best front and somehow got through the study. No one acted as though anything was any different. *These guys trust and respect me,* I thought. *Would they still trust me if they knew about my drinking? What if they knew I was a fake?* I was a hypocrite. Worse, I was a drunk who acted spiritual and led a Bible study! To everyone in the room, I gave the impression that I was an upstanding Christian.

God must really be getting sick of me, I thought.

Even a Live Dog Is Better Off than a Dead Lion!

After my unforgettable night in jail, my life spiraled from bad to worse. Often I left my office discouraged and full of self-pity. I just drank and drove around aimlessly. Julia lived in fear that I would kill someone. She prayed that if I had a wreck I would be the one killed and no one else. Knowing I was a Christian, she prayed this way and believed I would go to heaven. As my drinking continued to drag on, she (and most of my friends) doubted my Christianity.

I, however, never doubted my relationship with Christ. I knew God loved me and accepted me. I expected to slip into heaven by the skin of my teeth. I probably would have had nothing to live for had I doubted my salvation. I knew that the Lord had an answer for me; maybe one day I would find it. For months, I hung onto a single verse from the Bible: Ecclesiastes 9:4, which says, "Anyone who is among the living has hope—even a live dog is better off than a dead lion!" *(NIV).*

Some may have thought my many disasters would help me come to my senses. Bondage, however, doesn't respond to common sense, logic or clear thinking. Alcoholics Anonymous calls such actions "insanity," which they define as "continuing to do the same thing and expecting different results."

One year after my jail experience, the church discipline committee called me to meet with them for my continued drunkenness. This same church had supported me financially during seminary. They sent me to a secular treatment center, but I was drunk a week after I got out. I eventually lost my job and all our money and savings; I lost the respect of my friends, family and my wife. Finally, in January of 1985, Julia kicked me out of the house. When she did, I was almost glad because I was consumed with guilt and despair. Her rejection was easier for me to handle than her love. Ironically, kicking me out of the house was the most loving and redemptive thing she could have done. It paved the way for my healing and restoration.

Kicked Out of My House

Shortly after Julia kicked me out of the house, I left for my second treatment center. It had been one and a half years since my episode in the indigent hospital. Everything in my life was pouring down the drain. I had run out of options to try or promises to make to Julia. I couldn't persuade her otherwise. She didn't believe my words or promises. I wouldn't have believed them either! Julia had reached her limit. Her attitude wasn't vindictive or spiteful, but the pain in her eyes was almost unbearable. Again and again, I had violated and broken our relationship. I didn't know if I would ever see her again when I walked out the door. There was no question that she had given up on our marriage—and me.

I headed for a Christian treatment center that operated as a ministry and charged no fee. It was the only option I had left. My insurance hadn't covered my stay at the secular treatment center a few months earlier. As I tried to pay off my bills from that program, I almost had to file for bankruptcy.

As I went out the door, Julia's last words were, "Don't call me, don't even write me. I don't want to ever see you again." Her words were painful, but I couldn't blame her. I had reached my lowest point and felt as though my world had caved in.

Though I didn't fully grasp it at first, and though it seemed unlikely at the time, the process had started to bring me into my full inheritance as a child of God. The Lord wanted me to experience the victory, peace, freedom and joy that Christ had purchased for me. At the time I had no clue of such freedom because I didn't know my position as a child of God. I had no concept of God as my loving heavenly Father, but I would learn that God accepted me just as I was. The Lord loved me and would do whatever it took to bring me to the end of myself. Only after I reached the end could I experience life— real life, His life, divine life, Christ's life as my life. The journey had just begun.

Julia's Perspective

Editor's note: In the last few pages, you've read about the downward spiral of Mike Quarles's life. Where was his wife, Julia, in the midst of these experiences? Most spouses of alcoholics face their own issues and struggles. At the conclusion of each chapter, Julia will tell her story about the same period in their lives.

RING! I was tossing in a fitful sleep when the phone rang in the middle of the night. *Should I even answer it?* When I had finally fallen asleep, I knew Mike hadn't come home yet. *Was this Mike calling?*

"This is Officer Daniels at the Birmingham jail," the deep voice said. My heart raced as I listened. He told me the police had picked up Mike during the night. "Mike hurt himself and we took him to a local hospital. Later this morning, he'll be back at the jail. You can come pick him up around nine o'clock."

As the officer told me the details, his voice held real concern. "Mrs. Quarles, has this ever happened before?" he asked.

I assured him that it was the first time. I told him how Mike was struggling with a drinking problem. "He wants to stop but can't seem to quit," I said.

"Mike looks like a respectable businessman and not the kind of person we usually pick up. I'm sorry you're having this problem," he said.

After I hung up the phone, my tears fell uncontrollably. The tears came from embarrassment, humiliation, frustration and anger. My anger swelled at Mike for causing it, at God for allowing it and at myself for still being in a marriage that had gone down this far. I tried to go back to sleep, but tossed and turned. Finally, at a respectable hour I called one of our friends at church—Craig, the assistant minister.

After telling Craig about the call, I asked if he would take me to get Mike. I didn't know the location of the city jail and was afraid to go alone. Later as we drove to the jail, we tossed around some questions we had been discussing for two years. Why does Mike get drunk? Why can't he control it? Why can't he quit?

For me, these last three years in Birmingham had been an emotional roller coaster. And now this. What was going on? To enter the city jail and bail out my husband made me feel humiliated. The $20 fine was nothing compared to the emotional cost.

When we arrived, the officer on duty told us that Mike was in transit from the hospital to the station. Craig and I waited in silence. There was nothing else to say. I looked around at the other women in the station. I seemed to be the only woman *without* pink foam rollers in her hair and fuzzy slippers on her feet. I seemed a bit out of uniform, but thought each of our hearts were probably in the same shape—hurt, full of fear about our future, embittered and embarrassed. I felt sorry for the others as well as for myself.

After we bailed out Mike, Craig drove us to the Hilton parking deck so we could pick up Mike's car. During our drive home, Mike repeated several times that the bartender or someone must have slipped something into his drink to make him sick. I was mad at Mike for being in a bar, but felt sorry that he had been victimized. Once again, instead of taking decisive action to end this way of life, I fell victim to Mike's excuses. Rather than doing anything about it, I decided never to tell anyone. I hoped no one would find out. I rationalized that we could just go on with our turbulent life. Every day I hoped and prayed that this day would be *the* day Mike would be free from this bondage. It was ruining our lives.

On the Edge of Disaster
How did we get to this horrible place? As Christians, we had made a commitment for our lives and marriage to count for the Lord.

In June 1980, three years before Mike's terrible night in the hospital, we moved back to Birmingham. He enjoyed the challenge of rebuilding his business as a stockbroker. I found it exciting for Mike to be in the business world. Maybe our years of stress and frustration had ended.

Because Mike was no longer in the pastorate, he said it would be OK for us to have wine with our meals or for him to drink a beer every now and then. The alcohol didn't pose any problem for me, although we had never kept any liquor in our house. The first time we had wine with dinner Mike had three or four glasses. A few nights later when I looked for the bottle to serve it again, the wine was gone. Mike told me that because the wine was almost gone he had polished off the bottle.

We had an extra refrigerator in the basement. I began to notice cartons of beer would suddenly appear—then vanish. When was he drinking these beers? *Why* was he drinking? "Mike, if having beer around makes you drink, then let's not buy it," I suggested. But this new pattern continued.

One Saturday morning during football season, Mike picked a fight with me. Then he stormed out of the house. I was confused and upset. Why would he do this? What had I done? My afternoon and evening were miserable because I had no idea where he was or what he was doing. Finally Mike came home; he seemed drunk. Or was it my imagination?

That winter, Mike began to call home around dinner time several times a month. He would say, "Julia, I've got to work late and I will have to miss supper." It sounded reasonable to me, but when he came home around midnight he would be drunk. Had Mike lied to me about working?

"Oh God," I prayed, "don't let this be real!" I wasn't sure how I should react. Maybe Mike just needed my love and encouragement. Did he drink from the stress of his business or my failure as a wife? How could I help him stop drinking?

Progressively it became worse. Some nights Mike didn't call at all. Then he wouldn't come home until about midnight or later. Each time, he walked into the house drunk.

Mike's Drinking Was My Fault

What in the world was going on? We were a nice Christian couple. We didn't drink—much less get drunk. None of our friends drank. For years, I had complained about Mike's failure as a godly husband and father. Maybe it drove him to drink. I felt guilty.

In response to his drunken binges, I redoubled my efforts at being a good wife. When Mike called to tell me his excuse about working late, I tried to bribe him with steak dinners— "date nights," special plans—anything that popped into my mind. Nothing worked. My feelings of frustration increased. *What might happen as Mike drove around drunk?* Thoughts of him killing someone filled my mind with fear. I felt as though I was a failure as a wife. His drinking was my fault.

Mike had some responsibilities he didn't like so I decided to do them for him. For example, Mike hated paying bills, balancing the checkbook or working in the yard. I began taking on these responsibilities, thinking Mike could enjoy being at home. I would show Mike how capable I could be. I was strong. I could handle all of this.

As the leader of a small women's Bible study group, I was afraid one of them—or someone else in our large church—would find out what was happening with Mike. I was also involved in a prayer group for the women leaders, but it was impossible for me to ask for prayer about this situation! Who would understand? I couldn't tell anyone my secret. I was also teaching a Bible study in our neighborhood. What if they found out? I counted the weeks until I finished the quarter of teaching, and kept quiet about Mike's drinking.

The majority of Mike's clients and coworkers were Christians. I didn't want to hurt his business. If his business suffered, I would suffer.

I couldn't tell our family or friends. If I didn't understand Mike's drinking, how could I explain it to someone else? Many nights I turned on the "700 Club" television program. The cohosts, Pat, Ben and Denuda became my regular companions. Often I called their prayer line to pray that Mike wouldn't have a wreck and kill someone. I also asked for prayer that God would deliver Mike from this bondage to alcohol. The people at the other end of the prayer line were a great source of encouragement to me.

Please Help Me, God!
On the nights when Mike didn't call or show up, I sat on the sofa in front of the window and watched the cars driving up our street. Everyone else's husband would be home by 6:30 or 7:30 P.M.—everyone's husband except mine. Where was Mike? When I finally realized he wasn't coming, I lay on the sofa and cried. Sometimes I got hysterical imagining what might happen as he drove around drunk. "Please help me, God! Who can I talk to about this?"

God began to provide friends. Each of these people had someone in the family who had an alcohol problem. Our friends in Atlanta, Jack and June, were always available to pray with me on the phone for Mike's safety. Many nights when I was upset, I called them and confided in them. They always stopped what they were doing and prayed for us.

Another support person was a young mother named CeCe from my Bible study. She would say, "OK, Mz. Julia, Mike has decided how he is going to spend his evening, now how are you going to spend yours?" Through CeCe, I understood that I couldn't do anything about Mike, but I could do something about me. She insisted on not hanging up the phone until I told her what I was going to do. She suggested I vacuum my house or clean a closet or play music and ballet dance. Anything physical helped pass the hours and helped me be tired enough to attempt some sleep.

One of my other prayer warriors was Mary Adley. This dear African-American woman worked for me during the final months of my first husband's illness and through my years as a widow (my first husband died of cancer). Mary understood my plight because her husband, Josh, had been an alcoholic. Years ago, God had delivered Josh. Firsthand, Mary knew that God could deliver Mike from this situation. She often prayed with me on the telephone. Many times she called to tell me she and her mother who was in her nineties were "turning their plates over" for Mr. Mike. These two women fasted and prayed for Mike. Mary was a constant source of encouragement to me. She helped me view my situation as a spiritual battle. I needed to quit looking at my circumstances and look to the Lord. She often told me this.

To me it was critical to maintain our Christian "front." We attended church regularly, sitting in our usual seats near the front. Sometimes we shared a hymnbook. Occasionally I thought, *God will strike us with lightning for our hypocrisy.* We didn't want to give up church services though and stay at home.

My Personality Changed

By the second year of this turmoil, in 1982, I reached a point where I hated to talk to anyone I knew—whether in the grocery store or on any errand. It felt hypocritical to tell people, "We're fine, just great." Some days I stayed home all day. It eliminated the possibility of seeing anyone. Other times after a bad night I lay in bed all day. I didn't want to face life. My personality changed. I was becoming a hermit.

Maybe I needed a job. It would fill the empty spaces of my life and give me a place to hide what was happening. *Besides,*

I thought, *it would be nice to earn some spending money for myself.* Although Mike earned lots of money, he spent it on himself. My brother-in-law, Dan, worked with New Life, a friendship evangelism ministry, and needed a secretary. He needed a part-time person to work about 20 hours a week. It became a perfect job for me. No clock to punch and I recovered my sense of responsibility. Now I was "too busy" for Bible classes or prayer groups. The job salvaged my self-esteem a little as well as gave me a purpose in life.

I'm Not Leaving
Nothing worked for Mike. He prayed, read his Bible and begged God to help him stop drinking. I felt so sorry for him because I believed he wanted to quit. Mike's life reeled out of control and it scared both of us. My response was to continue loving, accepting and encouraging him. As I "hung in there" with him, it wore on me. Many nights when he came home drunk he would sit on the bed beside me and just sob. He would say, "Why can't I stop this? It's controlling me! I don't want to be doing this. Why don't you just leave me and get out of this mess?"

I said, "Listen, this is horrible, but I know God can change it. I'm in this nightmare with you. I'm not leaving because I want to be here to enjoy it when it finally gets good."

How could this be happening to someone like me? I was in my forties and had been a Christian for 17 years.

I grew up in a loving, secure, church-going family in Birmingham. My life had always been "religious." Each day I read devotional books, but never the Bible because it was boring to me.

After I graduated from Birmingham Southern College in 1958, I married my college sweetheart, Bradley Fulkerson Jr. We both sang in our church choir and considered ourselves Christians. In the fall of 1965, during his senior year at medical school, Bradley noticed a small lump under his arm. When he had it removed, the tests concluded that it was a malignant melanoma. Radical surgery was performed and no more tumors were found. We thought he would be fine and we could continue with our lives.

The cancer scared us and we started thinking about life and death. One of our friends, Carol McCarty, sent her pastor, a young man from a new Presbyterian church in the area, to come and talk with us. When Frank explained to us that salvation is a free gift from God, that we can't earn it, only accept it, we realized we had never made this commitment. For several weeks, Frank visited us and patiently answered our questions. In March 1966, Bradley and I committed our lives to Christ.

That fall when Bradley was an intern at a local hospital, the cancer reappeared. This time the cancer was in his lungs. The doctors told us that Bradley had three months to live, but he lived for another two and a half years. As a couple, we had a crash course in trusting God and leaving everything in His hands. We had joined Frank's church and had many friends as well as a supportive family. They helped us to know Christ intimately through Bible study, Scripture memory and prayer. We were surrounded with love, acceptance and encouragement.

Bradley died in April 1969, and I knew he had gone to heaven. God gave me great peace. Many people, including several in our family, came to know Christ through those years. I was a young widow and had a seven-year-old son, Bradley III. I learned to lean on God as my way of life. The Lord became my companion, my comforter and confidant during those years.

During the next several years, I often spoke at Christian Women's Clubs across the southeastern part of the United States. I told the women about our triumph over death and about God's sufficiency and faithfulness. In addition, I taught Bible studies for teenage girls and single mothers.

Three years later at our church, I met Mike Quarles. Mike had an exciting testimony and was attending seminary. Although Mike seemed to be the kind of man I would like for a husband, I had no desire to marry again. Through persistence, however, Mike pursued me and won me. We were married in May 1973 after his first year at seminary. Both of us wanted our marriage to honor God.

Now, 10 years later, we were riding home from the jail with our pastor. It didn't seem real, but it was. I didn't think our life could get much worse, but it did.

Programmed for Addiction

It was a warm summer afternoon in Tuscaloosa, Alabama. Some men came and cut down a tree in our backyard. They chopped the wood into small pieces, but left it scattered across the yard.

"Those ?X!* workmen," my father fumed when he came home. "Now, I'll have to take part of my Saturday to move the wood."

As a teenager in the middle of my summer break, I planned to be home all day. I thought, *I'll help Dad and move those logs for him.* For the greater part of the day, I worked to stack the logs in a neat pile against our house. Although tired, I felt proud of my hard work and initiative. I had completed the job without anyone asking me!

That evening when my dad came home from work, I was sitting in our den. He walked in and asked, "Who in the hell stacked that wood against the house?"

"It was me," I said. "What's wrong?"

"That's the dumbest thing you've ever done," he replied.

"Dad, I thought we'd burn those logs in our fireplace this winter," I protested.

Dad shook his head in disgust and frowned at me. "Haven't you ever seen junk pine?" he said. "It's not worth burning. Besides, like bees to flowers, pine attracts termites. Can't you do anything right, Mike?" Dad turned and stormed out of the house. For the next two hours, he moved the wood away from the house.

Maybe Dad is right, I thought. *I can't do anything right.*

Four Failure Patterns in My Life

Growing up in a middle-class family, I was the oldest of three children. As the foreman on a maintenance crew at a large chemical company, my dad was hardworking and financially responsible, but one of the angriest people I've ever known. He had a quick temper and little patience, which made him prone to violent outbursts. My dad ruled the home with an iron hand. He was strict with everyone, including my mother. If I ever raised any objections to his commands, I paid for it dearly.

Because my dad was a gifted mechanic, he could create almost anything with his hands. He took his talent for granted and had minimal patience with everyone. Whenever we'd attempt to screw in some bolts or try to fix something, Dad took over saying, "You can't do anything right." Because he repeated the message so often, I believed him—after all, he was my father. I decided that I was a complete klutz, especially when it came to anything mechanical.

As a child, I developed my belief system from messages I received from significant people, especially my parents. When I was small, my dad came home from work tired and upset. In his frustration, he told me, "Get out of my way, you worthless kid."

Because I was just a child I couldn't analyze my situation and understand: Dad is just upset, tired and acting like a jerk. Instead, I internalized the message: I'm worthless and my dad doesn't want me in his way.

A tormented and insecure man, my father was chronically unfaithful to my mother. Also, he abused alcohol and disciplined us in a rage. All of us were physically abused, but my mother received the brunt of it. Each of us lived in fear of his tirades and beatings. As we grew older, Dad withdrew from the family. In his later years, he came home from work, made a large drink, then went into his bedroom, locked the door and took a nap. Mother served his meal in their bedroom. For the rest of the evening, Dad watched TV.

As children, we weren't permitted to go near his room. If anyone woke him from his nap or disturbed him in any way, all hell would break loose. My dad was unavailable to me and he never nurtured me. Repeatedly my dad taught me that I couldn't do anything right and was unacceptable.

In response to my dad's harshness, my mother became extremely overprotective and solicitous. Often my mother used a phrase such as, "Mike, let me do it for you." I know she meant well, but because Mom had done it for me I thought I couldn't do it myself. I was treated as an irresponsible person and not allowed to make my own choices. The message I received was: You are deficient as a person. My feelings of inadequacy were regularly reinforced from both my mom and my dad.

I don't remember any love between my mom and dad. In the house they fought violently in an ongoing war. Scattered into the arguments were a few moments of peace and calmness. Several times my dad turned over the kitchen table, scattering food across our floor and breaking dishes. I could not bring my friends home to such a miserable situation. Using any excuse, I stayed away from home as much as possible.

In some of my most vivid childhood memories, I remember lying in bed at night and listening to my mom and dad in one of their violent arguments. Once my dad chased everyone out of the house with a loaded shotgun. I lived in fear that one morning I would find one of my parents had killed the other one. Today as I look back, I'm convinced it's a miracle no one died a violent death.

My brother is two years younger and my sister four years younger than I am. As children, we responded to our home life in a predictable manner. As the oldest, I learned to fight and rebel against our alcoholic father and his abusive authority. My brother became the people pleaser and did anything to placate Dad. My sister learned to withdraw, hide and stay out of the way. Of course, we adopted these same patterns for dealing with stress in our adult lives.

Some people think an alcoholic should be told: "Stop drinking; that is sin." The alcoholic already knows that, but what can be offered to replace the alcohol? Some try the pious platitude: "Just trust Christ." Telling someone to do right does not give that person the power to change.

In most things, I performed better than did my brother and

....

My patterns were based on how I saw myself (identity), and how I attempted to meet my own needs by my own resources (flesh). They set the stage for me to become an alcoholic.

....

sister, but "trouble" was my middle name. If something was done wrong, my parents looked for me. More often than not, I was guilty. These guilty feelings I developed while growing up were built into my belief system. Although I was a better student than my brother and sister were, my parents would say, "Why can't you behave and act like your brother and sister?"

I couldn't answer those questions. Deep down I believed something was wrong with me and feelings of guilt were always with me.

As a child, I didn't introduce myself by saying "Hi, I'm Mike Quarles. I'm unaccepted, inadequate, insecure and guilty. Something is wrong with me." In the recesses of my soul, however, these feelings were there. Like everyone, I longed to have my basic needs of love, acceptance and approval met. I developed my own patterns in how to deal with life, solve my problems, become a successful person and meet my needs. These patterns were based on how I saw myself (identity), and how I attempted to meet my own needs by my own resources (flesh). They set the stage for me to become an alcoholic.

Rebellious to Authority
Early on I learned to *defy authority*. My dad used his authority in an abusive and capricious manner. It taught me to hate

authority. I questioned it, challenged it and disobeyed it. Although I knew it was for my own good, I couldn't submit to authority. At 18, I joined the navy and became possibly the only person in history to get put on report for "smirking." When I was a recruit in boot camp, the petty officer in charge entered our barracks and began to read the riot act about the condition of our quarters. During his tirade, he turned to me and said, "Quarles, you're on report."

"For what?" I asked, "I didn't say a word."

"For smirking," he replied. He was right. I couldn't hide my contempt for this uneducated bumpkin, who probably couldn't hold a "real" job. Now he was telling me what to do. This same pattern kept me in trouble. I had difficulty submitting to and respecting the authority of my employers.

I found it hard to submit to God when I became a Christian. How could I trust God for things I didn't understand? As a "Lone Ranger Christian," I trooped off on my own and didn't contribute to the Body. The necessity for believers to be connected to the Body would be a painful lesson I would be forced to learn.

Irresponsible
Another pattern I developed was *irresponsibility*. Although my mother didn't plan it, she trained me to be irresponsible. She didn't allow me to suffer the consequences of my wrong behavior. Many times, Mom lied to Dad so I would stay out of trouble.

My dad asked, "Was Mike home by midnight? Had he been drinking?"

Mom assured Dad that I had come home on time and had not been drinking; although many times she knew it was two or three o'clock in the morning when I staggered through the front door. If mothers want to train their children to become addicts, they should do everything for them and not let them suffer the consequences for wrong behavior. In almost every area of life, this trains children to be irresponsible.

Throughout the book of Proverbs, wayward sons and sluggards are described. These passages teach that destruction is the path of those who are not disciplined. Proverbs 19:18 says,

"Discipline your son, for in that there is hope; do not be a willing party to his death" *(NIV)*. Ecclesiastes 8:11 also addresses this topic: "Because the sentence against an evil deed is not executed quickly, therefore the hearts of the sons of men among them are given fully to do evil."

These feelings of failure and inadequacy made me fearful to try anything, even when something was assigned to me. Instead of facing the fear, I procrastinated. I returned to the University of Alabama after I left the navy. I made the dean's list for the first three semesters. Then my priorities shifted from studying to partying, drinking and dating girls. My final year I almost didn't graduate because I missed so many classes and was chronically late with my required assignments.

One professor told me, "I've never seen someone with so much ability who put so little of it to use." This professor's message about my ability didn't sink in. Instead, it reinforced my inadequacy.

Quitting

Another pattern I developed was *quitting*. Programmed for failure, I knew that quitting was always a possibility. On the high school basketball team the coach announced that some players would be cut from the team. I naturally assumed I would be released, so I immediately quit. That way, I wouldn't have to face rejection and failure.

About the time I turned 18, I had a life-changing experience. Two of my best friends and I decided to celebrate our high school graduation by getting drunk. The alcohol changed my personality. I lost my inhibitions in a new experience and enjoyed myself. Instead of being shy with girls, I talked, joked and laughed with them. I began to cut up with the guys and become one of them. At least temporarily, the alcohol liberated me from my shell of self-consciousness, insecurity and worthlessness.

The exact same experience didn't phase my two friends. For each of them, drinking was a negative experience and never became part of their lives. These friends found their worth and acceptance in ways I couldn't. One of them had everything material—wealth and all its trappings, popularity with the girls, was a member of the state championship basketball team and president of the student body.

Although my other friend didn't have material possessions, his family was one of the most loving and affirming I have ever known. This family didn't scream at each other or put each other down. To my amazement, these people appreciated each other. Like a safe haven to get away from the raging storm in my home, I spent as much time as possible with this family. They introduced me to Christianity. It was years before I responded.

Earn as Much Money as Possible
My middle-class neighborhood was only a few blocks from some of the most affluent parts of town. This is where my friends lived and they allowed me to sample the lifestyle of the wealthy. My best friend was a surgeon's son and lived in a mansion that included a gardener and a full-time maid. This friend had every advantage money could buy—fancy cars, designer clothes, plenty of spending money, fabulous vacations and country club membership. How I envied him! Money took care of everything. His family didn't seem to have the problems of my family. Their wealth gave them a stature and a confidence I didn't have. I hated never having enough, always scrimping and being told, "No, you cannot go to the beach with your friends because we don't have the money." When I grew up, I determined never to be in that predicament.

Shortly before I graduated from college, I clearly remember sitting in a classroom thinking, *My goal in life is to earn as much money as possible.* This simple and shallow goal drove my life for years.

Life After College

Alcohol became a major part of my life during the next 10 years. I was never far from it. In my first few years after graduating from college, I used alcohol for enjoyment and fun. Later it became my hobby and favorite pastime. When things didn't go well, I used alcohol to commiserate. When there were events to celebrate or I needed to relax after a hard day, alcohol was there. When I failed, alcohol salved my conscience and allowed me to escape when stress increased. My socializing, entertaining and recreation revolved around alcohol. When I had a choice about social events, I attended primarily based on whether alcohol was available. Sometimes I got into arguments with my first wife, Denise, (not her real name) about attending a particular social event. If I knew no alcohol would be served, I wouldn't go.

Like the social events, I selected my friends with the same criteria. "Do they drink alcohol?" was my primary question. If a

....

The major pattern I used to meet my needs was based on a *drive to succeed.* Success became "life" for me. If I was successful, I felt accepted and worthy.

....

friend wasn't inclined to drink, I had no interest in his company. Among my main group of friends, our favorite weekend activity was to cook on the grill *and* drink. Our goal was to delay our wives as long as possible while they urged us to begin grilling the steaks so we could eat. The longer we could delay, the more we could drink. For us, it was a game. Like every alcoholic, my drinking wasn't just a bad habit; it was a way of life. I didn't permit anyone or anything to interfere with it.

Galatians 5:19-21 says drunkenness is one of the "deeds of the flesh." A person becomes an alcoholic after drinking such a large volume for so long that he or she no longer has a choice. Alcohol liberated me from my paralyzing inadequacies and insecurities. I thought it added something I desperately needed; I wouldn't give it up easily.

In High Cotton and Loving It
The year after I graduated from college, I went to work for

Merrill Lynch and became a stockbroker. As I began to earn money, I acquired all the perks—country club membership, a red Jaguar, then a big house with a pool. For vacations, I went skiing in Colorado and Vermont and traveled to Miami when Alabama played at the Orange Bowl. Then I traveled to Dallas for the Cotton Bowl. As they say in the South, I was in "high cotton" and I loved every minute of it.

I joined a private club located on the top floor of my building. Most afternoons I couldn't wait for the stock market to close. Then I would jump on the elevator to my club and drink, reveling in my success. I would sit at the bar with the guys, telling everyone about my success and swapping war stories.

I told my drinking buddies, "I like money because it enables me to buy what I want, do what I want and go where I want." Inside, I knew people looked up to anyone with money. I believed money gave me the acceptance and worth I had longed for since I was a small child.

Running Scared

The major pattern I used to meet my needs was based on a *drive to succeed*. Success became "life" for me. If I was successful, I felt accepted and worthy.

During my early days in the brokerage business in Birmingham, I called on Rab Brown, a trust officer at the First National Bank in Tuscaloosa. This kind gentleman was old enough to be my father. At first, Mr. Brown didn't rebuff my attempts to solicit business. After several meetings, Mr. Brown turned to me and said, "Mike, let me give you some friendly advice. You're young and have your whole life ahead of you. I suggest you try something besides being a stockbroker. I've been around a lot of stockbrokers in my time and you just don't have what it takes to be successful. You have to be outgoing, forceful and aggressive. You're just not that way."

His words cut me to the core. How dare Mr. Brown tell me I didn't have what it takes! I'd show that old patronizing fool—and I did. I pushed and drove myself. I worked nights, then got up early and I worked weekends. In downtown Birmingham, I was the only stockbroker who made cold calls at *every* office in *every* major office building. Why?

Bear Bryant, legendary football coach of the Alabama Crimson Tide, used to say, "I run scared for every game. That way I never let up." I was running scared. Deep down my identity said I was a failure. As I ran scared, I tried to prove to others—Mr. Brown the trust officer or my dad, whomever—that I was OK. I desperately sought acceptance and worth.

Many times during the years, I've thought about Mr. Brown's advice. Actually, looking back now, his words were excellent and right on target. Twenty years later, E. F. Hutton hired me to open a Birmingham office as their manager. The company didn't give me its normal aptitude test, but waived it because of my success record in the business.

Later, the management asked me to take the test for a file about successful stockbrokers. I took the aptitude test. Later the person in charge of testing called. "You didn't fit the expected profile," he said. My profile was almost exactly the opposite of the typical broker. My main distinction from other brokers was exactly what Rab Brown pointed out—I wasn't outgoing, forceful and aggressive enough. The test projected that I would do better as a counselor or trainer. I climbed the ladder of success because I was driven to meet my basic needs.

I Could Make Things Happen
When I was growing up, I convinced myself that if I tried hard enough, I could make things happen. I listened to Napoleon Hill's tapes and read every self-help book about success that I could find. "Where there's a will there's a way," was my life motto. I determined to be the captain of my soul and master of my fate. By age 29, I became the top stockbroker for Merrill Lynch in Alabama.

After seven years with Merrill at age 32, I left at the top to start my own brokerage firm. Because clients had confidence in my abilities, they invested $440,000 in my company. Things were going my way. One of my associates said, "Mike works hard and plays hard." In reality, he described a man driven to perform, who drank to excess and put his own needs above everything—and everyone—else. I neglected my family. After I pushed myself on the job all week, I partied and drank on the weekends. Then I relaxed in front of the tube and had little left for anyone else.

I thought I was on top of the world. As the founder, president and controlling stockholder of my own brokerage firm, my life was typified by an oversized, handmade, custom-ordered desk. The front of this desk had a large *Q* carved into it; the desk symbolized my perceived success. Contrary to my feelings, the desk told me I had made it. I was worth something.

My fire-engine red Jaguar had a burled, walnut panel and black leather seats. It always attracted attention and I loved every second of it.

On the crest of Shades Mountain in Birmingham, my family and I lived in a 5,000-square-foot house, including a large swimming pool. Our downstairs was one big party room, containing a fireplace, a complete kitchen, a dressing room and bath leading to the pool. Stereo speakers were scattered throughout the downstairs. My favorite place was just off the party room; I called it my study. In one corner stood a large circular cabinet that looked like a free-standing Greek column. I kept it stocked with Jack Daniels whiskey, Chivas Regal scotch, Beef-eaters Gin and various other liquors. Of course our downstairs refrigerator was full of cold beer. In my study, I spent many hours just drinking to escape my fractured relationships or personal moral failures.

In my fantasyland, all was not well. My marriage to Denise was failing, the stock market was going downhill in a wheelbarrow and my company was rapidly losing money. I applied the lessons from those self-help books, but the bleeding couldn't be stopped. Many days I entered my office by six in the morning and worked until midnight. Nothing helped. One major problem was a fast-dealing, free-wheeling partner. He had talked me into doing business with a certain client, contrary to the warnings of other people. When he didn't pay for a large block of stock, this client left us holding the bag for $80,000.

One night I left my office to eat dinner and was listening to another Napoleon Hill tape while driving back to my office. I faced another late night of work. I thought, *This isn't working; it doesn't make any difference what I do, I can't control it. "Where there's a will there's a way" isn't true.*

Headed to Hell

A few weeks later, I attended a cocktail party at a friend's house in the affluent Mountain Brook area. As we sat on the beautiful garden patio, I enjoyed a large gin and tonic along with our light, bantering conversation. Summer was ending and the cool temperature was pleasant. As the alcohol relaxed me, I forgot my problems and joined in the conversation.

One of the men said, "My brother has gotten religion and is always preaching to me. He says that I'm going to hell if I don't turn to Christ." He laughed and said, "I guess I will go to hell." Everybody laughed—except me.

I became lost in thought. I didn't know if there was such a thing as life after death. Of one thing I was certain: if there was a hell, I was headed there. Because of my lifestyle, I was the kind of person who would be in hell. The thought of spending eternity in torment staggered my mind. Hell would never end and it shook me to the core. I broke out in a cold sweat. Only a few seconds had passed. No one around me knew I was consumed with the idea of hell.

I couldn't handle these distressing thoughts. So I thought, *There is no such thing as life after death—when you die, you die like a dog. That's the end of it.* I pushed any dismal thought about hell out of my mind. Years later, the man who made the statement about his brother died in his early 50s of acute alcoholism.

Although I tried to quit, I couldn't stop thinking about life after death. For the first time, I considered the meaning and purpose of life. Sometimes I would see older people and think, *Do you just live 70 or 80 years or so and that's it? If so, life is just a farce. There's no meaning or purpose.* My thoughts consumed me. To my amazement, I lost any interest in my company and my business.

Life Seemed Meaningless

Some days I sat at my desk and stared blankly out of the window. For the next several weeks, I left the office early and went to the country club. In a corner of the restaurant, I stared at the tennis courts regardless of whether anyone was playing or not. I felt numb, empty and barren. My life seemed meaningless. I had no clue what to do about these feelings.

I hadn't been near a church in years. My mother stopped making me go to Sunday School when I was a teenager. Then I stopped attending church altogether.

Denise badgered me into going to a Sunday School party with some of her friends a few years earlier. When we arrived, I was pleasantly surprised to discover a tub of iced-down beer. I thought, *Now this is my kind of church.* So our family joined the church. The congregation was small and theologically very liberal (though I didn't know it at the time). For a while, I attended and enjoyed getting to know the people. The adult Sunday School class was called "Current Events." We discussed such topics as "Is God on America's side?" Some of the people, such as the arts editor of the local newspaper, plunged into deep philosophical discussions. To me, these discussions were a bore. Because of my drinking the night before, I preferred to sleep late on Sunday mornings. Usually I needed the sleep.

A New Class Called "The Bible"

One Sunday morning in September 1970, as usual I woke up having a hangover. I felt a highly unusual desire to attend church. The church was starting a new Sunday School year and had announced a new class called "The Bible." I thought, *The Bible is supposed to have all the answers. I'm going to that class.* I don't know where the thought originated; I had never read a Bible nor knew anything about it.

Six people attended this Sunday School class. A widow in the church had become a Christian and wanted to share her newfound faith. She received permission to teach Campus Crusade's "10 Basic Steps to Christian Maturity." During her teaching, she discussed a personal relationship with Christ and "being washed in the blood of Jesus." I found it embarrassing because no one had ever talked to me like that.

Years earlier, three people had talked about Jesus to me in a *one sentence* testimony. Each had an effect. Two former fraternity brothers told about turning their lives over to Christ. For them, it had made a great difference. Also, when my company was struggling financially, I met a man who had an office on our same floor. Recently, he had begun a little one-man personnel placement business. His business wasn't financially feasible so he decided to close the operation. One day I saw him in the men's room and asked, "John, what are you going to do for a job?"

"I don't know," he replied, "but I've turned my life over to Christ. He has always taken care of me. I know He will now." As I walked down the hall to my office, the thought went through my mind, *That's what you ought to do.*

No, I reasoned, *only weak people follow Christ—like John who can't make it in business. Christianity is a crutch and I don't need that.* I continued my pursuit of the elusive butterfly to "make it."

Something, however, intrigued me about that Sunday School class lesson. The lesson clearly described sin—not only as wrongdoing (murder, lying, theft, adultery and so on). Rather, the teacher defined sin as also choosing to go your own way and living your life independent of God. She told us about Jesus and His death on the cross as the payment for our sins. Then she taught about our need to receive Him as forgiveness for our sins and the only means to peace, freedom, fulfillment and joy. It was the first time I had ever heard this news.

I began to get hooked and planned to return next Sunday, but on the following Saturday night we attended a drunken blast—my favorite activity. I got blitzed. Sunday morning I woke up, hopped out of bed and started to dress for church. Although shocked, my wife began to do the same thing.

Besides getting to church with a major-league hangover, that Sunday a major miracle took place that I'll never forget. In the Sunday School class, the teacher continued to present the gospel clearly. She described a 1923 meeting at the Edgewater Hotel in Chicago, Illinois. Some of the world's most important financiers attended this meeting: a member of the President's cabinet, the president of the International Bank of Settlements, the biggest investor on Wall Street, the president of the largest steel company, the president of the largest utility company and the president of the New York Stock Exchange.

Twenty years later, where were these important men? Each

one had either committed suicide, gone bankrupt, gone insane or spent time in prison. Although each person had learned to make a living, he hadn't learned the meaning of life. The story hit me like a bombshell! I thought, *These men have attained what I am striving for and giving my life for. What good did it do for them? There must be life after death for there to be meaning and purpose in life.*

A Simple Prayer During a Hangover
That fall day in 1970, after lunch, I finished reading the lesson booklet. In the final pages, it described how to receive Christ as Lord and Savior, then suggested a prayer. At that moment, I believed the gospel, prayed the prayer and received Christ. My life was committed to Him. No bells rang. I didn't feel warm and tingly all over. I still had a hangover and I lay down and took a nap. Inside, though, I knew I had done business with the Lord. My life would never be the same.

I had discovered the answer to life. I hit the ground running in my spiritual life. Two weeks after my conversion, I attended a weeklong Campus Crusade Lay Institute in Lake Yale, Florida. Right there in Florida, I knocked on doors and shared the gospel exuberantly, but probably not with a lot of tact. Several people prayed with me to receive Christ and I was really pumped. Surely this is what every Christian did! The news about Jesus was something I wanted to share with everyone. After all, I had found meaning and purpose to my life!

Unfortunately, my wife at the time didn't share my enthusiasm. My changed attitude completely turned her off. "I've got to get out of here," Denise said to me. I drove her to Orlando, Florida, and she took a plane to Birmingham, Alabama. I returned to Lake Yale and continued to devour the new teaching about Christ. On my trip back to Birmingham a few days later, a church in Tallahassee, Florida, asked me to stop and share my testimony. When I arrived, I discovered they had arranged for me to conduct the whole service. I found the experience thrilling.

Back in Birmingham, I discovered my minister and the church leadership didn't share my enthusiasm. I chastised them for their lack of understanding. One day, I made an appointment with a denominational executive and proceeded to confront him about his lack of preaching the gospel during a message at our church. I patiently explained to this pastor how babies didn't receive the Holy Spirit when they were baptized as he had stated.

My Wife Didn't Share My Changed Life
I began a Bible study in my home and invited many big-name evangelicals in Birmingham to share their testimonies, then I would present the gospel. My overzealous attitude turned many away from the gospel—including Denise. On the positive side, God began a revival in our church and many people became Christians. I was a catalyst, but the revival began with a widow, who in the face of an unfriendly environment, faithfully shared the truth to a handful of people.

I became a sensation overnight. People wanted to hear my testimony—about how a hard-driving, heavy-drinking, money-hungry stockbroker had become a Christian. Eagerly I hit the testimony trail. I shared my story whenever and wherever possible. I changed my church membership to a large evangelical church and became increasingly active.

Another stockbroker, also a Christian, had worked with me at Merrill Lynch. One day he said, "Mike, I heard you got saved, but I couldn't believe it. I have prayed for your salvation for years, but I didn't have faith to believe you would be saved."

I was in a dinner club one day with another friend who was a Christian. Later he told me that my conversion was difficult for him to believe. To him, I was one of the most arrogant and obnoxious people he had ever met. Of course, at our parties, I was always drunk.

Shortly after my changed lifestyle, I sensed that God was changing the direction of my life and wanted me to move into full-time ministry. Having Denise's agreement (and I thought her blessing), I sold my company and my stock in it. Then I applied and was accepted at Reformed Theological Seminary in Jackson, Mississippi.

After we signed a purchase agreement for a small house in Jackson and returned home, Denise informed me she wanted a divorce. After my initial shock, I asked what could be done to stop her from divorcing me. Denise said, "Don't go to seminary and sign over all our assets into my name." Looking back, this was not one of my wisest decisions, but I fulfilled both requests.

Within a few months, Denise divorced me anyway. I don't want to give the impression that she was totally to blame. She wasn't. For 10 years, I had been a miserable excuse for a husband. The worst part for me was losing my children. At the time, my son was nine and my daughter was three. When my divorce was final, I rode around in my car and wept. I knew my life would never be the same. To miss watching my children grow up was the greatest loss of my life.

As I tried to cope with my personal situation, I worked several different jobs, but my heart was still directed toward ministry.

A New Family and a New Direction

In June 1972, two years after accepting Christ, I entered Reformed Theological Seminary. During the spring, at my new church, I met a young widow, Julia Prater Fulkerson. Her husband had died of cancer in 1969 and she had a 10-year-old son. Julia seemed to be everything I had wanted and more. Besides being beautiful, outgoing and having a winsome personality, she loved the Lord Jesus. She taught women's discipleship groups and spoke at Christian Women's Clubs across the southeastern United States. I fell head-over-heels in love with Julia, then finally persuaded her to marry me.

We eagerly looked forward to serving the Lord as a couple. We were married in May 1973, after I completed my first year of seminary. We trusted God in simple faith to bless our marriage and use us in a wonderful way. It didn't work out exactly as we had hoped; both of us had a lot to learn.

Still Driven to Succeed

I believed I had thrown off my old methods to meet my needs when I became a Christian. These old self-centered ways were apart from Christ, but the change didn't happen easily. I didn't learn overnight to go to Christ so He could meet my needs. Some of my obvious patterns such as materialism and heavy drinking had seemed to drop away. When I entered the pastorate, however, I spiritualized my flesh pattern of driving for success.

Now my goal wasn't to earn money, but to do something for God—build a successful and growing church. I became adept at counting the number of people in the service before I got up to preach on Sunday mornings. If the attendance was up from the previous Sunday, I felt pretty good. If the attendance was down, however, I didn't feel good.

My preaching must be the problem if attendance is down, I thought. *Why aren't the people coming? What am I doing wrong?* My self-worth and self-acceptance rose and fell with the Sunday morning attendance. Success continued to drive my life, but in a different venue. The Christian community gave me all the encouragement I needed for this quest. At pastors' meetings or whenever I ran into someone new, those who learned I was a pastor would inevitably ask such questions as, "How big is your church? How many members do you have? Are you growing? Is attendance up?" In an endless supply, I read church-growth books and books about how to increase church attendance. My life cranked into overdrive.

I used all the determination from my days as a stockbroker to set out to build a successful church. I tried everything, but it didn't lead to success. My success in making cold calls on strangers as a stockbroker were significantly better than in getting the members of my church to move out into their neighborhoods and reach new people for Christ.

I had been an active member in one of the most successful churches in our denomination before I attended seminary. Now in my new church, I tried the same successful methods from this church (and from anywhere else). I attempted a variety of church programs such as visitation evangelism, world-missions emphasis, home Bible studies, discipleship groups, prayer groups and Vacation Bible School. I tackled the various disciplines of the spiritual life such as prayer and fasting. I studied scriptural principles and attended every seminar I could.

From the pulpit and one-on-one, I begged, berated, challenged, and threatened but without results. These people were content with the status quo. I couldn't say anything to persuade them otherwise. I bitterly described my last church as "rampant apathy and unbridled lethargy." The church had become my enemy. It stood in the way of meeting my needs.

My Formula for Living the Christian Life Had Failed
I had started my Christian life with great zeal and commitment. In faith, I believed nothing could stop me. I wanted to become everything the Lord wanted and to faithfully serve Him in ministry. From the day I became a Christian, I pursued education and preparation for ministry, attended seminars and read literally hundreds of books about the Christian life and ministry. I was a diligent student of the Bible and memorized chapters of the Bible. I prayed and fasted. It was my custom to spend at least one hour in the Word and prayer daily. My motto hung on my wall, "Only one life, 'twill soon be past, Only what's done for Christ will last" (by the great missionary to Africa, C. T. Studd). If someone had told me when I became a Christian in 1970 that I would become an alcoholic, I wouldn't have believed it.

Slowly I came face-to-face with a sad but obvious conclusion: the Christian life was not working for me. My church was going nowhere—fast. If Julia had not been married to the preacher, she would have attended another church. I admitted that if I hadn't been the pastor, I wouldn't have attended my own church. My need to build a successful church, coupled with my understanding of the Christian life, led to disaster. I had become a legalistic and harsh person. I demanded that Julia and the children attend every church function. I didn't want them to do anything to embarrass me. My formula to live the Christian life had failed. I believed I had failed God, my wife and family, my church and anyone who believed in me.

Somehow my commitment and countless activities didn't work. My marriage was failing. My children didn't respect me and my personal thought life was a mess. Finally I came to grips with reality and admitted that I was unfit for ministry. I could make only one possible decision. In 1979, I resigned my pastorate.

I was discouraged and disillusioned. My vision had died along with my dream to make my life count for Christ. My anger raged at God, at my wife, at the church, but most of all at myself. After my resignation, in my last sermon I used the

....

What was my church's problem? *I* was the problem. Instead of ministering God's truth, love and grace along with focusing on people and their needs, I tried to meet my needs. I wanted to build what I considered to be a "successful" church.

....

text from Revelation 3:16. It describes how Christ spit the lukewarm Christians out of His mouth. I really blasted my congregation.

What was my church's problem? *I* was the problem. Instead of ministering God's truth, love and grace along with focusing on people and their needs, I tried to meet my needs. I wanted to build what I considered to be a "successful" church. When this success didn't happen, I saw myself as a failure. The stage was set to turn to alcohol. It would medicate the pain of my deep, unmet needs.

Julia's Perspective

Editor's note: The turmoil in Mike's life wasn't easy for Julia to face. In the following paragraphs, Julia tells her story about their life together.

I had never wanted to be married to a pastor, but I tackled my new role wholeheartedly. Outwardly, I did everything I could to help Mike. Mike was an excellent Bible teacher. We saw people become Christians because of his ministry. Others were discipled and were growing in their faith because of Mike's teaching, but these results were never enough for him. Mike only looked at what didn't happen rather than at the positive occurrences. It is the old story about the half-full glass. Mike looked at the glass as half empty instead of half full.

Sometimes Mike talked about giving up and trying something else. I always tried to marshal reasons why he should continue. Mike always presented such a strong case about moving on to the next place. He overpowered me verbally so I would give in.

My Disappointment in Our Marriage

During the first six years of our marriage while Mike was in seminary and in the pastorate, I complained about how he was a disappointment to me as a husband and as a father. He never measured up to my expectations in either category.

Mike was demanding and critical of the children and me. We felt his pressure for us to "do right" and to make him look good. I was good at "acting spiritual" in public when my heart was hard with anger or breaking from rejection. I tried to cover up my miserable feelings in front of the kids. During these years, we sought counseling regularly but it never seemed to help us.

When Mike stood on the brink of resigning from his last pastorate in Pensacola, Florida, I returned to Birmingham and talked with my Christian counselor. She challenged me about my wishy-washy behavior in our marriage. She said that for years I had been coming to her and was trying to blame everything on Mike and wanted out of the marriage, but never had grounds.

Mike always accused me of having a "packed bag" mentality, and he was right. My counselor brought me to the point of decision. She said, "You need to decide if you are going to make a commitment to the marriage and quit complaining about it or be willing to get out of the marriage. No one forced you to marry Mike. You need to take responsibility for your own actions." I felt like a wave in the sea, blown and tossed about by the wind; double-minded and unstable in everything (see Jas. 1:5-8).

The next day, I spent time alone with the Lord, my Bible and my thoughts. It was something like a courtroom where I argued my case, then God argued His case. Finally, late in the afternoon, I reaffirmed that God was God. He was in control and big enough to take care of me and my marriage. I wasn't going to be a quitter and give up on God or on my marriage. In my own mind, I had been too much of a critic about Mike's performance in our home. As a result, Mike couldn't believe me when I tried to praise him or compliment him.

That afternoon, I recommitted myself to God, to Mike and to our marriage. I prayed, "No matter what kind of husband Mike will be, I am going to stay married to him, Lord. I want to honor You through my commitment." I was determined to be *with* Mike and *for* Mike.

Mike had driven to Birmingham from Pensacola. We stayed with Lucy and Dan, my sister and her husband. I told them about my transaction with the Lord. The next day Mike and I drove to Atlanta to visit our friends, Jack and June Fagan. They took us to the North Georgia mountains for a few days. We talked everything through with them and with each other. Mike decided to carry through with his decision to resign from his pastorate. He wanted to return to business.

We went back to Pensacola with one heart and mind as a couple. Fortunately, my son, Bradley, was living with his uncle and aunt in Hilton Head, South Carolina, for the summer. He was working for his uncle's construction company.

Our congregation was upset about Mike's resignation. As their shepherd, Mike was loved and respected. Through a weekly Bible study in our home, we had enjoyed ministering with several young couples from a nearby naval air station. They begged Mike to reconsider his decision, but he was determined to make this change.

Mike accepted an offer with a stockbrokerage company in Atlanta, Georgia. This move marked our fifth in six years of marriage. Bradley would be in the senior class at the Christian school where he had attended eighth and ninth grade. Maybe now Mike would settle down into something that fit his vision and dreams. Well, I was with him for the long haul—no matter what.

Within a couple of months, Mike realized he had made a mistake trying to restart his business in Atlanta instead of Birmingham. After some inquiries, he was able to transfer to the Birmingham office and live with his mother. Bradley and I stayed in Atlanta. I was not going to move again so soon, much less move Bradley in his senior year.

Bradley and I had one of the best years we ever had. Mike being gone all week caused the stress level in our house to plummet. I could give myself totally to being a mother of a high school senior. I joined a prayer group with four other mothers of seniors. We spent a day each week praying for our kids, studying the Bible, having lunch, laughing and talking. I went to all of Bradley's sports activities without worrying about Mike being around to criticize us. I had forgotten how much fun life could be!

Mike was usually in an awful mood when he came home on the weekends. Bradley started spending time away with friends. I was sad that our home wasn't a comfortable place to be, but I was glad for Bradley to be with a loving family. I had no idea what was going on with Mike and he wouldn't tell me. Remembering my commitment to our marriage, I just tried to love and encourage him.

Who would have ever thought our worst years were ahead? I never knew my commitment would be so tested, but God did test my commitment, and I clung to the Lord for His guidance and comfort.

Who Will Set Me Free?

It was official. I resigned the pastorate at my church on July 2, 1979. As I drove from Atlanta to my home in Pensacola, my emotions were in turmoil. My resignation made my dream of serving God in a ministry evaporate. This vision for service was the *only* thing in my life that I desperately wanted. It seemed unreal, but it was over. The elders at my church accepted my resignation and I announced it to the congregation.

A few of the members were genuinely sorry I was leaving, but the majority accepted it in stride as though they weren't surprised. The long-term members knew that pastors come and go, but the church goes on. I hated giving up, but I believed I had no other choice. As a friend of mine suggested, I had to "come to grips with reality." Except my reality was a mess. My marriage was shaky and my children didn't respect me. I had little ministry left.

How could I have failed so miserably? When I gave up my business, I believed I had turned my back on the world and everything it offered. Considering that sort of sacrifice, wouldn't God bless me, my ministry and my family? Why did I leave my business in the first place? I should have stayed.

Now the previous seven years of my life looked like a waste. I was forced to start over again. I should have known better. Why did I think I had anything to offer God and the ministry?

Failure and I were on close speaking terms. Throughout my life, failure always lurked around the corner. My fear of failure became a self-fulfilling prophecy. I thought, *I stepped out of my league and tried to accomplish something spiritual.* There was only one thing I knew best—selling stocks. Couldn't God have kept me from such failure? Where was God during these years? And where was He now? I thought I knew the answer—my failure had overcome God's grace. Today I know that message is a lie of the enemy, but in 1979 it was ingrained in my belief system.

In some sense, I was relieved that my attempt at ministry had ended. For years, I dreaded failure in ministry. Now I could quit struggling; it was finally here. I didn't have to put on the mask of a pastor and act as if my life had no problems. I could return to being a regular guy—a struggling Christian like everyone else. When I resigned from the ministry, I decided to loosen my personal standards. So what if I missed a quiet time or two? It wasn't the end of the world. If I wanted to drink a beer or two, what was the big deal? I had looked around and observed many other Christians who didn't maintain such restrictive lives.

After my resignation, I sent more than 50 letters in response to newspaper ads for jobs. I didn't land one single interview. Finally I gave in to the pressure and sent letters to about a dozen brokerage companies in Atlanta. Rather than returning home to Birmingham, I decided to go to Atlanta. I felt like such a failure that I couldn't face my friends back home. In Atlanta, I would plan a new start where I didn't know too many people. Each brokerage company responded to my letter. I landed interviews with 10 of the 12 companies. Two weren't hiring at that time. It felt good to be appreciated and wanted. In the stock business, I had an excellent record and had proven myself as a producer. My interviews went well and it appeared I would have my choice of several companies. I narrowed my selection to two companies. I planned to return to Atlanta with Julia the following week and make the final decision.

Out of Control—Again

As I turned off the interstate for the last leg of the trip into

Pensacola, a wave of depression came upon me. I didn't want to return to the stock business, but here I was again. In another sense, I felt some excitement about making a fresh start. I thought about Julia. *She's in Birmingham visiting her family and won't be home until the first part of the week*, I thought. *It will be OK to stop for a drink because it is Friday afternoon. Thank God it's Friday!* I stopped at a small bar to throw back a beer or two. During the last couple of months, I had done this several times, but I had managed to keep everything under control. This time I lost it.

After a few beers, I decided to indulge myself. I asked the bartender about some local action. Who would ever know? He directed me to a place located a few miles north of town. The "action" turned out to be a roadhouse featuring a country and western band. The atmosphere and music matched my mood perfectly. I sat listening to the sad hillbilly songs and drank myself into oblivion. Finally when the place closed, I stumbled to my car.

Although extremely drunk, I thought I was heading toward my home. About an hour later I was in the middle of nowhere, and had no idea of where I was or which way was home. I drove for another hour and came to Atmore, Alabama. I had left the roadhouse in Flomaton, Alabama, which was less than an hour from Pensacola. Now I ended up another hour away in Atmore, after two hours of driving. I had difficulty focusing on my driving and began weaving all over the road.

Out of nowhere, a siren sounded. Looking in my rearview mirror, I saw the blue lights. *Oh no, it can't be; now I'm drunk and about to be arrested for drunk driving. What a great end to my ministry!* I sent up a quick SOS prayer, "Oh God, please, please don't let them arrest me."

I'll never know why, but God answered my prayer. Perhaps the officer felt sorry for me. He took me to an all-night restaurant. "Give this man enough coffee to sober him up," he told the waitress. After a couple of cups of coffee, I still wasn't sober but managed to drive home. The sun peeked over the horizon as I turned into my driveway. *Hope no one sees me*, I thought. When I drifted off to sleep, I hoped to wake up and find my nightmare had ended. It hadn't.

Culture Shock in Downtown Atlanta

I settled on a company in Atlanta and began working as a stockbroker. I knew immediately it wasn't going to work. We couldn't afford a house near my office so I had to commute more than an hour to reach downtown. It forced me to get up early each morning, then drive half an hour and catch a bus. In the rush hour traffic, I rode more than an hour on the bus.

Life in downtown Atlanta was totally foreign to me. The unfriendly people rushed past on the street and the buildings seemed barren and without any distinct features. Up and down the streets were a wide assortment of people—panhandlers, street people, pickpockets, prostitutes and an assortment of petty thieves. These people who were looking for handouts were extremely aggressive and often grabbed me by the arm.

Crime reeled out of control and the police seemed helpless to curb it. Someone was murdered every day in downtown Atlanta that summer of 1979. One noon hour, a man was shot to death on the sidewalk right outside our building. Another man worked late and was killed in our parking lot. Everyone downtown seemed to carry a gun or mace or some equivalent. I purchased a can of mace and made sure my hand was on the trigger inside my pocket whenever I ventured outside.

The environment there kept me uptight constantly; I couldn't sleep at nights and spent a lot of my workday looking at my watch and wishing 5 o'clock would arrive. Then I sneaked a few drinks. I experienced full-scale "culture shock." At one time I had been appointed as a missionary to Taiwan. Now, as an ex-minister, I wasn't surviving in downtown Atlanta; and I had tried to be in ministry! Who was I kidding?

Back to Birmingham

Rather than persist for months, I decided to bite the bullet and move back to Birmingham. Our company had a Birmingham office and I transferred there. We had one hurdle to jump before moving. Our son Bradley was a senior at a local Christian high school where he had attended eighth and ninth grades. We agreed that Julia and Bradley would stay in Atlanta so he could finish the school year. Then they would join me in Birmingham.

We made the decision about Bradley's school in November 1979. I would be on my own for seven months. My mother lived alone in a small one-bedroom apartment. During the week, I moved in with her and slept on a living room sofa bed, then on the weekends I commuted to Atlanta.

It felt good to return to the familiar location and my many friends. No one seemed concerned that I had left the ministry. Everyone accepted that I had returned to my business. Their attitudes helped me a lot, but deep down I thought about my own failures. Through my hard work, my business began to build. Soon I had a solid base of clients and was beginning to make a decent income.

A Growing Sense of Guilt About My Drinking

Because I was living away from home, it gave me an opportunity to drink whenever I wanted without any interference from Julia. I began to take full advantage of my situation. Once I began drinking, I didn't know when to stop. I hardly ever stopped until I was drunk. When I had a couple of drinks, I usually lost control.

I knew what the Bible said about alcohol. I was convinced nothing was wrong with taking a drink every now and then. At the same time, I knew what the Scriptures said about drunkenness. I could quote Ephesians 5:18, "Do not get drunk on wine, which leads to debauchery. Instead be filled with the Spirit" *(NIV).*

I could justify drinking a few beers here and there or a glass of wine with a meal, but I knew my lifestyle was impossible to justify from the Bible. Whenever I had too much to drink, I thought and acted in a way that wasn't godly. I always ended up doing things that made me feel ashamed. My sense of guilt and remorse continually haunted me. I couldn't hold back from getting drunk several times a week. Throughout my drinking, I never rationalized it away. I knew it was wrong and hated what alcohol did to me. This demonic stranglehold plagued me without any rest.

Sometimes I managed a few days or a few weeks without a

drink, but I knew soon it would happen again. It was the anticipation that weighed on my mind. Then when I did get drunk, my tortured mind filled with accusations and recriminations I now know were straight from Satan.

....

I resolved to do whatever it took to beat my problem. As a Christian, I belonged to the Lord. In the next five years, I tried everything I knew, everything anybody told me or I had read. Julia says I earned a D.D.— a Doctorate in Drunkenness.

....

My business was going better than I expected. Despite my success on the outside, I was miserable and failing on the inside. I didn't want to be a drunk and I hated myself for what I had become, but I couldn't stop. I resolved to do whatever it took to beat my problem. As a Christian, I belonged to the Lord. Scripture told me I could have deliverance and freedom. I sought and pursued it with all of my being. I wasn't going to give in to my problem. In the next five years, I tried everything I knew, everything anybody told me or I had read. Julia says I earned a D.D.—a Doctorate in Drunkenness.

The following are some of the things I tried:

1. Pastoral counselors
2. AA and five separate sponsors
3. Christian 12-step group
4. Christian counselor
5. Secular counselor
6. Addictions counselor
7. Antabuse drug
8. Read every book about addiction
9. Public confession
10. Christian psychiatrist
11. Secular psychiatrist

12. Christian psychologist
13. Secular psychologist
14. Healing-of-memories session
15. Baptism of the Holy Spirit session
16. Deliverance session
17. Accountability
18. Biblical confrontation
19. Called before the church discipline committee
20. Secular treatment center
21. Group therapy
22. Christian treatment center
23. Willpower
24. Promises to God and to my wife
25. Prayer
26. Bible study
27. Scripture memory
28. Fasting
29. Evangelism
30. Discipleship

Nothing worked!

Because I was a Christian, I screwed up my energy to apply what I learned. Almost from the first day I became a Christian, I had been taught that the secret to the abundant life was *"doing"* right. They taught me that a key was to spend time with God in a "quiet time" of Bible study and prayer. Through this time, I thought I could learn what God wanted and get Him to strengthen me for action. I didn't view this time with God as spending time with my loving heavenly Father. My time with God was a duty where I got something from God, which applied to my daily situation.

Although discipleship and quiet times can be valuable growing experiences for the Christian, I mistakenly believed that if I would spend enough time in the Bible that I would change. I neglected faith and saw this time with God as a duty to perform.

One of the formulas I used for my quiet time was called the nine *P*s. Using a selected Bible passage, I went through it nine times. First I perused it, then pondered it, then pushed it, then pulled it, then penetrated it, then pounded it, then pulverized it and so on. Before I was finished, I should have been able to get from God what I needed. Jack Miller, president of World Harvest Mission and a proponent for sanctification by faith, calls this method sanctification by osmosis. We mistakenly think that if we spend enough time in the Scriptures, they'll change us. It didn't work for me. Scripture says the truth will set us free, not just spending time in the Bible.

Often I spent two hours in "quiet time," then before dark that same day I was drunk. I studied at least one hour every day and often two hours. I memorized many scriptural passages, then quoted them during times of temptation. It never worked.

In the book of Proverbs I saw many verses about drunkenness and irresponsibility. As I searched for deliverance I outlined the whole book. For hundreds of hours I studied the Bible and looked for scriptural principles of deliverance. I tried the gamut of spiritual activities such as fasting, praying, begging and pleading. Sometimes I gave it up and other times I gave it to God.

Then I thought maybe I would find my answer in other evangelical Christian groups. I tried the gamut of them—discipleship groups, charismatic meetings, revivals, prayer meetings and praise gatherings. Some Christians encouraged me to attend a healing-of-memories session. Others said I needed a deliverance session. I tried anything and everything I was told. Possibly I could find release from my bondage with a new insight in an area of the church that was completely different from my Presbyterian background. Each of these groups included believers who had a sincere dedication and commitment to Christ. I, however, didn't find a program or discipline that released me from my bondage to alcohol.

I also went to a variety of Christian counselors in Birmingham. I read every book I could find about alcoholism and addiction. Like Naaman the leper in the Old Testament stories (see 2 Kings 5:10), if someone had told me to wash in the Jordan River seven times, I would gladly have done it. Or if someone had told me to swim the Jordan, I would have given it a shot. Each day I lived in an almost unbearable state of misery, anguish and despondency. My hope began to dim that I could ever attain freedom from alcohol. Instead I redoubled my efforts at trying.

"Get Your Mind Off Your Own Problems"

The first time I met with my pastor about my problem, he devised a unique solution. "You need to get involved in our visitation evangelism program," he said. "As you get your mind off your own prob-

....

People told me I needed accountability. Accountability is a good concept, but it doesn't give freedom.

....

lems and help others, it will make a difference." From what I had been taught through the years about Christianity, I accepted his counsel.

My brother-in-law Dan Allison jokingly categorized this philosophy in this way, "If what you're doing isn't working, then double your efforts." Dutifully, I joined the program and each week with my partner knocked on doors and shared the gospel. A few years later, I learned that my partner, a young businessman, had a major drug problem. I wonder if he struggled with drugs back then and had been counseled to try the evangelism program. It didn't work for either of us.

Other people told me I needed accountability. So I gathered a group of strong, mature Christian men. Each man made a commitment to work with me about my alcoholism. Five men, including my two brothers-in-law, met with me weekly and checked on my activities and decisions. It worked for a few weeks and then fell apart because no one could watch my every action.

Accountability is a good concept, but it doesn't give freedom. On a Christian radio station I heard a man tell about how when he traveled he overcame a problem with lust and pornography. His solution was to take someone with him on each trip. It might keep him externally accountable and out of trouble, but kept him internally still in bondage.

Another time on television I watched Gloria Steinem describe how she overcame an eating disorder. "How did you do this?" the interviewer asked.

Steinem said, "I don't keep food in the house anymore." Her solution is creative, but did not really free her from bondage to food.

I Tried Alcoholics Anonymous

Craig, the assistant pastor at my church, took the greatest personal interest in my problem. Our church had never addressed such addictions before so Craig began a Christian 12-step group. I was a charter member and probably should have been the honorary founder. I received much support and encouragement from these groups, but I didn't find my freedom.

After several weeks, I believed that Alcoholics Anonymous (AA) was more effective than our Christian 12-step group because their focus was clearer and their philosophy was distinct. Our Christian 12-step group tried to incorporate the methods and philosophy of AA and also bring Christ into the program. Our Christian 12-step program accepted a key premise of AA: "Once an alcoholic always an alcoholic." If we confessed that we were alcoholics, used the AA methods and sought help from Christ, then we could deal with our problems. To me, it appeared that Christ was an add-on to the program and not the centerpiece. I accepted my identity as an alcoholic, but I never learned my true identity "in Christ." I settled for a method of coping, but it stopped short of real freedom. I was extremely frustrated! Where was the truth that would set me free?

One day I sat in Craig's office. "What should I try next?" I asked.

"Maybe you should attend some AA meetings," Craig suggested. The idea hit me right between the eyes. It seemed to be an admission that Christ wasn't enough. I needed something else to become free from my addiction. Or maybe worse, I was admitting that I couldn't make the Christian life work for me. By this time, though, the evidence was overwhelming.

Craig leaned forward in his chair and with characteristic intensity said, "I believe you need to do whatever might help you—whatever it is, whether secular or not. The Bible does say that if your right eye causes you to sin, gouge it out and throw it away and if your right hand causes you to sin, cut it off and throw it away. You need drastic and radical action."

I didn't interpret this passage the same way, but who was I to argue? At this point, I wasn't sure of my name. My life was so out of control that I had no certainty where I would be during the next hour. Why not try AA? I was headed in a direction that would soon land me on the streets or in an institution. In a run-down section of Birmingham, I stood outside a dilapidated concrete block building that had been painted white. Soon my AA meeting would begin. I leaned into the wall with my head down and thought, *I hope no one recognizes me.* A wide assortment of people milled around, looking glad to be there as they laughed and joked with each other.

A few who waited were women, a couple were business types; some young people looked as though they had spent many years in the drug culture. Many of the men appeared to fit into the roughest bars in town. *I would be more comfortable in any of those rough bars—instead of standing here,* I thought.

Suddenly a voice behind me said, "Mike, it's good to see you. I'm so glad you're here." When I turned around, the guy looked vaguely familiar. As we talked, I learned he was a member of my large evangelical church. Joe didn't go to church anymore. He brought me up-to-date on his story. About the same time I became a Christian, Joe and his wife also found Christ. Then not long after that, they left town to go on staff with Campus Crusade for Christ. He hadn't been around in a long time, but I remembered them. After a few years with Crusade, Joe developed a drinking problem and had resigned from the ministry. They returned to Birmingham.

As his drinking intensified, Joe's life had gone from bad to worse. Now his wife had filed for divorce.

"Joe, I'm not sure I'm supposed to be here", I said, "but I have a drinking problem and wanted to find out for myself."

He looked straight into my eye and said, "This is right where you need to be. This is what you've been looking for all your life. You couldn't find this in Christianity or the church." His words sounded strange, but I didn't want an in-depth conversation, so I didn't pursue it. We planned to have lunch later that week. At the meeting time, everyone filed into a large room. Except for the straight-backed chairs arranged in a circle, the room was bare.

I learned about the four kinds of AA meetings. This particular meeting was a sharing session where anyone could share anything—struggles, victories or feelings. Another focus is on discussion meetings where a topic is selected from "The Big Book" —*Alcoholics Anonymous.* "Step" meetings discuss one of the 12 steps. Finally, in other meetings someone shares a personal story.

As we settled into our chairs, the meeting started in the pattern I learned was the same for every AA session. Each person introduced him or herself, saying, "My name is (Mike) and I am an alcoholic." This is a crucial part of the program and part of the indoctrination. A person admits the problem of alcohol and then confesses that he or she is an alcoholic. The program teaches "once an alcoholic, always an alcoholic." Then, only two choices can be made for life—to quit drinking or to die. The most proven way to quit drinking is through AA. Its program is simple and effective.

As I attended the sessions, I learned AA's underlying philosophy. Here's how it works: As an alcoholic, you were born that way and will always be that way. The disease is deadly and if you ingest alcohol, you lose control. Through its teaching it is well documented that those who continue drinking will eventually destroy everything—mental health, social relationships, family, finances, career, emotional health, physical health and life. The choice is yours—quit drinking through following the AA program or die. The fear of losing everything meaningful to you should compel you to stop drinking. The argument is convincing.

The majority of AA literature and meetings emphasizes the disease aspects of alcohol. I have concluded that it is really an *issue of identity.* Everything revolves around this alcoholic person who will never change. Instead, the focus is shifted to what a person can change—his or her behavior by doing everything he or she can do to stop drinking. Honesty compels me to say that this program works if abstinence is the ultimate goal. Through attending hundreds of AA meetings, I met hundreds of people who have stopped drinking—yet none of them said they were free. Most openly admitted that their bondage continued.

Honesty is the hallmark of AA, but internal change and lasting freedom isn't the goal or purpose. The focus is to stop drinking, and from my perspective, AA does the best job of anybody. It has done a better job of addressing the problem than has the church. Although many families are better as a result, I learned that only Jesus Christ can reveal the truth that sets a person free (see John 8:32,36), and enable the person to be a new creation in Christ (see 2 Cor. 5:17).

My friend Joe became my first sponsor. He told me that in AA I would find what I couldn't in Christianity or the church. He was dead serious and sincere. For Joe, AA had become his church; he attended an AA meeting at 11:00 A.M. on Sunday. As he and most of the others said, "AA isn't a program, it's a way of life." Joe along with many others believed they had been rescued from a life of hell. Now AA was their life.

During one of Joe's fervent sales pitches, I asked, "What do you believe God's purpose is for you?"

Without a pause, he said , "For me and every other alcoholic like you, God's only purpose is not to drink".

"That's it?" I asked incredulously.

"That's it," he assured me. From my knowledge about the Bible, I couldn't believe that was God's purpose for me. I did admit the quality of my life would drastically improve if I stopped drinking. I hoped God had more for my life than that though!

Most people gave lip service that AA was a spiritual program, but everyone knew it was not a Christ-centered program. If I or anyone tried to mention Christ or the Bible, we were quickly reminded that this wasn't the place. AA made no attempt to direct people toward the person or work of Christ. AA, however, was the best secular program the world could offer.

During the next couple of years, I attended hundreds of AA meetings and had five different sponsors. But for me, it didn't work. Did I faithfully "work the program," as they encouraged? Probably not, because I was looking for more than AA had to offer. Maybe if I had worked the program, I would have stopped drinking, but I wanted to do more than just stop drinking. I wanted freedom. Deep inside, I knew my problem wasn't drinking alcohol, losing control or getting drunk.

One of my AA sponsors was a doctor. He prescribed the drug Antabuse for me. If you take Antabuse and then drink, you get violently ill and can even die. I tried it for a short period. It didn't work. Twice I was violently ill. I gave up on that treatment.

"There's Really Nothing Wrong with You"

If I knew the guaranteed disastrous results, what drove me to drink? What were the strongholds built over a long time period that resulted in this crippling bondage? Most importantly, how could I be set free to live the life of peace and joy that God promised?

I tried seeing Christian and secular psychiatrists, and Christian and secular psychologists. After listening to my story, a psychiatrist told me, "You just have a problem like everyone does. You just need to deal with it the best way that you can; there's really nothing wrong with you." He was trying to encourage me, but his words were devastating. If nothing was wrong, then why was my life going downhill in a wheelbarrow? I wanted answers, not positive platitudes or words of encouragement. He told me there were no answers. I left his office and drove straight to a bar.

After hearing my story, one psychologist told me, "You are more comfortable with discomfort and being upset. This seems to be a way of life that you choose."

"OK then, how do I make some different choices?" He couldn't tell me.

I continued reading every self-help book I could find. Several of the books were written by an author who had spent many years working with alcoholics. I found the books encouraging so I contacted the author in New Jersey. We arranged a time for me to fly there and spend three days of intensive counseling with him. I found this counselor extremely encouraging. Through our conversations, I saw some new aspects about my past and my childhood. I felt challenged in my relationship with the Lord and left there uplifted and inspired. But it didn't stop my drinking. Throughout every session of counseling, advice, confrontation, challenge, rebuke, admonition and instruction, no one ever said, "The problem isn't you, it's the lies you believe about who you are."

No one ever said, "The answer isn't what you do, but what God has done."

One person after another told me to "do this...try this...work on this...don't do this...refrain from that...restrain from that...or avoid that."

Christian Confrontation

At the end of the summer of 1984, my brother-in-law decided to follow the biblical admonition and confront me. Then he returned with another Christian brother. They talked to me in love and in obedience to the Bible. I found it humiliating, but it didn't help. I wondered if he would go the next step according to the Bible. Sure enough, I was called to face the church discipline committee. For five years, I had struggled with my drinking. I attended this church when I was called into the ministry, then they supported me for the three years in seminary. Their promising preacher had become their prodigal son.

When I was notified about the meeting, I considered killing myself, leaving town or turning my back on this church and not attending their meeting. In the end, I submitted to what I thought God wanted and went to the meeting. When I walked into the room, four elders from the church and the assistant pastor were seated at a round table. I knew each of these men well from prayer groups, Bible studies or visitation evangelism. Stan invited me to sit at the table with them. He began the discussion, saying that my drinking had come to their attention and couldn't be neglected.

Although I was humiliated and embarrassed, I admitted it was true. They assured me their intentions were to help and become part of my solution. Then they admitted they had no idea what to do and would be seeking advice from Craig, the other assistant pastor and David, another recovering alcoholic in our church. I hated to learn this was their plan. I knew exactly what Craig and David would recommend. As a physician who had become an alcoholic, David had gone through a secular treatment program and AA to find his sobriety. David believed the AA philosophy of "once an alcoholic, always an alcoholic." In addition, David thought everyone struggling should go through secular treatment and commit him or herself to regular attendance at AA. I dreaded going through a secular treatment center.

A Secular Treatment Program

Later when I met with Craig and David, my worst fears came true. They recommended I enter a secular treatment center. In their most convincing tone, they said it was my best option. I wasn't convinced, but I had no alternative options. I felt trapped. I would probably have to go, but already predicted that the treatment wouldn't do any good.

For the next few days, I prayed and searched the Scriptures. Surely God had an answer. I didn't need to go into a secular treatment center for 30 days. Another problem I faced was the cost. The treatment would involve a large sum of money, which we didn't have. My insurance didn't cover treatment for alcoholism. The men at the church assured me that they understood and promised to help financially.

Julia firmly opposed my going into the treatment center. Although she didn't like the financial burden, her main objection came from hearing the stories of other people. Through the Al-Anon program for family members of alcoholics, she heard about people going through the treatment program yet still drinking or leading miserable lives.

After a few days of prayer and Bible study, I was convinced that I didn't need to go into treatment. I would do whatever it took to stay close to the Lord and not drink. On a Wednesday

....

Somehow I believed the lie that I could live the Christian life through determination and resolve. If I just had enough commitment, then I could make it work.

....

morning, I met with our pastor. I presented my case with all the eloquence and force I could muster. He shared his doubts. For the last five years, Drew knew I had tried every other option. Nonetheless, he listened attentively but remained neutral. He didn't give his blessing nor completely reject the idea. Like everyone else, he wanted me to be free from alcohol. I left our meeting encouraged and determined to change my behavior.

Before sundown of that same day, I was thoroughly drunk. It was another classic example of "the spirit indeed is willing, but the flesh is weak" (Matt. 26:41, *KJV*). I was locked in bondage to alcohol. The Bible says, "The just shall live by faith" (Rom. 1:17, *KJV*). Somehow I believed the lie that I could live the Christian life through determination and resolve. If I just had enough commitment, then I could make it work.

After getting drunk that evening, I was completely undone. My good intentions hadn't even lasted through the daylight hours. I had absolutely no idea how to fix my problem. I decided to go to the secular treatment center. I called Craig and told him about my decision. "You've made the right decision, Mike," Craig assured me. Inside I felt as though I had received a death sentence. Now I couldn't deny it. I was a hopeless, helpless, incurable alcoholic who could never change. For me, the Christian life didn't work.

Maybe My Answer Was in a Secular Treatment Center

Craig drove me to the treatment center on a fall day in September 1984. As I checked in, I had to admit my "Christian" attempts simply hadn't worked. I determined to plunge into the program full force. I wanted it to work. The center had an interesting mixture of people: young men and women in their 30s hooked on cocaine; older men in their 50s and 60s who were hard-core alcoholics; doctors, lawyers, businessmen, laborers, housewives, students, retirees, as well as some people from wealthy families.

To my shock, I found a young man from our church who owned his own business. He was addicted to prescription drugs. We encouraged each other because we claimed to be "committed Christians." I felt mixed up about my identity. If I was a Christian, I was a pitiful excuse for one and had become an embarrassment to myself, my family and the church. My dreams about serving God and being a godly man had crashed.

The secular treatment center revolved around a program of unrelenting indoctrination. They wanted to convince me that I was "an alcoholic with a deadly disease and headed to certain devastation and eventual death or institutionalization." My only option was to follow their instructions.

To some people, nothing is more offensive than a recovered drunk. Just about every member of the staff was in this category. They believed in their program and used any means to project their message. They focused on reeducating each person about the dangers of alcohol and drugs. Finally, they wanted me to accept my alcoholism for life and then determine to work their program for the rest of my years. They used fear of the consequences of drinking as the principal motivation for their program to succeed. To the alcoholic, they presented no other choice.

Each day we watched many films and listened to a variety

of lectures and testimonies about the tragic consequences of alcohol and drugs. Each of these experiences was designed to break down any resistance from the patient. They wanted us to admit that our state was hopeless and incurable. Our only means for survival with alcohol or drugs was to never forget that we were and always would be alcoholics.

"Group therapy" was the cornerstone of this program. For about two hours each day, I met with a small group of men. This group was designed for us to admit our problems, then accept our condition as alcoholics. A trained therapist led these sessions and encouraged and practiced brutal confrontation. At times these sessions evolved into ugly discussions—definitely not pleasant or uplifting. I hated them.

Although honesty and openness about our problems is essential along with the need to accept responsibility, I believe to take people to the end of themselves is God's responsibility—not ours. Through group sessions, many men were brought to a state of brokenness. Unfortunately the staff gave these men nothing to replace the way they had found acceptance and worth for many years.

Because of the relentless pressure, eventually I admitted (at least I thought I did) that I was an alcoholic who had an incurable disease. I needed to deal with this "death sentence." In the program I became a model patient and worked with diligence. I avoided the label "recalcitrant" because they recommended that these patients stay an additional week or two. I wasn't interested in staying one minute longer than required.

When I left the treatment center, I was determined not to drink. Every day I tried to attend a meeting. I went to AA meetings and I also went to group therapy meetings for former patients of the treatment center. In less than two weeks, however, I was drunk again. Feeling worthless, I stopped AA and the group therapy meetings. I avoided contact with anyone. The pressure to stop drinking mounted, and in response I trouped off and got drunk. Afterward I wallowed in guilt, remorse and despair. The next day I was drinking again. My cycle continued.

One day Julia told me, "The kids will all be here for Christmas and I want them to enjoy being here. Let's just get through this holiday. I'm not going to try and deal with anything else right now." Somehow we made it through Christmas, but it was the worst one of my life. I was trying to survive without hope.

My Ultimatum from Julia

In January 1985, Julia presented an ultimatum. "I can't continue living this way for a day longer," she said. "If you ever drink again, you will have to leave." I agreed with Julia that something had to be done. Because drinking was my problem, I promised to leave if I ever drank again. Within a few days I had violated my promise—drunk again. We established one week as the time limit. I had seven days to locate another place to live.

Where would I go? One possibility was to move to an apartment on the south side of town and continue my life of drinking. If I lived alone and no one gave me a hard time, then I could drink as much as I wanted when I wanted. I didn't want that. Underneath, I yearned for freedom, but I had no idea how to find it.

In December, my grandmother had turned 105. Julia showed me an article in a Christian magazine that asked for stories about people in this age group. While reading the article I noticed an ad for Hebron Colony of Mercy, a Christian treatment center. I didn't know such places existed! I phoned and ask for information.

This particular center was temporarily without a director. They recommended another center nearby called Bethel Colony of Mercy. I phoned and talked with Mike Stewart, the director. The center had a 60-day program without a charge because it operated as a ministry. Part of the cost for the program was absorbed as residents worked for about six hours each day. During the mornings, they attended Bible study and listened to tapes by well-known evangelicals. They also worked through the *Navigator's Design for Discipleship* workbooks. Their overall program seemed solid.

I didn't have any other place to go. Here was another opportunity I hadn't tried. Perhaps it held my answer. Inside me, a small light of hope began to shine.

A Christian Treatment Center

About midnight on January 17, 1985, I boarded a Greyhound bus and rode throughout the night to Bethel Colony of Mercy in Lenoir, North Carolina. I was the only person on the bus so it gave me a lot of time for reflection.

Am I the same person who drove a fancy car and lived in a huge house that had a swimming pool? Did I really graduate from seminary and pastor a church? Was I the manager of a prestigious brokerage firm and a respected Christian businessman in Birmingham? My biggest problem was wrapped up in identity. For years I had tried to discover my identity in my performance and in many other places. My identity wasn't in Christ, but it would take more months for me to find my true identity.

At about 5:30 A.M., my bus pulled into Charlotte. I had a three-hour layover until another bus left for Lenoir. Because I had enjoyed the fast, jet-set lifestyle, I knew a bus wasn't the best way to travel. As I was waiting at the bus station, I was overcome with grief and remorse about my ruined life and destroyed marriage along with anything else worthwhile. I struggled to pray. In my eyes, the Lord probably wanted me to crawl off into a hole somewhere and die.

Finally my bus pulled into Lenoir during the middle of the morning. The town didn't have an official bus station. Instead, people were dropped off at an old gas station. At a pay phone, I called Bethel and learned I would need to wait a few more hours to be picked up. The center's only truck was out on another errand.

I ordered a sandwich at a nearby drugstore lunch counter. I left my belongings at the gas station and wondered if it was safe but didn't care. Finally around 2:00 P.M., two men arrived. They were both in the Bethel program. Picking me up was a part of their job. A normal treatment program lasted two months, but I learned that these men had been there a lot longer.

Why would anyone stay longer than the required time?, I wondered. From my perspective, two months sounded like an eternity. As I rode with the men, I thought, *I'll be out of here when my time is up.*

These two men were among the most trusted in the program. They had been given the most responsible job: to drive a vehicle and pick up materials. Besides me, they were the only two who hadn't lost their driver's licenses. These old-timers filled me in on the place, the staff, the food and the other men. They talked with the characteristic cynicism and biting sarcasm that only drunks and addicts seem to master. After they picked me up they had more errands left to accomplish. About four in the afternoon, we made it to Bethel. After traveling for 16 hours, I felt physically and emotionally exhausted and completely depressed.

Located on a few acres outside of town, Bethel was surrounded by lower-middle-class neighborhoods. The property comprised three buildings. The dormitory consisted of 10 rooms, housed two people per room, and one communal bathroom for showers, commodes and sinks. It was definitely not the Hilton! The second building was an old house that had been converted into a dining room and some staff offices. The staff included a director and his assistant. The final building (also an old house) included a meeting room for morning Bible studies and for watching a little TV during the evenings. Because I arrived late on Friday, it would be Monday morning until I would meet with the director for my intake interview.

During that first weekend, I met most of the men. None of this motley bunch were still married; all of their wives had left them. Many had come straight off the streets and many of them had criminal records. As I looked around, I saw a tough group of guys. Why were they at Bethel?

Many of them were exactly like me—they didn't have any other place to go. Later I learned many of these men entered the program to escape the cold January weather. Some days I wondered, *What am I doing here?* Usually my self-esteem was so broken that I believed "This is where I belong."

On Monday morning I met Mike Stewart, the director, for my intake interview. He was a graduate of Columbia Bible College and Seminary and I had more in common with him than anyone else there. Mike took an interest in me. My seminary training and time in the ministry caught his attention. I begged Mike, "Please don't tell anyone else that I have been a pastor." In my own way, I was trying to fit into the program.

When he broached the possibility that I could return to a ministry in the future, I couldn't even talk about it. The whole idea was too painful. I had sunk too low to return to a ministry. God was finished with me. In my mind, I couldn't be of any use to God or anyone else in the future. At the time, it seemed like Mike cracked a cruel joke.

When I completed my sordid story of failure, the interview had ended. Mike assigned me to manage the laundry room. It contained one washing machine and one dryer. I would wash and dry clothes for these 20 alcoholics, addicts, street persons and chronic offenders. For the next two months, I became a part of this group. Many of them came into the program carrying a plastic bag full of the filthiest, most soiled clothes I had ever seen. These clothes had not been washed for months. Washing filthy clothes seemed an appropriate task for me.

Bethel became a place of refuge, retreat and renewed hope. I plunged headlong into the program. I worked the discipleship workbooks and attacked my job of washing and drying the clothes. The Bible studies were meaningful along with my times of counseling with Mike and the assistant director, Don Loss. Mainly, I received renewed hope that God had an answer for me. For the first time in many months, I began to experience a little peace and joy.

I also renewed a commitment to my marriage at Bethel. Having a new sense of determination, I wanted to make my marriage work regardless of what it took. Counseling sessions with Don and Mike challenged me to take responsibility for my failure as a husband. I'd never made my marriage a priority. In a fresh sense, I began to appreciate my wonderful wife. In letters to Julia, I began to tell her about my growth and feelings for her and our marriage. Julia was reluctant to be encouraged. I couldn't blame her.

Many times I had built up Julia's hopes, then each time I crushed them. Though sometimes we talked on the phone, Julia refused to write or visit or express her love for me. It hurt me deeply, but I understood.

After I had been in the program for five weeks, on Valentine's Day, February 14, 1985, I received a package from Julia. She had baked some chocolate chip cookies and included a short note, which said, "I love you, will you be my valentine?" I was ecstatic—there was hope for our marriage. For the first time in many months, she said she loved me. My two months at Bethel were well worth it. Throughout the rest of my time in this program, I looked forward to going back and being with my wife. Maybe we could start over again.

Julia's Perspective

Editor's note: Mike Quarles tried a gamut of treatments to escape alcoholism. As he tried these different options, what was going on in the mind of his wife, Julia? This is her story about this same period in their lives.

The move back to Birmingham in June 1980 seemed like the best one we had made. For the first time, we moved into a new house and I enjoyed decorating it. Randy and Audrey, Mike's children from his first marriage, came to spend the summer with us. Mike hired Randy and Bradley to landscape our front yard, which was nothing but red clay. They worked hard all summer planting trees and shrubs. The weather was sweltering and the temperature rose to the low 100s every day. They got up early to begin work.

Audrey spent her day keeping her brothers supplied with water and lemonade. Late in the afternoon, they went to the pool or played tennis. Now that Mike was no longer a pastor, his critical attitude of me and the children changed. It was a good summer for us as a family.

When the kids went back to school, Mike began coming home very late some evenings. He would be irritable and hostile. *The change from ministry to business is just getting to him,* I thought. Every now and then, however, when Mike walked into the house it seemed as though he had been drinking. I thought, *I must be going crazy to think that Mike is drunk.*

For about a year and a half, we lived in confusion and stress. He would come home drunk. The next morning, Mike would apologize and promise it would never happen again. I believed him—then in a few weeks he would drink again. His guilt and remorse ate at my heart. Finally I realized he couldn't quit on his own. The drinking controlled him. I was scared and didn't know what to do.

Mike rarely drank on weekends and we would have a good time together. I began to think the problem had ended, but then many Monday nights he didn't come home until the middle of the night. Although Mike didn't drink often, I lived on eggshells trying to prevent it. He was usually able to control it when Bradley was at home or if Randy and Audrey were visiting us during the holidays. Mike didn't drink during these times, but was short-tempered and unpleasant to be around. It was like living with Jekyll and Hyde.

When we realized the extent of the problem, Mike began trying to get help. Both of us were willing to try anything. Each day, I assured Mike of my love and commitment. I bent over backwards to keep Mike from having any reason to get mad at me. I didn't fight back. I overlooked his irresponsibility and neglect. Then I stuffed my feelings deep inside. For my way of thinking, I was being the kind of godly wife described in Proverbs 31. I tried to admire him and respect him and build him up, but nothing seemed to help Mike.

As Mike continued to get drunk, I didn't respect myself for my actions or for what I was enduring. I tried anticipating Mike's desires and to meet his every demand. It was like trying to fill a bottomless bucket.

One day Mike decided he could control his drinking if he didn't drive. He handed me his car keys, "Julia, will you drive me to work in the mornings and pick me up about five o'clock every evening?" I agreed to try it. The first few days were fine. Then one afternoon, when I arrived at Mike's office, he wasn't there. Hiding my embarrassment, I tried to casually inquire about his whereabouts from his secretary.

"I don't know where Mike went," she said. "I'll ask some of the other brokers." No one knew where Mike had gone. My insides began to tremble. I didn't want to arouse any suspicions so I casually said, "Oh yeah, I forgot. He told me he had a meeting after work. Sorry I bothered ya'll. Bye!"

I quickly walked out and got into my car before I broke into tears. Where was Mike? How embarrassing for me to show up at his office when he wasn't there! Why hadn't he called and told me not to come? I felt hurt and mad! I wanted to look for him but had no idea where to begin my search. Home was my safe place. I wanted to be there but didn't like being there alone. I feared that one day I would receive a phone call and learn that Mike had done something horrible such as kill someone while he was driving drunk. My imagination worked overtime during such times. Back then I didn't understand how Satan works in our minds and gives us thoughts we think are our own. I was at the enemy's mercy.

Somehow I pulled through those empty and lonely hours. Finally I lay down on the bed in our guest room. When I heard a car pull up in our driveway I was sleeping fitfully. Through the curtains, I saw Mike climb out of a small but obviously expensive convertible sports car. He was drunk again! I was furious!

Had Mike gone crazy? Where did he get that car? Despite my questions, I didn't want to see him. I locked the door of the guest room and tried to get some sleep. At least Mike had arrived home safely, once again, and hadn't killed anyone.

The next morning Mike sheepishly told me, "I decided to leave the office early and go out to get just one or two drinks. I called a cab at the office and it took me to a dealership. I took that car out on approval."

"How could you have done such a thing?", I screamed. "What if you had wrecked that car? Don't you ever consider the consequences of your actions?" Then I turned ballistic and confronted Mike about his selfish actions. "Do you ever think about how your drinking affects me? No, you don't! All you think about is yourself and what you want." The idea marked another failure. Mike was so ashamed of his actions that he just listened to my angry criticism.

People with Whom I Identified—Al-Anon
I constantly searched for the solution to our problem. I made appointments with every guest speaker who came to town and focused on marriage or the family. Every single speaker had the same advice for me.

"Your husband has a disease," the person said. "He can't help it and you've just got to accept it." Then the person suggested I go to Al-Anon, which was designed for family members of alcoholics, to learn from others how to live with my situation. Al-Anon didn't sound like a Christian organization.

Surely my answer wasn't outside the church. The repetitive advice finally made me give in. I called our pastor, Drew, and he gave my name to two other wives in our church. He knew these women were active in Al-Anon. One of them invited me to attend a meeting.

The Monday night meeting was held in a church not too far from my home. I felt nervous about walking into the meeting but the people were friendly. To my surprise, I saw several people I already knew. I learned that Al-Anon meetings were coordinated at the same time as an AA meeting in a nearby room.

About 50 people attended, who were mostly women. They represented a broad spectrum of ages and races. As I listened to their stories, I learned they too were living—or had lived—in this insanity of alcoholism. I wasn't the only one! Each one seemed free to say anything about feelings or situations. They encouraged each other and accepted each other. I felt like pinching myself to see if I was awake. This was exactly the kind of meeting I had been trying to find. Although the meeting was held in a church, it wasn't like any Bible study or prayer group I knew. These people understood my misery and uncertainty.

I discovered that Al-Anon had a meeting somewhere every night of the week. I picked up a schedule for our section of town. Meetings were also held on Friday, Saturday and Sunday mornings. I began attending different ones. Each session followed the same format in the Al-Anon handbook. In each one, the number of people and atmosphere was different. In most meetings the room was filled with smoke. Because I have asthma, I could hardly breathe sometimes. (Some parts of the country now advertise smoke-free meetings.) During the meetings, these people talked about God, but they defined God as whoever or whatever you thought he was. They were not talking about the God of the Bible. Each one's view was respected and I decided that because I knew God as my heavenly Father He could take care of me at these meetings.

During some meetings I heard more foul language than I had ever heard in my life, including from women. It made me realize I had lived a sheltered life. Though it was difficult for me to admit, at this time in my life I had more in common with these people than my Bible study or home fellowship group. At these meetings, I didn't have to be an actress. Also I knew whatever I said would not be repeated outside the meeting. Slowly I became an active participant in Al-Anon. I found several Christians and even some neighbors and became friends with them. (Now many Christian groups that use the 12-step program offer meetings in which foul language and smoking are not acceptable.)

Occasionally, Alcoholics Anonymous sponsored an "open meeting" combined with the people in Al-Anon. Someone always told a "story" about becoming sober. I loved hearing those stories; however, I heard more about the drinking world than I ever imagined or wanted to hear. I decided greater involvement with Mike would show my seriousness about helping him. Sometimes we attended a meeting together and I enjoyed those times. But Mike didn't last long attending with me. Soon I returned to going on my own. Sometimes before the Monday evening meetings I met some of the people at a cafeteria for dinner. I made lunch appointments with other women or just went for coffee to their homes for friendship. To me, it opened a new world of people who understood this insane life.

It upset me when I heard spouses talk about mates who had been sober for years, but who were still miserable and it was difficult to live with them. These mates still wanted a drink. I wanted Mike to be sober, but I wanted more than that. I wanted him sober *and free*. At some point, I determined if Mike would become sober—and AA had a great record at helping people become sober—then God could work to get Mike free. I would just take one step at a time. For now, Mike's sobriety was *my goal*.

During this time I was discouraged to learn about mates, children or parents who had gone to a local long-term, secular treatment center. Many people were still drinking or they were sober, but were miserable and living with them was difficult. These centers were expensive and no one in Al-Anon recommended them. I learned the success rate at these centers was low. AA had a much better track record, and was free. "Those who will attend 100 meetings in a row," they said with confidence, "will get sober and will stay sober." This 100-meeting mark became *my goal for Mike*.

My frustration would build when Mike wouldn't attend a meeting with me. Other times he would try to string a bunch of meetings together, then wouldn't come home one night. Mike never cooperated with my plan for him. Should I give up? How could I? Our life was falling apart and I had to hold it together! Finally I decided to attend Al-Anon whether or not he went to AA.

Mike diligently sought God for an answer and didn't give up his search. He decided that his answer wasn't AA so he looked elsewhere. Inside, I knew Mike didn't want this way of life any more than I did. He was really trying to find what would work to make him quit.

Sometimes I prayed, "When are you going to help us God? What is Your secret for sobriety and peace? Why does it seem to elude us?" The heavens seemed silent.

For a couple of years I went to Al-Anon. We always introduced ourselves saying, "I'm (Julia) and I'm a co-alcoholic." I didn't like saying that. Instead I wanted to say, "I'm Julia and I'm a Christian who is married to an alcoholic." But I carried on with the program. Sometimes I sat there thinking, *Well God, is this the mission field you have for me?* I hoped not. Would I have to attend these meetings for the rest of my life? I immediately threw the thought out of my mind. Nonetheless, this seemed like the only place to get help while I lived through this nightmare. I am thankful for the friends I gained during this time, and for a place to go where I could be honest.

Was Mike a Christian Alcoholic?

Can a person behave like this and still be a Christian? I wondered. Maybe that was Mike's problem; maybe he really wasn't saved. One morning I had a cup of coffee as I talked with my friend from Bible study, CeCe. It felt safe to talk about things with CeCe. I knew she wouldn't condemn me or Mike.

"Yes, Christians can behave this ungodly," she assured me. "But Mike's remorse is a good indication that he's saved." As we talked, I admitted that through Al-Anon I had met many wives whose husbands didn't have any remorse about their behavior. Mike's remorse and guilt seemed to eat him alive. It was hard for me to admit he was a Christian, whether he acted like one or not. Why didn't God stop this madness?

One day Mike and I learned about Ralph, a minister from Florida who worked with many alcoholics. Mike called Ralph and told him about our situation. He said he would be passing through Birmingham soon during a trip to Tennessee. "Could you stop by and counsel us?" Mike asked.

"I'll consider it only if you'll be sober for the week before I come," Ralph said. Then he added another condition to his visit, "And you'll have to follow my instructions exactly." We agreed to these conditions.

"And there are consequences if you do drink, Mike," Ralph said. "If for some reason you break the promise and drink before I come, then Julia will move out of the house." Mike agreed to this condition.

This will work, I thought. *Surely Mike won't drink knowing I'll be moving out.* I also agreed to the terms.

A few nights before Ralph arrived, Mike didn't come home. I was devastated. This was awful! Would I have to move out of my own house? This was crazy! I wasn't causing our problems. Couldn't he control it for one week? My determination grew. It was his problem so he would have to move out.

The next day, Mike called Ralph and told him what had happened. He strongly advised me to move out. "And Mike, I won't be stopping by to see you." Both of us felt ashamed and abandoned by Ralph and by God. Who could help us? We felt sorry for each other and for ourselves.

At the time, the term "co-dependency" didn't mean anything to me, but it fit our situation exactly.

My Cover-Up

For me it was important to cover up Mike's alcoholic lifestyle. I wanted Mike's business to succeed. If Mike lost his job or clients, I was afraid of losing our house. In my eyes, I should have been awarded a trophy for "Best Actress" in Birmingham. Alone I attended supper-club dinners. Other times when we were hardly speaking and I had to go to a family member's house, I created excuses for Mike.

When our son Bradley came home from Auburn University during the weekends or holidays, I tried to hide the problem. Usually Bradley asked, "Mom, what's wrong here? What's going on?" I left out any specifics when I talked with Bradley. Instead I explained Mike and I were having a "little problem" but we were working on it. I could see in his face that Bradley didn't believe me, but what else could he do? Mike never drank when Bradley was there. There was no way for Bradley to believe or understand Mike had a drinking problem.

When Mike's kids, Randy and Audrey, came for Christmas, Mike made a real effort at coming home every night. Then one night, he didn't make it. I concocted some excuse for him, then tried to act as though everything was all right. Inside I was very upset. It was hypocritical and I hated the deception. I worried that they would ask me a direct question about Mike's drinking. I wouldn't have lied, but I didn't want to tell them their Dad was an alcoholic. I maintained a gentle balance between doing or saying anything so Mike would not lose their respect, and I wanted to discourage them from following his alcoholic example. My life was full of deception and I hated myself for doing it. I felt trapped.

My Foolish Attempts to Help Mike

To help Mike stop drinking became my obsession, and I did some foolish things. One day I came out of the grocery store and noticed Mike's car parked in front of the liquor store next door. Quickly I locked my car and got into the front seat of his car. When Mike came out of the liquor store and saw me, he was furious.

"Get out of my car, Julia," he demanded. I refused, so Mike took off and drove around town recklessly to frighten me. Although I was terrified, I tried not to let it show. I begged him to take his beer home and drink there. I was afraid Mike would drive around drunk and kill someone.

Finally Mike agreed and returned home. Later I learned how horrible it was for him to get drunk at home when he didn't want to be there. Mike changed into a completely different person—not the same man I knew and loved. I fled the situation and locked myself in our guest room.

Another afternoon Mike had left to play tennis at our country club. On the spur of the moment, I decided to meet him afterward and eat dinner. When I arrived at the club, his car was parked near the clubhouse door. Mike was coming out with a six-pack of beer. When he looked up and saw me, Mike jumped into his car and took off. I chased him in my car trying to catch him. On a two-lane road full of curves, we drove about 80 miles an hour. As I drove, I screamed at God to help me and protect us. I wanted God to stop him. Finally Mike lost me and I drove home in a hysterical condition. I couldn't believe I had risked my life by driving so recklessly to catch him. Here I was sober and Mike was drunk, but I acted just as crazy. Maybe both our lives were out of control!

On yet another evening, I decided to go looking for Mike. From his canceled checks, I knew which bars he often frequented. Located on the south side of town, I drove to the area. Although frightened, I was determined to bring Mike home. I found his car parked on a nearby street. I moved it to the next block into a parking lot behind a store.

Because I had Mike's transportation in my control, I entered a bar. Immediately I felt out of place. Everyone stared at me as though I had just arrived from Mars. Then Mike saw me and said, "Get out of here!"

He took off running—and I ran after him. Wildly we weaved through people on the sidewalk, until finally he ducked into another bar and lost me. I burst into tears. I felt like a fool.

Slowly I walked down the sidewalk as I was crying. Then I looked around me and noticed the party atmosphere and the people who had been drinking. I was frightened. Locating a pay phone on the corner, I called a friend from Al-Anon. After telling her where I was and what I was doing, I asked her to pray for my safety. Instead, this friend talked me into coming to her house for the night. Then I wouldn't have to return home feeling upset. The whole scene was insane.

Through these four years, I had to unlearn much of what I had taught and had been taught, particularly about the role of a godly wife. Wrongly, I believed that through godly behavior I could bring someone out of such a bondage. Through trial and error, I discovered that most of my actions only perpetuated the problem. Because of my commitment to the marriage, I believed I had to tolerate any kind of treatment and behavior. Unknown to me at that time, God in His love didn't expect me to put up with Mike's irresponsibility and sinful behavior.

On an Endless Merry-Go-Round
Toward the end of the fourth year, I prayed that I could keep up my "acting" and we could get through the summer. Bradley was graduating from Auburn University in June. He was engaged to Susan, his high school sweetheart from Atlanta and they planned a big wedding in July. The wedding fulfilled one of my dreams and I wanted to enjoy all the festivities. Again and again, I begged God not to let anything horrible happen to Mike or me that would remove our joy during this time. God was faithful and everything went smoothly.

The next month my acting came to an end. Mike was called to meet with the discipline committee at our church. They sent him to a secular treatment center. For a long time, I opposed this treatment because of the enormous cost and because of its awful recovery record. Nevertheless, he went. When Mike was gone, it was difficult for me. I felt forsaken by the people at the church who knew he was there. None of them ever called to encourage me or check on me. I threw myself into the program in any way possible and tried to make it work. I attended "family week" with Mike and learned about expectations for me.

When Mike came home, we attended the daily follow-up meetings. Quickly Mike tired of these sessions. Within two weeks of coming home, my worst fears came true. Mike drank again. Seven thousand dollars washed down the drain! I had told them it wouldn't work!

After Mike's drunken spree, I ran out of energy and initiative to encourage him. My Super Woman role began to crumble. I began to feel as though I was on an endless merry-go-round and couldn't escape. My friends at Al-Anon assured me that I could get off, but I had to make the decision for myself. I hated to give up; Mike and I had been through so much. Would this mean I was giving up on God? I would never do that. The Lord was my life.

I finally faced up to the reality that my entire life was headed in a negative direction. I was worn out physically, confused spiritually and exhausted emotionally. We lived on the verge of bankruptcy. Divorce hadn't been an option, but despite my commitment to the marriage, I couldn't live like this much longer. I needed to decide how to salvage myself while I still could. *Bradley, Randy and Audrey need at least one parent who is sane for them*, I thought. Some day there would be grandchildren and I wanted to enjoy them. I *couldn't* decide for Mike, but I *could* decide for Julia.

As I carefully considered it all, I faced the possibility of losing our house, living in a small apartment and working full-time. Every one of those hurdles for daily life looked better than my current level of stress and uncertainty. Maybe Mike would have to be on the streets, but I gave up trying to stop the inevitable. My own efforts during these years hadn't helped. I struggled and wanted to give up. Finally I told God, "Mike is Your problem, Lord. I want to concentrate on salvaging my life." Unknown to me, God had been waiting for me to reach this point for a long time.

After another night of Mike's drinking, through my tears I said, "I love you Mike, but I've made this decision for my good and for our children. We've run out of possibilities. I won't be there for you, to cook your good meals, clean your clothes or to carry on your responsibilities." Then I presented an ultimatum. If he drank again, he would have to move out. I didn't plan on divorce, but for now a separation. Mike looked so understanding that it almost broke my heart. Again he assured me he was trying to stop. I believed his words, but he didn't know how to end his horrible addiction.

"I will honor your decision," he said.

That Friday night Mike didn't come home. By that time, my tears were all cried out. Around nine o'clock, I called a nearby friend who knew about our situation. I asked her if I could come spend the night. Without asking any questions, she told me to come right to her house.

The next morning, I stayed with her until almost noon. I tried to put off the inevitable. When I arrived at our home, Mike sat at the kitchen table. His face was sad, and he looked up and said, "I know what you're going to say; I'll leave." "I'll give you a few days to find a place, then you'll have to go," I said.

That day, Kay and Walter called and invited us for dinner. Even when things were bad, they often invited us to their place. I told Kay things were the worst ever between us. She said, "Julia, you've still got to eat. Ya'll come on over."

During dinner, Kay and Walter acted as though nothing was wrong, but we told them what we were facing. They helped us through our first night of this new agony.

Within a few days, Mike learned about Bethel Colony. He packed his bags to go there. Then our friends Jack and June called to suggest that we come to Atlanta and stay for a couple of days. Jack offered to take Mike to the bus station for the midnight bus to Bethel. It helped just being around their love and acceptance for a few days.

The night Mike was going to leave we went out for ice cream after dinner. With a heavy heart, I told Mike, "I don't want you to call or write me during these 60 days." In my mind, our marriage had ended.

My New Life
The next day I felt as though Mike had died. It was the death of our marriage and everything I had tried to hold together for eleven and a half years. I couldn't do anything else for Mike. Instead I tried to face reality and get on with my own life. June took me out for lunch and then to get my hair done.

The next day I drove back to Birmingham for my new life—alone. I looked forward to the peace, quiet and lack of stress. Again and again I quoted, "Be content with what you have, because God has said, 'Never will I leave you; never will I forsake you'...'The Lord is my helper; I will not be afraid. What can man do to me?'" (Heb. 13:5,6, *NIV*). Those words from Scripture gave me strength for the days ahead.

Each evening I came home from work, built a fire and settled down in my chair near the fireplace. After years of thinking God must not like me because He let my marriage be so awful, I needed to sit and think about my relationship with God. I had tried hard to please Him. All I wanted to do now was imagine myself sitting in His lap, having His arms around me and holding me. It was hard to believe that He loved me, but I needed to believe that He did—just because the Bible said so.

I began to face some issues in my life that had been overlooked. Most of our focus had been on Mike and his drinking problems. Compared to Mike's issues, mine didn't look so bad, but God lovingly showed me His concern about my heart, which held a lot of anger, hate, bitterness and envy. Although these feelings might have been backed by good reasons, God showed me they could destroy me if they went unacknowledged and unforgiven. As I faced them and agonized about them, I began to ask God to make me able to forgive Mike.

Those days were wonderful. God slowly changed my heart. Instead of slamming down the phone when Mike called, I began talking with him. I could tell God was also working in his life. Finally I took a big step and decided to send him a valentine. I wanted to let Mike know I was beginning to be willing to start over with him again.

As I made a conscious choice to forgive Mike, I found a new sense of enjoyment for my life. I realized I could trust God and know He was in control. Mike was God's problem, not mine. It freed me from being the controller and being a victim of my past.

Jack and June offered to take me to visit Mike. I was nervous about seeing him, but he was very different. Mike was interested in me and laughed and seemed more easygoing. He didn't complain about where he was and the people who lived with him. I respected Mike's attitude in that situation. God had to be changing him for this to be happening. The four of us had a lot of fun together that weekend. It made me anticipate Mike's homecoming in a few weeks.

The Sentence of Death

We were under great pressure, far beyond
our ability to endure, so that we despaired
even of life. Indeed, in our hearts we felt the
sentence of death. But this happened that
we might not rely on ourselves but on
God, who raises the dead.
—2 Corinthians 1:8,9 (NIV)

When I returned to Birmingham in March from the treatment program at Bethel, I felt encouraged that God had worked in my life. Now I could continue a normal life with my wife and *not* drink. Because I had worked through several issues, I felt better about myself. I was beginning to understand repentance—a missing aspect in my life. I saw myself as "the problem" and took responsibility for myself and my failures. In a fresh sense, I made a commitment to my wife and my marriage, which felt good. I believed my answer was through God. He would enable me to live a life of freedom—without alcohol.

A Ministry—Again

Going home, my first order of business was my job situation. In the middle of the worst of my drinking times, I had changed brokerage firms from E. F. Hutton to Morgan Keegan. I thought the change of scenery would help and that I could escape my management responsibilities at Hutton. Instead, the opposite happened. My business fell sharply and my drinking escalated. I had worked for the new company for less than a year and three of those months I had been in two different treatment centers. The management at Morgan Keegan was not impressed.

When I returned from Bethel, my boss and I met for breakfast. He told me, "Mike, the firm has given up on you and we no longer need your services." I wasn't surprised because I had heard rumors from my colleagues that I would lose my job. My years in the brokerage business had worn on me. I was ready for a complete change, but what? I had no idea and was afraid to try anything different. I checked with some other brokerage companies and J. C. Bradford was willing to give me a chance.

I lasted less than four months at the Bradford firm. I had no enthusiasm or energy for the brokerage business. As my clientele observed my whirl through two treatment centers and three brokerage firms in less than a year, my business was completely decimated. I had no heart to solicit new clients. I couldn't even pick up the phone and call anyone. When you can't pick up the phone in the brokerage business, you are out of business. I had no option but to face the facts and leave. I probably would have never left on my own, but now I had no choice. For the next three months, I took a stab at financial planning, but it was similar to the brokerage business. I put little energy and enthusiasm into the business so I didn't make any money.

During this period of struggling with my job, I didn't return to alcohol. Instead, I began to have a ministry with other alcoholics and addicts. People saw a change in me and began coming to talk with me. This counseling role began to take a lot of my time and matched my interests. I had wanted to be in ministry again for many years because I believed I had something to offer.

My brother-in-law Dan worked with a friendship evangelism ministry called New Life, headquartered in Knoxville, Tennessee. Dan was the only staff member in Birmingham so he suggested I work with him and pursue my ministry to alcoholics and addicts. The board of directors approved the position.

One of the benefits of this job was working near Julia. She worked as the secretary and for the first time we worked in the same office. Since God had dealt with me at Bethel and I had made a commitment to Julia and our marriage, our relationship had greatly improved. It wasn't perfect, but both of us had renewed hope in the marriage and in each other. Each of us was making a concerted effort to make it work. As we did, it began to bring results and we began to think we were on the right track.

In the fall, I joined New Life and began a biblical, Christ-centered ministry to alcoholics, addicts and their families. Through my experiences, I knew Christ-centered help for these people was virtually unavailable. In a short time, ministry filled my days. My main help was letting people know a "Christian alternative" to the secular approach. The bulk of my activities consisted of counseling and sending people to Christian treatment centers. In the next three years I sent more than a hundred people to Christian treatment centers.

I loved returning to ministry and helping people, but something was still missing. Often in my thought life I would be overcome with strong feelings of guilt or insecurity. Many days I felt convinced of my failure and doubted I could help anyone. I sat at my desk or drove around aimlessly. Finally the inevitable happened. On one of these days I had the urge to take a drink or two. It would take the edge off my nerves. I gave in to the overpowering urge, but decided to drink only three beers. I didn't get drunk, but I was overwhelmed with guilt. How could I minister freedom to people struggling with addictions if I wasn't free?

I hid the experience from Julia and no one else knew about it. I resolved it wouldn't happen again, but I had opened the door to alcohol. Every month or so I repeated the secret pattern. I didn't go to the bars because someone might have recognized me. Instead I drove around in my car and drank. Sometimes I parked somewhere and drank. Each time I promised myself and God, "This will never happen again." But it always did.

The Drunken Counselor to Alcoholics

Finally I got so drunk one night that I couldn't hide it from Julia and Dan. Both were extremely understanding. They encouraged me to deal with the problem, yet continue in my ministry because it seemed to help many people. I wanted to continue my ministry, but more than anything I desperately wanted to be free. Would I ever be free? Others were looking to me for the answers. Where was my answer?

One afternoon I noticed a copy of *The Wittenberg Door* on Dan's desk. *The Wittenberg Door* is the Christian's counterpart to *Mad* comic books or the *Far Side* comic strip. It pokes irreverent fun at many things the evangelical community considers sacred. This particular issue included an interview with a Catholic priest named Brennan Manning. Manning had been an alcoholic at one time. I began to read the article. I didn't agree with everything Manning said, but to me, he presented a fresh concept of God. It bowled me over as he portrayed God's unconditional love and acceptance of us. Throughout the 16 years of my Christian life, I viewed myself as a dirty, rotten, guilty sinner who needed to shape up. I believed God was getting sick and tired of me and my antics. No one had taught me anything different.

Now Manning had the audacity to say that our performance doesn't affect God's love for us. No matter what we do, God accepts us and loves us unconditionally. Manning wrote:

> The only lasting freedom from self-consciousness comes from a profound awareness that God loves me as I am, not as I should be. He loves me beyond worthiness and unworthiness, beyond fidelity and

infidelity, He loves me in the morning sun and the evening rain without caution, regret, boundary, limit or breaking point; that no matter what I do, He can't stop loving me. When I am really in conscious communion with the reality of the wild, passionate, relentless, stubborn, pursuing, tender love of God in Jesus Christ for me, then it's not that I've got to or I must or I should or I ought; suddenly I want to change because I know how deeply I am loved.[1]

The words flowed like pure water poured out on a man dying of thirst in a dry, parched desert wasteland. I drank them in and God's love penetrated into the depths of my being. God was *for* me—not against me. The issue wasn't about my changing to gain God's love and acceptance. Instead God loved me so I could change. Manning said, "The biggest

....

As my concept of God began to heal, my relationship with the heavenly Father took on a new dimension. Instead of viewing myself as a slave trying to perform for God, I saw myself as a dearly loved son.

....

mistake we can make is to say to God, 'Lord, if I change, you'll love me, won't you?' The Lord's reply is always, 'Wait a minute, you've got it all wrong. You don't have to change so I'll love you; I love you so you'll change.'" Deep within me, these words rang true.

I couldn't sit still. I walked around the building silently praising God with a song of worship in my heart. Through the years of my Christian experience, I had heard about God's unconditional love and acceptance—through reading and teaching others about it. But for me, this day marked my first opportunity to understand and experience it firsthand.

Like Mark Maulding, my friend at Grace Ministries, says, "If someone tells my wife that I love and accept her, that is all well and good; but if I tell her I love and accept her, it's altogether different; it gets through to her and makes contact." God had made contact with me. I felt unconditionally loved and completely accepted—without any dependence on my actions. An article in *The Wittenberg Door* introduced me to God's grace and I took an essential step toward true freedom.

As my concept of God began to heal, my relationship with the heavenly Father took on a new dimension. Instead of viewing myself as a slave trying to perform for God, I saw myself as a dearly loved son. Almost all of the defeated Christians I've met and counseled see themselves as slaves to God. They don't view God as a loving heavenly Father who accepts them with all their faults. Many have a wrong concept of God and see Him as a:

- Stern taskmaster;
- Harsh judge;
- Disapproving boss;
- Distant ruler.

Manning is correct when he says, "The single most important need today is the healing of our image of God. So many of us have images of God that fill us with fear, anxiety, and apprehension. But Paul says in Romans, 'The Spirit you have received is not a Spirit of slavery leading you to fear, but a Spirit of Adoption that allows you to cry out Abba [Daddy] Father.' It is true that we make our images of God. It is even truer that our images of God make us."[2]

If the answer is found through our relationship with God, how will we ever come to God and receive it when we see Him as disapproving or unaccepting? We cannot bond with someone who is unapproachable.

Learning About God's Unconditional Love

During this period, Julia and I left the large evangelical church where we had been members since becoming Christians. We joined a smaller neighborhood church in the same denomination. At this church, we met Charlie and Ruth Jones and immediately we became close friends. At the same time, all four of us were learning about God's unconditional love and accepting grace. For many hours, we sat and talked about the changes in our approaches to life. Through a set of audiotapes, Charlie and Ruth introduced us to Dr. Jack Miller, a Presbyterian pastor from Pennsylvania. Dr. Miller taught about God's grace and the practical outworkings of it for the Christian, things I had not heard before. I devoured a set of Dr. Miller's tapes that taught through Galatians.

As I listened to these tapes, I clearly caught the concept from Galatians that as Christians we are dead to the law and can live under grace. Throughout my Christian life, I had read and heard this truth, but now I began to understand it. Because I was released from a life under the law, it released me from a performance treadmill. It startled me to learn that I had been living in the barren wasteland of legalism my entire Christian life. Besides living under this legalism for myself, I had imposed it on everyone else around me—my wife, my children, the congregations where I pastored and my friends. It shocked me to realize my wrong beliefs about God and Christianity.

Almost immediately I wrote to each of my three children to confess that I had been a harsh, unloving, legalistic father. I confessed that I had given them the wrong idea about Christianity and God.

Surely this is the missing piece in my life and what I need for freedom and completion of my Christian life, I thought. Although this truth was a major puzzle piece, I still wasn't free of my alcohol problem. I didn't drink every week and sometimes I lasted months without a drop, but inside, I knew that sooner or later when the pressure built up I would turn to the only thing I knew would relieve it. These binges tore down everything I had tried to put back together.

The majority of alcoholics don't drink every day. In my case and in many others, the drunken binges are periodic, but sufficient to disrupt a person's whole life. Although I understood

God's love and acceptance despite my actions, it didn't take care of my low self-esteem and life-controlling problem. Underneath the veneer, I was the same old person who couldn't quite get it together.

Where were the answers for my alcoholism—or was I doomed to bondage for the rest of my life? Maybe I would have to be satisfied with the knowledge that despite my failures, I was loved and forgiven and one day going to heaven. Other Christians told me that I'd have to be satisfied with this knowledge. I continued to search for a more fulfilling answer.

Depressed and Sitting in a Chair for Weeks

All the stress occurring in our lives made Julia feel the need to get away for a few days. She left to visit her best friend, Rachel Sugg, in Dothan, Alabama. One afternoon while Julia was gone, I stopped on the way home from the office and fell into my old pattern—I had a beer or two. Many beers and hours later, I drove home in the early hours of the morning. I had been drinking the entire night. This was the first time I had stayed out all night. I was an ordained Presbyterian minister who had a ministry to alcoholics and addicts and I was trapped in the same bondage as the people I counseled. I felt like the world's biggest hypocrite!

For the next few hours, I slept fitfully. Then I got up full of remorse and self-loathing. Something had to be done and I knew my next step. First I would notify Presbytery, confess everything, then be kicked out. Next I would call the ministry where I was working, confess everything and resign. Finally I planned to call the little Presbyterian church where I preached on Sundays, confess to them and resign. I couldn't continue living this way. Maybe I needed to make a full confession and be purged.

That morning, I telephoned Julia in Dothan and confessed to her. "I'm going to resign everything," I told her.

She got upset. "Mike, please don't do anything impulsive. Wait until I get home and we can talk it over," she said. But her words fell on deaf ears. I had made up my mind. I hung up the phone, then made my various calls, completed the confessions and resignations.

Somehow it didn't have the desired effect. Immediately I plunged into a deep depression. I didn't have a job or any prospects for one. My ministry to alcoholics slid down the drain with my reputation. I had no other place to go and nothing to do. For the greater part of each day, I just sat in my chair in our living room. Julia says I spent so much time there that I wore out the chair fabric.

I didn't watch television, read a book, magazine or newspaper. I sat staring blankly ahead. Bible reading—forget it. Prayer—no way. I just sat in the chair. My mind was in neutral and I had only vague and hazy recollections.

I felt completely devastated and without hope. My options had been eliminated. I had no interest in *anything*. During these weeks, Julia also felt discouraged, but she rallied to the occasion and tried to encourage me. My brother-in-law Dan also tried to lift my spirits. Every now and then, Charlie came over and tried to cheer me up. But their words made no difference to me. Nothing held meaning. Sometimes I wished for the courage to end my life, but I knew I didn't have it.

I wanted to be drunk this entire time, but I had no money for alcohol. Instead I sat in my chair. Every once in a while, I got a few dollars and got drunk. After a few more weeks, I reached a point where I dreaded to leave our house. My life reeled out of control; if I began drinking I didn't know where I'd end up. I longed to be normal. This became my only wish. I quit trying to be a godly man or to serve God through a ministry. I had even given up on being a Christian. Everything was out of my reach.

During these dark days, if God had physically appeared and said, "Let's make a deal. You can be normal; not a good Christian, just normal. I'll give you a job. You can show up for work, then come home at night and be a halfway decent husband" I would have agreed in a New York minute. My life held no hope. By far, this was the most painful part of my life, but it was exactly where God wanted me.

Jerry Clower, the Mississippi comedian, tells a story that illustrates my pain. One night Jerry and his good buddy

Marcel went coon hunting. At the top of a pine tree they see this big she-coon, and Marcel shinnies up the tree to shake it out. When Marcel climbs up the tree, their dogs on the ground are barking and going crazy. After Marcel reaches the animal, he discovers it's not a she-coon, but a souped-up wildcat, a lynx. That lynx attacks Marcel and is about to tear him up. Then Marcel hollers down at Jerry, "This thang is killin' me, shoot!...shoot!" Jerry hollers back, "I'm afraid to shoot, I might hit you." Marcel answers, "Shoot up here amongst us, one of us has got to have some relief!"

Finally Broken

Jerry's story described my situation perfectly. Like the prodigal son, I was without hope of advancement, acceptance or even tolerance. I just wanted to get out of the pigpen. God, however, had me right where He wanted me. As Earl Jabay, a counselor, says, "It's only when we've spent our last buck and

······································

In our performance-based society, the majority
of us have bought the lie of the "American
dream" and center our identities in what we
do rather than in who we are (in Christ).

······································

shot our last bullet that we are ready to do it God's way." I had finally exhausted all my resources and options. At my point of spiritual bankruptcy, I was finally ready to let God do what He wanted to do all along. Second Corinthians 1:8,9 says, "We were under great pressure, far beyond our ability to endure, so that we despaired even of life. Indeed, in our hearts we felt the sentence of death. But this happened that we might not rely on ourselves but on God, who raises the dead" *(NIV)*.

Is there a price for freedom? I, and many others, have found the price tag is to completely give up on myself and come to the end of my resources to find freedom in Christ. I gave up trying to live by my own strength and resources. I gave up on my plans, and my agenda. Freedom comes when we give up living life in our own resources and trust Christ to be our life. I hadn't fully trusted in Christ to be my life or looked to Him to meet my needs. As long as there was one more program or one more self-help book, I traveled that road. I tried to set myself free and I could not. I completely bought the lie that my freedom and success were dependent on what I did, not on what Christ had already done for me.

I was searching throughout my Christian experience for an identity. Many people find their identities in their jobs. If suddenly their jobs are lost and they can't find another one, they become prime candidates for major depression. Surveys reveal that retired, elderly white males have the highest incidence of suicide. In our performance-based society, the majority of us have bought the lie of the "American dream" and center our identities in what we do rather than in who we are (in Christ).

When I speak about this period of my life in my talks, people often ask, "Does that mean I have to become a drunk and lose everything if I am going to be free?"

"No," I always say, "but it helps." Everyone doesn't have to become a drunk and lose everything, *but* everyone does have to come to the end of him or herself.

The means God uses to bring us to the end of our resources is different for everyone. A physician I know experienced a gradual decline of self-reliance and quietly broke free from himself and found his sufficiency in Christ. On the other hand, his son was hooked on drugs, went through great depression and teetered on the verge of suicide before he came to the end of himself. In his "Victorious Christian Living" tapes, Dr. Bill Gillham tells about his arrival at the end of himself. Others around him didn't know it was happening. My experience was full of failure, pain and public humiliation. Julia experienced a lot of pain, but it wasn't public and open. God used my experience to bring her to the end of herself.

Someone has said God lets us experience as much misery as

we want. The people in AA say, "It takes what it takes." My tragedy wasn't the process of experiencing the pain and failure of brokenness. It was worth it. The real tragedy is when a person never gives up and continues in his or her own strength. These people never experience God's freedom. One of our close friends is a lovely, vibrant Christian lady. For many years she has suffered bouts of major depression and has spent some time in mental hospitals. During one of her struggles, I encouraged her as she lamented her weaknesses. "Yes, you and I are weak," I said, "but I believe we're the fortunate ones. Those who appear strong or think they are, don't know how desperately they need God. Some of them can stray away from Him and not know it. That's not true for you and me. If we move away from depending on God we crash and burn. It's ugly. On our own, we know we can't make it and are forced to depend on Him."

After I had failed and fallen again, I talked it over with my brother-in-law Dan. He said, "You are fortunate. If you get away from God, you mess up so badly you and everyone else knows it. Because of my stability, I could move away from God and neither I nor anyone else would know it for months or more." He's right about me. Beyond a shadow of a doubt, I desperately need God. Without the Lord, I can do nothing. If I move away from Him, it's a prescription for disaster. An old Southern expression says, "He has been broken from sucking eggs." Behind the saying is a story about a young boy who lived on a farm. For some reason, he enjoyed punching a hole in the eggs and sucking out the insides. One day, this boy selected a rotten egg. It broke his habit of sucking eggs. In terms of trying to live the Christian life on my own resources, I have been broken from sucking eggs.

Why Is Brokenness So Difficult?

Why is it so hard to come to the end of ourselves? One possible answer can be illustrated by a man I counseled who had struggled for many years with alcoholism. Steve lived one of the most shallow and empty lives of anyone I have ever known. When we met he still lived in the same house with his wife. Although married, they hadn't lived together as a couple for more than eight years. At the age of 56, Steve had no close friends and little relationship with his children or other family members. He didn't seem to have any hobbies or outside interests.

He did have one thing—money—and lots of it. He had inherited millions and retired from his job at age 52. Every day his routine was the same. He slept until the early afternoon, then had lunch. He would drive to his health club and enjoy the whirlpool, sauna and steam bath. After a massage, Steve returned home and began drinking. He continued drinking until after midnight when he fell into bed in a drunken stupor and slept until the next afternoon. Every day of the week, his routine was the same.

Because money was no object, Steve lived in a mansion on top of a mountain, drove a BMW and had the finer things of life. Once Steve told me he had spent almost a half million dollars at secular treatment centers for his alcoholism. Steve claimed to be a Christian, but he resisted giving up on himself and trusting God. After one of our meetings, he said "Mike, I guess I'm just too weak to live the Christian life and trust God."

I told him, "Steve, that's not your problem. You aren't too weak. You're too strong to give up and trust God." With his millions, Steve searched for another program or plan or treatment center to try.

Just before I met Steve, he had gone off to Miami on a drunken binge with a couple of his cronies. At a fashionable restaurant, he almost choked to death on a piece of steak. His heart had stopped beating. His doctor said it was a miracle he didn't suffer brain damage. Steve told me, "I believe God was trying to get my attention." Unfortunately God never got Steve's attention. A few months later, Steve choked to death on a sandwich in his home.

Besides the rich, lower-income people are also stuck in the mire of alcoholism. When I was at Bethel, the Christian treatment center, several of the men had literally come off the streets. One morning I was complaining that I hadn't slept much the night before. The snoring from my roommate kept me awake most of the night. With contempt in his voice, this man said, "You'd never make it in a flophouse." In his eyes he was stronger than me because he could survive in a flophouse and I couldn't.

Nine out of ten people who live on the streets choose to return to the streets after they've been to a treatment center or some other shelter. Many make this choice rather than having a sure job or living with relatives. Why? Living on the streets is the ultimate form of independence. A person isn't responsible to anyone or anything. No one tells the person what he can or can't do. At Bethel, these street people looked at me with disdain. They were strong enough to live on the streets with nothing but their own creativity. They were right. I couldn't live in that fashion. I'm not strong enough.

I was the biggest barrier to my freedom—my pride, my strength, my plans, my goals and my agenda. Is there something else to try? If it works, then I can say I did it. My only qualification for writing about this subject is my failure. This failure paved the way for my brokenness. Only then could I experience all God had for me.

In the previous chapter, I listed more than 25 ways I attempted to escape the bondage of alcoholism—without success. Of course my list isn't exhaustive. It seems every day something new comes along to try. But these alternatives don't work. The *only* way anyone will have freedom, peace, joy and fulfillment is through Christ alone. It won't be Christ *plus* any program, treatment center or support group, but Christ can and does work through such programs, if they will teach us who we are in Christ, how to walk by faith and rely on Him.

Many of the means I tried were good, but doomed to fail from the start. Why? Following are four reasons:

1. I tried to change my behavior instead of the underlying belief that determined my behavior.
2. I focused on me and what I should do instead of focusing on God and what He had already done.
3. I relied on my own efforts instead of trusting God and living by the power of the Holy Spirit.

4. I accepted a failure identity instead of appropriating my true identity in Christ.

I lived under the law through my own efforts instead of under grace by faith in the power and wisdom of God. The results of living under the law are clear in Romans 7:5, "For when we were controlled by the sinful nature, the sinful passions aroused by the law were at work in our bodies, so that we bore fruit for death" *(NIV)*. We've believed a saying that isn't in the Bible—"God helps those who help themselves," which is a quotation from Benjamin Franklin. Instead, God

....

I was broken when God brought me to the
end of myself. Only then could I look
to Christ as the means for my
acceptance and worth.

....

doesn't help those who help themselves, but leaves them to their misery and to their own devices until they come to the end of their resources and trust in Him.

I was broken when God brought me to the end of myself. Only then could I look to Christ as the means for my acceptance and worth. Without this brokenness, I couldn't find freedom and victory. It doesn't occur for the self-sufficient or the self-reliant. These people are not broken and will fight it to the end.

Through my counseling, I've looked into the tear-stained faces of many distraught wives and mothers. They've asked me, "When will they ever stop?"

I patiently answer, "When they reach the end of themselves and their own resources." The spouse and/or the parents are usually the addict's top resource. As long as they continue to be a resource, they enable the person to continue in their addiction.

The most loving and redemptive action from Julia during

my struggle was to finally say, "I'm not going to put up with this anymore." Then she kicked me out of the house.

My failure and brokenness was the best thing that ever happened to me. It was a prerequisite for finding peace and the fulfillment in my life today.

In her book *Living Confidently in God's Love*, Hannah Whithall Smith says, "It is always a painful process and often a most discouraging one. The process continues until all that can be shaken is removed and only those things which cannot be shaken remain. Through this shaking the deliverance for which we prayed is accomplished. Through it all, we will be brought into the secure place for which we long."[3]

My addiction was the most painful and agonizing experience of my life. I am thankful for it. *But* I would not like to go through it again. As my good friend Mike Harden, the director of a Christian treatment center in Cumming, Georgia, says, "I wouldn't take a million dollars for my experience of brokenness, but you couldn't pay me five million to go through it again."

Julia's Perspective

Editor's note: As Mike bounced from ministry to drunkenness to ministry, Julia was trying to cope with her life and marriage. This is her story from the same period of their lives.

Work—My Attempt to Help Mike
In Mike's counseling ministry to alcoholics, he shared office space with our brother-in-law Dan. Because I was Dan's secretary, I worked for Mike as well as for Dan. Sometimes I thought, *God, you've sure got a sense of humor. Not long ago, I didn't want to see Mike again. Now I'm working for him.*

Six years earlier, a counselor had told me I needed to decide what I wanted to do about staying married to Mike. Her husband had an office in our same building. One day as she was going to her husband's office she walked past our open doorway. She did a double take, stopped quickly and stepped inside our office. Mike and my desks were side by side.

"Am I seeing things, or what?" she asked with a quizzical look on her face. We laughed and said, "Only God could've arranged this."

I still worked only 20 hours a week. It was all the ministries could afford, but we needed more monthly income. For years in our marriage I had been "the responsible one." *It's up to me to handle this,* I thought. For several years, I had toyed with the idea of a career as a real estate agent. After all of our moves, I thought I knew a lot about this business. Besides, I was almost 50 and wanted to take the plunge before I got older. Heading off to real estate school, I pursued a license. While attending school, I continued working part-time for Dan and Mike. Mrs. Super Responsibility at her best!

After my training, I got a job with a local realty company. The owners were Christians so their influence was felt in the office atmosphere and business policies. Only a few years old, this company was still small. Although I was older than most of the agents, they accepted and respected me. I jumped right in and worked diligently to build my business.

Because I got paid only when I closed escrow on a house, my paychecks were few and far between. I was highly motivated to work hard because we needed every dime I brought in. Many days I found the work frustrating—especially the competitive spirit and the disappointments when something didn't work out. Overall I enjoyed my job and the various people. It felt good to be a part of this important business and to gain the respect of others for my work.

My life passed in a whirlwind. Whether at the real estate office or at home or in Mike and Dan's office, the work seemed to be piled everywhere. Many mornings I rushed out the door and didn't take time to read my Bible or a devotional book. As I drove from our house to the highway, I prayed, "Oh God, this morning I've messed up again and didn't have a quiet time. Please forgive me. Please protect me and guide today anyway. I do love You and I'm sorry I didn't get up earlier. How can You love me? But the Bible says You do. I promise I'll do better tomorrow." In my heart, I wanted to do everything perfect but I never could. I hoped that God heard my "on the run" prayers.

I wanted my work to make Mike proud and relieve our financial burdens. He still seemed to struggle and to be frustrated. *If only I could make more money*, I thought, *then he could concentrate on being free.* Some days I felt as though I carried the weight of the entire world on my shoulders. *God will meet my needs and give me strength*, I reassured myself. *If that's so, then why do I get so exhausted? Why can't God get Mike completely straightened out, then convict him to be more responsible?* Sometimes in desperation, I prayed, "Lord, let me make some huge sales, then we can get out of debt." It didn't happen so I resolved not to be a quitter and to keep going. Someday it would work out.

Bradley and Susan were expecting a baby in January 1989. This brought me great joy as I anticipated becoming a grandmother. Any free time was filled with knitting little caps, sweaters and booties and making receiving blankets. I fixed one corner of our guest room with a crib and other baby necessities.

Mike tried to be a good husband. Each morning, he helped me get off for the office by making coffee and fixing my breakfast. When I was gone Mike unloaded the dishwasher or folded clothes. Although small things, they showed his good intentions. He dabbled in meal preparation and discovered his cooking skills, specializing in soups and stews. As with other things, Mike didn't cook halfway. Instead of a small pot of stew, Mike made five gallons at a time. I learned to appreciate a pot of soup simmering on the stove when I came home from work. We froze the extra so our freezer was well stocked. We just had to zap it in the microwave for a quick supper. To accompany Mike's soups, I began making bread and rolls. We made a good team in the kitchen.

As Mike began counseling alcoholics and addicts, our life was so much better than during those chronic drinking years. I began to quit worrying about whether or not Mike would come home at night. My trust had to be in God, not Mike. Occasionally Mike drank. I was upset and frightened, but so was he. What was going on? What else could be done?

I Needed to Get Away
By September 1988, I was growing weary of trying to always

be strong and optimistic. I needed to get away from him for a few days. I drove down to Dothan and visited my friend Rachel. From her and her husband, Joe, I felt love and acceptance for Mike and myself—no matter what. I felt safe in their home that had no tension. During these days, I slept, read, knit, prayed and began to relax.

Then one morning Mike called. He said the night before he had been out on a bad drunken spree. Mike was so devastated from the experience that he planned to confess his sin to the ministry, the church and to Dan. I begged him not to do it. "Mike, there's no need to go public with this and throw away everything you have gained," I said.

He wouldn't listen to any of my reasons. I knew he was resigned to this course of action.

The call crushed me. How could this happen? *Lord, haven't we been through enough?* I thought. I was furious at Mike both for drinking and then for confessing and resigning from the human race. I hung up on him and started sobbing. For a while I couldn't tell Rachel what was wrong. I never wanted to go home again. What was left? Maybe Mike should move to the south side of Birmingham, be a drunken bum and let me go on with my life.

Comfort in the Psalms

I began to question the Lord and ask, "God, what is happening? Where are you? Don't you care about us?" Through the years I had always found solace in the Psalms. Many of these psalms describe God as my shelter, my refuge, my shield, my companion, my comforter and my provider. I buried myself in God's Word. A variety of promises became special to me as I read:

"You will show me the path of life; in Your presence is fullness of joy" (Ps. 16:11, *NKJV*).

"Keep me as the apple of Your eye; hide me under the shadow of Your wings" (Ps. 17:8, *NKJV*).

"I would have lost heart, unless I had believed that I would see the goodness of the Lord in the land of the living. Wait on the Lord, be of good courage, and He shall strengthen your heart; wait, I say, on the Lord!" (Ps. 27:13,14, *NKJV*).

"Many are the afflictions of the righteous, but the Lord delivers him out of them all" (Ps. 34:19, *NKJV*).

For many years, I had regularly prayed through Psalm 37:3-9 about trusting in the Lord, feeding on His faithfulness, delighting myself in Him, committing my way to Him, resting in Him and waiting patiently for Him.

Psalm 73:26 described me often, "My flesh and my heart fail; But God is the strength of my heart and my portion forever" *(NKJV)*.

Psalm 91 gave me encouragement about hiding under His shadow and trusting Him, not being afraid and His angels being in charge over me to keep me. Verses 14 and 15 say, "Because he has set his love upon Me, therefore I will deliver him; I will set him on high, because he has known My name. He shall call upon Me, and I will answer him; I will be with him in trouble; I will deliver him and honor him. With long life I will satisfy him, and show him My salvation" *(NKJV)*. I held on to these anchors in the midst of this storm.

After several days at Rachel's house, I realized I had to return to my business. I dreaded facing Mike and our life. When I got home I concentrated on my work. I decided that our survival was up to me. Mike sat in his chair. We hardly talked to each other and just went through the motions of eating meals together. My food seemed to stick in my throat. Mike sat and sat and sat in his chair—staring into space.

Was Mike a born loser? He had made great changes and learned a lot. He was beginning to get some respectability. Now he had blown everything. Was I stupid for staying in our marriage?

"What now, God?" Mike's reaction was depressing to me. I wanted to just sit in a chair too, but instead I burned off my anger and frustration with work. Later I learned that I was a "performer." Performers never give up.

I Will Trust God No Matter What
One night I was reading my Bible and I came across Psalm 37:23,24, "The steps of a good man are ordered by the Lord, and He delights in his way. Though he fall, he shall not be utterly cast down; for the Lord upholds him with His hand" *(NKJV)*.

The verses moved me to action. I walked into our den and sat down on the hearth next to Mike in his chair, "Listen to me, Mike. I don't know what's going to happen to you, but I want you to know that I'm going to trust God *no matter what*. I can't make it without Him. Even though it doesn't look as though He's in control, I'm going to believe He is." I told him about the promise I had read in Psalm 37.

I continued, "Micah 7:8,9 *[NIV]* says, 'Though I have fallen, I will rise. Though I sit in darkness, the Lord will be my light....He will bring me out into the light; I will see his righteousness.' Well, you stumbled but you can choose to get up and go on. I'm going on with my life with the Lord with or without you. For me there is no turning back." After my little speech, I walked back to our bedroom and fell across the bed.

"Oh God," I prayed, "I can't see You and it doesn't feel as though You are here. But I'm going to believe that You are here. You promised to never leave me nor forsake me so I'm going to keep hanging on to You."

A few years earlier, a friend in another ministry came through town and stayed with us. After telling him about our struggles, he said, "Never forget that God promises that He *will* complete the good work He has started in you" (see Phil. 1:6). He also reminded us about Psalm 138:7,8, "Though I walk in the midst of trouble, you preserve my life; you stretch out your hand against the anger of my foes, with your right hand you save me. The Lord will fulfill his purpose for me; your love, O Lord, endures forever—do not abandon the works of your hands" *(NIV)*. I underlined those verses in my Bible when this friend was with us. Now my eyes fell on those verses and I gained a new sense of resolve. I would hold on to the Lord. He was in control, not me.

Notes

1. *The Wittenberg Door* (1987).
2. Ibid.
3. Hannah Whithall Smith, *Living Confidently in God's Love* (Springdale, Pa., Whitaker House, 1984), p. 175.

The Truth Will Set You Free

Then you will know the truth,
and the truth will set you free.
—John 8:32 *(NIV)*

The Beginning of the Truth

I was resigned to sitting in my chair. I had no clue how to resolve my problem. I was hopelessly ensnared in the bondage of defeat. I had exhausted all of my resources. Dr. Bill Gillham, in his book *Lifetime Guarantee* says, "The problem is you don't know what your problem is. You think your problem is your main problem, but that's not the problem at all. The problem is you don't know what your problem is and that's your main problem."[1]

Gillham says we have not yet discovered that the Christian life isn't hard to live; it's impossible. Our behavior will always be consistent with our beliefs. People will not always live what they profess, but they will always live what they believe. To the alcoholic and the addict or anyone in bondage, it means their problem isn't drinking alcohol or doing drugs or whatever.

Their struggle is with misbeliefs or lies that cause their behavior.

Throughout my struggle for freedom from the bondage of alcohol, I never questioned my beliefs or my theology. I tried many different things, but throughout I stubbornly held to some established beliefs that prevented my freedom. Why? From my perspective, I had been taught the "truth." I was convinced my problem wasn't my beliefs, but my inability to put my beliefs into action.

Somehow, God broke through and raised a slight doubt in my mind. As I sat in my chair in depression, everyone had given up on me. Later my pastor said, "I didn't know anything else to tell you."

Finally my close friend, Charlie Jones, gave up trying to help me. As a last ditch effort, however, Charlie gave me some tapes. In a very unconvincing tone he said, "Here, listen to these, maybe they'll help you."

As I read the label on the tape album it said, "Victorious Christian Living" by Dr. Bill Gillham and his wife, Anabel. About a year earlier I had purchased the advanced set. After I listened to one tape, I had concluded his doctrine was off and I hadn't listened to another one. Now Charlie gave me the basic set in the same series. Immediately I thought, *I don't want to listen to these. His theology doesn't agree with mine.* I continued to cling to my old beliefs about truth.

Then another thought came, *Your theology is not doing you much good!* I decided to listen to the tapes with an open mind. Well, almost open. Because I had both sets, the basic and advanced, I would listen to the advanced. After all, I *was* a seminary graduate and had been an ordained minister. Surely I didn't need the basic tapes. So I began listening to the advanced set.

A Stormy Argument

In the meantime, nothing changed. Life was totally miserable and I was depressed all the time. I had resigned from the ministry and gone public with my problems on August 25, 1988. Now it was the first week of October. I had given up and wasn't trying to act civil around other people. The next

Sunday, Julia encouraged me to go to church. Everything about the service rubbed me the wrong way. When we left the church, we got into a big argument.

"You and all those other goody-goody Christians just go to church," I seethed. Then I vowed never to go to church again—not that one or any other. On the way home I decided to head off to the beach for a few days. There I could drink and enjoy myself. I wanted to get away from everyone who kept reminding me about my terrible problems.

I stormed into the house and threw some clothes into a suitcase. Julia begged me not to go. "I'll do anything," she promised. But I didn't listen to her. I was out of control though I hadn't taken my first drink. Both of us knew it would only be a matter of time until I sipped that first drink.

In the middle of our argument, our doorbell rang. I shouted, "Who in the blankety blank is that?" Sheepishly, Julia admitted that it was Charlie and Ruth. Sensing that a make-or-break argument was brewing, she had asked them to come to our house after church. She thought they could talk some sense into me.

I wasn't in a mood to receive *anything* connected to sense or reason. Charlie was shocked to see me so belligerent and irate. He had never seen me in this irrational state of mind. Despite Charlie's best logic, I wouldn't listen. Instead, I turned on my friend and cussed him up one side then down the other. Charlie was speechless.

Was I the same friend and soul mate with whom he had prayed and discussed the Bible for hours on end? Charlie drew back. I knew I had won my point and would be able to leave. Despite Charlie's hurt and crestfallen appearance, I couldn't feel anything for him. I was consumed in my desire for the moment. Everything took a backseat to my addiction.

As I walked with my suitcase to the car, Julia, Charlie and Ruth pleaded with me not to go. I ignored them and took off down the road. At a small store I purchased some beer and drove to the nearest beach from Birmingham, which was in the Pensacola area. The last church I pastored was located in that area.

By the time I reached Pensacola, I was already drunk. As I drove past the first bar along the road, I stopped. As I sat there drinking, I thought, *What if I run into someone from the church?* Then I decided I didn't care. I couldn't live the Christian life, so why pretend anymore? After hitting several bars and consuming a lot more alcohol, I could barely walk or drive. After locating a motel, I checked in and fell into the bed in a drunken stupor.

The next morning I woke up with a raging hangover. Looking around I discovered that I had slept in a rundown, cheap motel. I struggled out of bed and washed my face with cold water. Then I threw on some clothes and checked out as fast as I could. I had to get out of there!

I drove out to Navarre Beach and checked into the Holiday Inn. The tourist season is off in October so the hotel was practically empty. That night I went out to drink again. After a few beers I felt so bad and depressed that I returned to my room.

The next day I walked the beach and wondered about my future. Almost two months earlier, I had resigned from the ministry, but I hadn't been able to think about a job, much less search for one. *Where was I headed? Was I going to drink myself to death? Or maybe I would end up living on the streets? Probably the downtown mission where I used to teach a Bible study would be my next stop.* I shuddered at the thought of such a bleak future.

That night I called Julia and Charlie and tried to apologize. Neither one wanted to talk with me, much less accept my apology. Charlie was still bewildered about how I had fallen into such a low state. Both acted incredulous that I called from the beach and expected any sort of civil response from them. The next morning I checked out of the motel and drove back to Birmingham.

A Glimmer of New Insight from Scripture

On the drive home I noticed that the "Victorious Christian Living" tapes by the Gillhams were on my front seat. I had nothing else to do so I popped a tape into the tape player and began listening. This particular tape was a short message from Anabel Gillham based on John 14:20. In this verse, Jesus says, "On that day you will realize that I am in my Father, and you are in me, and I am in you" *(NIV)*.

The verse was unfamiliar. I had never seen it before, although I had read the book of John many times. The verse startled me with it's implications. What an unbelievable statement! If that verse was true (and I knew it was because I believed God's Word was true), then had I started to find the answer to my problems? Would Jesus meet all my needs? I thought, *If Jesus is in me and I am in Him and He is in the Father, then what else could I possibly need?* It seemed to be a conclusive and definitive answer for the Christian life.

For many years I knew that Christ was in me. This verse said that I was "in Christ." I must have read the term many times, but I had always understood it in a theoretical or positional sense. Maybe it's more than that; maybe it has practical implications. I had no idea how to make it work for me; but if it's true that I am in Christ and He is in me, I have everything I need to live the Christian life. Why should I have to worry about who I am or what anyone else thinks? What could I possibly achieve or possess or what status could I attain to give me a better identity than being "in Christ?"

There is no greater worth than being in Christ. This was Anabel's main point on the tape. She said, "Anything that comes your way must first come through the Father, then through Jesus. Then when it gets to you, it finds you filled with Jesus, so what is there to fear?" If I could grasp this truth, perhaps there was hope for me.

After arriving home, I looked up John 14:20. Sure enough, it was in the Bible. Beside the verse in my Bible, I wrote the date October 11, 1988. Then I asked God to make His words real in my life. When I walked into the house, Julia was leaving for work. She acknowledged me, but didn't slow down.

In the next two weeks, I fell back into my old pattern of living. I forgot about John 14:20. Like everything else I had tried, I couldn't make this new insight work for me.

True Freedom in Christ

On October 24, I got drunk again. The next morning Julia strongly suggested I visit Jack and June Fagan and give her a break. Her idea sounded good to me. I packed a few clothes and drove to Lookout Mountain.

By this time, I had finished the advanced tapes and began listening to the basic set. I drove along listening to the third tape called "Co-crucifixion Is Past Tense." Bill Gillham taught about our death with Christ from Romans 6:6, "Our old self was crucified with Him." He pointed out that most Christians don't really understand what actually happened at the Cross. If they understood it clearly, they wouldn't live in such defeat. We understand that Christ died for our sins, but few of us understand that we also died with Christ. Because of this death, we are "new creations because the old self, the person we used to be is no more, and we are 'in Christ.'" He used the phrase again—"In Christ."

Romans 6:6,7 says, "For we know that our old self was crucified with him so that the body of sin might be done away with, that we should no longer be slaves to sin—because anyone who has died has been freed from sin" *(NIV)*.

His words pulled me up short. I have died with Christ and I have been freed from sin? I knew that was what I needed, but how could I make that true in my life? Then Gillham said, "It isn't something you do, it's something that has *been done*; our death with Christ is past tense, the old person that we were 'was crucified,' and 'anyone who has died has been freed from sin.'" And then he said, "You 'died to sin' (Rom. 6:2), you are 'dead to sin'(v. 11). You don't act dead to sin, you don't feel dead to sin, you don't even look dead to sin. You think that's just a positional truth. Listen, if that's what God says about you, that's the truth about you."

At that moment the lights came on and I understood the truth. I knew I had died with Christ. The old sin-loving sinner had died and was no more. For many years I believed I was a sinner and acted like it. Now I knew that I was dead to sin whether I acted like it, felt like it, looked like it or anyone else believed it because God said I was. I also knew the truth that I was free, "Because anyone who had died has been freed from sin" (v. 7, *NIV*).

Jesus said, "Then you will know the truth, and the truth will set you free" (John 8:32, *NIV*). I had believed I was a hopeless, helpless alcoholic. For years I lived in bondage, but less than 24 hours away from being drunk, I knew without any doubt that I, Mike Quarles, was a child of God who was "in Christ." I had died with Christ, was dead to sin and had been freed from sin. At last, I was free. Praise God I was free at last!

"Yeah, Mike, That's Nice"

The new discovery of my freedom made an immediate difference in my spirit. I ran into Jack and June's house shouting, "I'm free." I grabbed the phone and called Julia. In my own way, I tried explaining what had happened.

....

Most Christians are trying to become what God says they've already achieved or God has already accomplished. I had been encouraged to "die to self," and struggled to make it happen.

....

"Yeah, Mike, that's nice," Julia said to humor me. She didn't finish listening before she terminated the conversation. To her I was on another wild goose chase. Her response didn't dampen my enthusiasm. I knew who I was in Christ and that I was free. Since that day, I have never doubted it!

For the next couple of days I stayed with the Fagans and reveled in my newfound freedom and joy. When I drove back to Birmingham, I was anxious to tell Julia, Charlie and Dan (and anyone who would listen) about what I had learned.

The solution to my years of deep struggle may seem too simple. How could my years of bondage be released by listening to a tape? Actually listening to a tape didn't set me free.

I believed the truth that was taught on the tape. Ever since becoming a Christian I had believed a lie about myself. It kept me in bondage.

In his conferences, Neil Anderson asks, "How many died with Christ?" Almost everyone raises a hand. Then he asks, "How many are free from sin?" Then he says, "It better be the same hands because it clearly states in Romans 6:7, 'Anyone who has died has been freed from sin.'"

All Christians died with Christ so all Christians have been freed from sin. If they don't believe they're free from sin, they'll probably not live like it. We act according to our beliefs. The central issue is always identity. If you don't know the truth about your identity "in Christ," it doesn't make any difference what programs you are involved in or what spiritual exercises you are doing.

If Christians are already free, why don't they live that way? Why are many Christians living defeated lives? Most Christians are trying to become what God says they've already achieved or God has already accomplished. I had been encouraged to "die to self," and struggled to make it happen. Yet Scripture couldn't be clearer. It says, "For we know that our old self was crucified with him" (Rom. 6:6, *NIV*)

Zig Ziglar relates an incident that illustrates how a wrong perspective can prohibit freedom: "Harry Houdini, the famed escape artist, issued a challenge wherever he went. He could be locked in any jail cell in the country, he claimed, and set himself free in short order. Always he kept his promise, but one time something went wrong. Houdini entered the jail in his street clothes; the heavy metal doors clanged shut behind him. He took from his belt a concealed piece of metal, strong and flexible. He set to work immediately, but something seemed to be unusual about this lock. For thirty minutes he worked and got nowhere. An hour passed, and still he had not opened the door. By now he was bathed in sweat and panting in exasperation, but he still could not pick the lock. Finally after laboring for two hours, Harry Houdini collapsed in frustration and failure against the door he could not unlock. But when he fell against the door, it swung open! It had never been locked at all! But in his mind it was locked and that was all it took to keep him from opening the door and walking out of the jail cell."[2]

Like Harry Houdini, most of us are working our heads off trying to get free when Christ has already set us free (see Gal. 5:1). For Christians, the door to freedom isn't locked—when Christ died on the cross the door was opened wide. We died with Him. Not only have we been crucified, died and buried with Christ, but we have also been raised up with Him and are now seated with Him in the heavenlies (see Eph. 2:6).

How can we walk through that wide open door to freedom? We need to understand and believe the truth. "It was for freedom that Christ set us free" (Gal. 5:1). If we believe that we have to work, sweat and strain, God will allow us to work, sweat and strain—until we collapse in frustration and failure as did Harry Houdini. That was exactly my experience.

Watchman Nee writes, "Oh, it is a great thing to see that we are in Christ! Think of the bewilderment of trying to get into a room in which you already are! Think of the absurdity of asking to be put in! If we recognize the fact that we are in, we make no effort to enter."[3]

Besides understanding my identity "in Christ," I had another life-changing insight. If I am a new creation "in Christ" (2 Cor. 5:17), then I am no longer a sinner and I don't have to sin. For many years I had been taught, believed and also preached that everyone, including Christians, had a sin nature. Several years earlier I had been reading *The Ins and Outs of Rejection* by Charles Solomon.[4] I was benefiting from the book, but about three-quarters of the way into it I noticed something unusual.

This guy doesn't believe you have a sin nature, I thought. Immediately I labeled him a heretic and didn't read the book again. My theology didn't accommodate this teaching; however, my theology wasn't doing me much good, as my alcoholic lifestyle demonstrated.

If my basic beliefs and theology were true, I would be walking in freedom. God's Word is clear, "Then you will know the truth, and the truth will set you free" (John 8:32, *NIV*). I believed I was a sin-loving sinner with a sin nature. I also believed I was a hopeless, helpless alcoholic and that's the way I lived. I "was" by nature a child of wrath (see Eph. 2:3). If my old self was crucified with Christ (see Rom. 6:6), who am I now?

The Bible says, "Therefore if any man is in Christ, he is a new creature; the old things passed away; behold, new things have come" (2 Cor. 5:17). I am a child of God (see 1 John 3:1) and a partaker of the divine nature (see 2 Pet. 1:4). A new "me" was raised up with Christ (see Rom. 6:5) and by the grace of God I have become the righteousness of God in Christ (see 2 Cor. 5:21).

Suddenly it all became clear. I had bought the lie from Satan and it kept me in a futile struggle with sin that couldn't be won. Sinners can't ever overcome sin in their lives. To me it was apparent that as an evangelical Christian I had done what I often accused liberals of doing. My theology and beliefs had been formulated on my experience instead of God's Word. Experience convinces us that we're sinners because we have sinned. I needed to throw out my presuppositions and turn to God's Word by having a fresh perspective. Who was I "in Christ" and according to God's Word? As I learned this my experience could change.

About the time I was understanding these new aspects about my identity in Christ, I had lunch with a friend who was ordained in my denomination. I asked him, "Do you believe that you are dead to sin?"

Leaning back in his chair, he said, "Well, theoretically." That's the problem. He didn't want to flatly dispute God's Word. At the same time, he obviously didn't believe he was dead to sin.

Bill Gillham says, "Some have called these positional truths (implying that this is the way it will be in the sweet by and by; it's 'just the position in which God sees us'). We believe this is just a subtle way of saying that these truths aren't worth much to us at this point, but after we die they will suddenly become a reality. God's Word says that the believer is in Christ and He ascribes certain characteristics to any man in Christ. If God says that is the way it is, then that's the way it is right now—present day REALITY!!! Christian faith is simply looking at things through God's eyes and agreeing with Him. This will then begin to control our performance and we can experience a victorious walk!"[5]

Another day I talked about it with Charlie at his house. Although Charlie gave me the Gillham tapes, he didn't agree with their teaching. Charlie said, "I just can't go along with that. I *know* I've a sin nature. I'm drawn to sin and I want to sin."

"Charlie," I responded, "you're saying that, yet the truth is that you gave up a secure, well-paying job with your father's company that you would have inherited one day. Instead you

....

> The key to knowing Christ is understanding that we died with Him. Without this understanding we try to become somebody we already are. We try to do for ourselves what Christ has already done for us. This is an exercise in futility.

....

started a faith ministry to spread the good news of Jesus Christ. Are you telling me that you really want to sin? Get serious!"

The key to knowing Christ is understanding that we died with Him. Paul says, "For you have died and your life is hidden with Christ in God" (Col. 3:3). Without this understanding we try to become somebody we already are. We try to do for ourselves what Christ has already done for us. This is an exercise in futility.

For 18 years of my Christian life I tried to act like a Christian in my own strength. Then one day it is as if God said, "Mike, your act is no good. This is what I think of your act—I have crucified it and you. I've taken care of it and you." God has no interest in improving our old nature or our natural life. He desires that we exchange our old life in Adam for a new life in Christ.

"Praise the Lord, I'm Dead"

Watchman Nee also struggled with this truth. He wrote the following in *The Normal Christian Life*:

> For years after my conversion I had been taught to reckon. I reckoned from 1920 until 1927. The more I reckoned that I was dead to sin, the more alive I clearly was. I simply could not believe myself dead and I could not produce that death. Whenever I sought help from others I was told to read Romans 6:11, and the more I read Romans 6:11, and tried to reckon, the further away death was: I could not get at it....For months I was seeking and at times I fasted, but nothing came through. I remember one morning—one I can never forget—I was upstairs sitting at my desk reading the Word and praying and I said, "Lord, open my eyes!" And then in a flash I saw it. I saw my oneness with Christ. I saw that I was in Him and that when He died I died. I saw that the question of my death was a matter of the past and not of the future, and that I was just as truly dead as He was because I was in Him when He died. The whole thing had dawned upon me. I was carried away with such joy at this great discovery that I jumped from my chair and cried, "Praise the Lord, I am dead!"[6]

My feelings will not always match the truth, *but* I choose to believe what God says is true, "For we know that our old self was crucified with him so that the body of sin might be done away with, that we should no longer be slaves to sin—because anyone who has died has been freed from sin" (Rom. 6:6,7, *NIV*). The truth set me free. My freedom came when I understood who I was "in Christ." I had always believed that Christians are "sinners saved by grace," but what do sinners do? They sin. We call a person in bondage to alcohol or drugs an "alcoholic" or an "addict." And alcoholics and addicts drink alcohol and use drugs.

God says that our identity has changed. "For you are all

sons of God through faith in Christ Jesus....there is neither slave nor free man, there is neither male nor female; for you are all one in Christ Jesus" (Gal. 3:26,28). It is not what we do that determines who we are; it is who we are that determines what we do. During those first days of learning this truth I was so excited I drew out the concepts on a sheet of paper. Until we see the old self as crucified, there is little chance to experience the freedom Christ purchased for us.

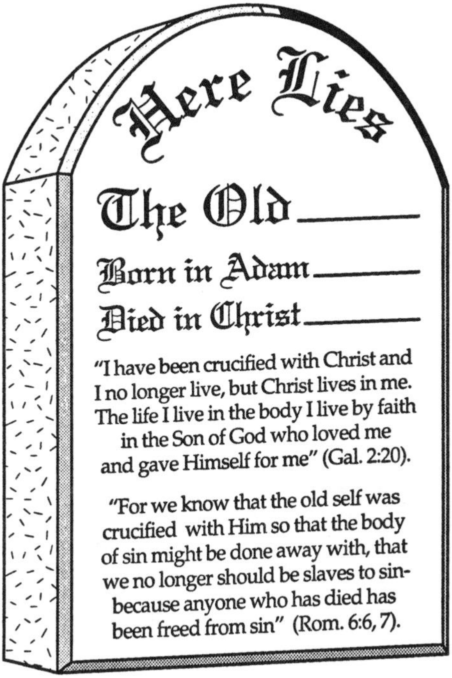
Here Lies
The Old
Born in Adam
Died in Christ
"I have been crucified with Christ and I no longer live, but Christ lives in me. The life I live in the body I live by faith in the Son of God who loved me and gave Himself for me" (Gal. 2:20).
"For we know that the old self was crucified with Him so that the body of sin might be done away with, that we no longer should be slaves to sin-because anyone who has died has been freed from sin" (Rom. 6:6,7).

Crucified-Dead-Buried-Gone

1. The person I used to be, the sin-loving sinner (see above)
2. Low self-esteem and feeling worthless (Col. 2:9,10)
3. Life-controlling problems and besetting sins (Eph. 4:20-24)
4. All coping and escaping mechanisms (Phil. 4:11-13)
5. Need to succeed and perform to be accepted (Jn. 6:29; 1 Cor. 1:30)
6. Desire for men's approval and meeting their demands (Gal. 6:14, 15)
7. The law and all its demands (Rom. 7:4-6, Gal. 4:4-7)
8. All the world's principles, customs and ways (Col. 2:20)
9. All sins, failures, mistakes, regrets (Rom. 4:7,8; Eph. 1:7)
10. Everything in my life that is not in Christ (2 Cor. 5:17)

Everything from the past is crucified, dead, buried and gone. We cannot fix our past, but praise God we can be free from it. This isn't wishful thinking. God has already accomplished it and all we have to do is believe it.

Bobby Patterson, one of my good friends, counsels at a nearby ministry. When he encounters counselees who have life-controlling problems, he asks, "Would your problems be over if you died?"

....

Neil Anderson says, "You are not primarily a product of your past, you are primarily a product of the work of Christ on the cross and His resurrection." Your beliefs determine how you live.

....

Without exception, they answer, "Yes".

"Congratulations," he tells them, "you've died!" Praise God, you have died. This is what Galatians 2:20 means. "I have been crucified with Christ and I no longer live, but Christ lives in me. The life I live in the body, I live by faith in the Son of God, who loved me and gave himself for me" *(NIV)*.

I am a child of God because of the finished work of Christ. I can't do anything to make it more true—God says it is true whether I feel it or not, whether I act like it or not. First Corinthians 1:30 says, "You are in Christ Jesus by God's act, for God has made him our wisdom; he is our righteousness; in him we are consecrated and set free" *(NEB)*.

This truth sounds incredible, but only God can save us and set us free from our past. He has taken care of everything. We can experience complete, full freedom from the past. First Peter 1:18,19 says, "For you know that it was not with perishable things such as silver or gold that you were redeemed from the empty way of life handed down to you from your forefathers, but with the precious blood of Christ, a lamb without blemish or defect" *(NIV)*.

Neil Anderson says, "You are not primarily a product of your past; you are primarily a product of the work of Christ on the cross and His resurrection." Your beliefs determine how you live.

Yes, some of us used to be alcoholics and addicts. Others still believe they are and still behave that way, but Scripture is clear that it is in the past for every born-again child of God. First Corinthians 6:11 says, "And such *were* some of you; but you *were* washed, but you *were* sanctified, but you *were* justified in the name of the Lord Jesus Christ, and in the Spirit of our God" (emphasis mine). Because of God, we have been washed (forgiven) of our sins. More than that, we have been regenerated; in other words, "born again" into a new creation. Also, we've been sanctified, from which we get the word "saints." The root word means "to make holy."

Also, we've been justified. This means we have been reconciled to God and made right with Him. The root word means "to declare righteous." We have received the righteousness of God by faith (see Phil. 3:9). Because of Christ's work on the cross we have "become the righteousness of God" (2 Cor. 5:21).

I Did Nothing; Christ Did Everything

How did I gain my freedom? The day before I received my freedom I was drunk. The answer is, *I did nothing.* I simply believed God. I died with Christ (see Rom. 6:6), and I am now free from sin (see v. 7). That was true the first day I became a Christian. It is true for *every* Christian. Every Christian was crucified with Christ, buried with Him and raised up with Him and is now dead to sin, and alive in Christ. We have to choose to believe what God says is true and walk accordingly by faith.

Does God have an answer for addiction? Yes, and it is almost too simple to believe. The prison doors have been opened wide. "It is for freedom that Christ has set us free. Stand firm, then, and do not let yourselves be burdened again by a yoke of slavery" (Gal. 5:1, *NIV*). This may seem overwhelming or too good to be true, but it is the gospel truth and it will set you free. In part two of this book, Neil Anderson will fully explain how we get into bondage and how we can all be free in Christ. I am thankful for the support I received from concerned people while I was in bondage, and I think the church can learn a lot from these caring people. Several issues contrast God's answer from man's answer as follows:

The Answer for Addiction by Mike Quarles

Man's Answer

A Program—Designed to change the behavior of the person (Gal. 4:9)

Result—Self-improvement (Gal. 6:3)

Need—To constantly work on doing the right behavior (Gal. 3:1-5)

Dynamic—Our commitment and performance (Col. 2:20-23)

Summary

Commitment—To subject myself to a program of:

Law—rules, steps, concepts and principles through:

Works—disciplined self-effort to:

Strengthen Flesh—improve self in order to produce:

Dead Works—behavior change

God's Answer

The Cross—to put to death the person who does the behavior (Rom. 6:4)

Result—New person with a new identity who behaves differently (Gal. 2:20)

Need—To understand who we are so our behavior will match up with our identity (2 Cor. 5:17)

Dynamic—The life of Christ (Col. 3:3)

Summary

Death—I agree with God's verdict on self and give up on myself and my resources and by:

Grace—appropriate what God has done and by:

Faith—appropriate my death and resurrection with Christ and by the:

Spirit—depend upon Christ's life in me to meet all my needs in order to produce:

Life—good works, the fruit of the Spirit

The Answer for Addiction by Neil Anderson

According to Man	According to God
Law	Grace
External Conformity	Internal Change
Change Behavior	Change Nature
Commit to Program	Commit to Christ
Work the Program	Walk by Faith
Alcoholic	Child of God
Reinforce the Flesh	Crucify the Flesh
Accountable to Man	Accountable to God
Live by the Flesh	Live by the Spirit
Sober	Free
Disease	Sin
Self-Improvement	New Creation
Guilty	Forgiven
Works	Faith
Bondservant of man	Bondservant of God
Rejected by mankind	Accepted by God
Try Harder	Rest in Christ
Go to the Meeting	Go to Church
Dependent on Self	Dependent on God
Physical Life	Spiritual Life
Fellow Addicts	Fellowship
Human Centered	Christ Centered
Higher Power	Personal God
Relative Truth	Absolute Truth
Meetings	Discipleship
Big Book	Bible
Human Counsel	Divine Guidance
"Stinking Thinking"	Peace of Mind

Julia's Perspective

Editor's Note: While Mike found his freedom in Christ, Julia was nearing the end of her rope as a performer. Mike's enthusiasm for the teaching about freedom was commendable, but was it just one more attempt to break free from the bondage of his addiction? Here's what was going on in Julia's life.

One Sunday after church I asked Ruth and Charlie to come to our house. For the last few days Mike had been irritable. I wanted to give Charlie a chance to talk with him. I felt uneasy when Mike was irritable. Mike was *not* happy to see Charlie and Ruth when they walked into the house. All of us sat in the den and tried to make conversation. Suddenly Mike got mad and stormed out of the room. "I'm getting out of here," he said. I panicked because I could interpret those words—Mike was headed for a drinking binge.

Charlie attempted to reason with Mike, but it was impossible. The three of us followed Mike down the stairs to our garage. We begged and pleaded with him not to leave. At one point I attempted to get his car keys, but this aggravated him even more. "I'm going to Florida for a few days," Mike proclaimed as he roared out of our driveway. Having horrified looks on their faces, Ruth and Charlie watched Mike leave as I dissolved into tears.

At the time our phone was out of order and I was glad. I couldn't receive any calls from Mike, the police or anyone else. I tried to work and act as if everything was completely normal.

A few nights later, late at night, I heard a loud knock on my front door, then the doorbell rang. When I opened it, there stood Joe, my kind next-door neighbor. Mike had called Joe's phone and wanted to talk with me. I was so embarrassed. At this hour Joe had been awakened and now he stood at my door in his bathrobe. Although I had no desire to talk with Mike, I didn't want Joe caught in this mess. I grabbed my robe and slippers and followed him. He had a phone in his garage. "Just talk as long as you'd like," he said. "Lock the door on the way out. I'm going back to bed."

When I answered the phone Mike began to rave about this wonderful Holiday Inn at Navarre Beach where he was staying. He couldn't wait to bring me there someday.

He has lost his mind, I thought. *I don't care where he is. Doesn't he know that?*

"I don't really care, Mike," I told him. "I don't want to hear from you and don't call back on Joe's line. EVER!" I slammed down the receiver and stormed back to my house.

The next day Mike returned home. He was all excited about some cassette tapes he had listened to on the drive home. Whoopee. Big deal. His enthusiasm and excitement just rolled over my head. I couldn't be bothered with the latest craze to end his addiction. I had my hands full working my job and keeping up appearances.

Was This for Real?

Mike's excitement diminished quickly. He seemed afraid to leave the house and continued to spend most of his time sitting in his chair. A few weeks later he went out on another bad drunken spree. I thought, *Will he ever be able to stop drinking?*

His actions and the resulting remorse and apologies didn't phase me. "Why don't you go visit Jack and June?" I suggested, "I need a break." These dear friends had recently moved from Atlanta to Lookout Mountain, Georgia. I needed a few days of peace and quiet. What a relief to see Mike leave!

Then he called me almost immediately after his arrival. Mike was talking like some sort of crazy person about some cassette teaching tapes. "I've found my answer," he proclaimed.

Internally I groaned. "Not another one," I told him firmly. "I don't want to hear this." I hung up. Immediately he called back.

"Julia, you've got to listen to me," he pleaded. "I'm coming back tomorrow so you can hear these tapes." I begged him to stay a few days. It seemed as though Mike wasn't listening so I hung up.

When Mike arrived home a couple of days later, he seemed different. I didn't want to notice, but some things were obvious. He was enthusiastic about what he had learned. He wasn't restless. He didn't sit in his chair staring into space. All he wanted to do was either listen to those tapes or talk about them. They were by Bill and Anabel Gillham from Texas. How could listening to some tapes have changed him so drastically?

Though I was skeptical, I couldn't help but be curious. He didn't push me to listen. He wasn't critical of me. He called Charlie and Dan daily to tell them what he was learning.

A few days later Ruth and Charlie came to our house. It was evident to them that Mike was a different person. He was attentive to me. He was excited about his life. He was reveling in this new discovery of being free. I didn't understand it, but it was a welcome change. Was this for real?

A Different Crisis

That same week we faced a different crisis. During Susan's six-month checkup, she and Bradley were told by their doctor that something was wrong with the baby. I was devastated for them.

Mike comforted me with verses from the Bible about healing and hope. He reminded me that Jesus is *Jehovah Rapha*, the God who heals. I began singing the praise chorus again and again, "I am the Lord who healeth you, I am the Lord, your healer." Mike helped sustain me in my distress. He had real confidence in God's love and mercy.

Two days later my prayer group met with me while Susan and Bradley visited a specialist in Atlanta. We kept thanking God for this baby and for what He was doing. In the early afternoon Bradley called and told me the specialist had done extensive sonograms and tests. Nothing was wrong with the baby. God had chosen to heal this child!

The next day Mike and I drove to Atlanta to rejoice with Susan and Bradley about this miracle. It culminated an incredible week of blessing.

Notes
1. Dr. Bill Gillham, *Lifetime Guarantee* (Eugene, Oreg: Harvest House, 1993), p. 10.
2. Don McMinn, *Spiritual Strongholds* (Oklahoma City: NCM Press, 1993), pp. 73, 74.
3. Watchman Nee, *The Normal Christian Life* (Wheaton, Ill.: Tyndale House Publishers, 1957), pp. 64, 65.

4. Charles Solomon, *The Ins and Outs of Rejection* (Littleton, Colo.: Heritage House, 1976).
5. Dr. Bill and Anabel Gillham, *Victorious Christian Living* booklet (Fort Worth, Tex.: Lifetime Guarantee, Inc., n.d.), p. 14A.
6. Nee, *The Normal Christian Life*.

Really Free

If the Son, then, sets you free, you are really free!
—John. 8:36 *(Phillips)*

Now that I was free, what next? Did my newfound freedom have any practical implications for daily living? When I got home from Lookout Mountain my life hadn't changed. In disgrace I had resigned from my ministry. The Presbytery was investigating my situation to determine what kind of disciplinary action should be taken. I didn't have any income, a job or any prospects for one. Julia didn't know if this freedom obsession was just another wild goose chase or what.

One morning after my return home I sat at my desk and reviewed all the facts of my current situation. Although my circumstances were unchanged and everything looked bleak, to my surprise, for the first time in my life, I felt at peace. I was beginning to experience peace and freedom—completely apart from my circumstances. The joy of Christ flooded my soul and I jumped up and shouted, "Hallelujah! Praise God!" Then I sat down and silently thanked God for a joy that no person could take away.

Then I had one of my all-time weirdest thoughts, *I hope I*

don't get a job anytime soon. For a while, I want to enjoy just knowing I don't need anything but Christ for freedom, peace and joy.
Malcolm Smith said that happiness depends on the happenings of favorable circumstances, but joy is found only in our relationship with God. We usually spend years looking for joy in all the wrong places. Then when we discover it's not to be found anywhere else, we are ready to find joy in our relationship with God.

> You have filled my heart with greater joy than when their grain and new wine abound (Ps. 4:7, NIV).
> You have made known to me the path of life; you will fill me with joy in your presence, with eternal pleasures at your right hand (16:11, NIV).
> Surely you have granted him eternal blessings and made him glad with the joy of your presence (21:6, NIV).
> Then will I go to the altar of God, to God, my joy and my delight (43:4, NIV).
> When anxiety was great within me, your consolation brought joy to my soul (94:19, NIV).
> The Lord has done great things for us, and we are filled with joy (126:3, NIV).
> Then you will find your joy in the Lord, and I will cause you to ride on the heights of the land and to feast on the inheritance of your father Jacob. The mouth of the Lord has spoken (Isa. 58:14, NIV).
> I have told you this so that my joy may be in you and that your joy may be complete (John 15:11, NIV).
> So with you: Now is your time of grief, but I will see you again and you will rejoice, and no one will take away your joy (16:22, NIV).

These are only a few of the verses about joy; the Bible contains more than 200 verses that focus on joy. Joy is part of the package. God wants us to experience His joy—joy to the fullest extent that no one can take away (see John 16:22). Our joy comes from our relationship with God and God alone. If I look elsewhere for this joy, it becomes elusive and soon fades into a vain hope. If we place our joy in a loving, supportive spouse or a well-paying, secure job or obedient children or anything else, our joy can be removed in an instant. None of these things are consistent. At a moment's notice, they are subject to change.

What Is Freedom?

Many people ask me, "What is freedom?" Freedom is the assurance that your needs for security, significance, love, acceptance and worth are always met in Christ. They can't be taken away by changing circumstances or personal bondages. Because we have Christ and He is in us and we are in Him, circumstances can't change that reality. Neil Anderson will explain more about this aspect in the second part of this book. Also, the "Steps to Freedom in Christ" in appendix A enable us to process our issues in the seven major areas where Satan robs us of our freedom.

I was free to choose. I learned that I could say yes to sin or no to sin, but I quickly discovered that I didn't feel dead to sin. Many times I felt very alive to it; but the truth is based on what God says, regardless of my feelings.

Now to me this short statement is the secret to living the victorious Christian life. God says I am dead to sin and freed from it (see Rom. 6:2,6,7). Because I am free, I can count myself dead to sin and alive to God (see v. 11). When I choose to not let sin rule in my body and not obey its evil desires (see v. 12), I offer myself and my body to God (see v. 13). Once I understood this truth, an amazing thing happened—I experienced victory in my situation. I was no longer hopeless and helpless.

My Difficulties Didn't Disappear

My problems didn't evaporate overnight. In the days that followed I went through many difficult times. I had pressures and stresses from finances, unemployment, possible discipline from Presbytery, and of course, my recent failures and loss of reputation. When Satan attacked me and reminded me about my bad deeds and how I needed release from my old ways, I chose to say no. Because I understood my identity in Christ, the old temptations and patterns of lust had lost their power.

Don't misunderstand. I had plenty of temptations and they

....

We experience freedom when we choose to believe God, then act on the basis of the truth *regardless of our feelings.*

....

continue today. Today, however, I can face these temptations from a position of strength. But what happens if I fall?

If you walked outside after a heavy rainstorm and fell into a large mud puddle, what would you do? Lay in the mud puddle for the rest of the day, or get up, clean off and keep on walking? I hope you would get up and keep on walking. Many Christians who experience problems don't get up. Yet the Christian life is a walk. If we fall, we can confess to God, get up and keep on walking. The truth that set you free is still true.

In counseling others I have listened to many people as they try to get their feelings to coincide with the truth. It's not going to happen (not for very long and never completely). After listening to people, I say, "If you are trying to match your feelings with God's truth, you'll never experience freedom."

We experience freedom when we choose to believe God, then act on the basis of the truth *regardless of our feelings.* When I counsel other Christians about who they are in Christ and their freedom from sin, to many it seems almost too good to be true. Some think I'm just trying to make them feel good.

"This is more than positive thinking," I tell them. Unless it's based on the truth, positive thinking won't stand the test of endurance. You'll soon be looking for another program. If we believe the truth, the truth will set us free. As Neil Anderson says, it is not positive thinking, but positive believing.

A New Freedom to Forgive

I was free to forgive. In September 1984, when the discipline committee at my church recommended I enter a secular treatment center, they knew their recommendation would cost money I didn't have. My insurance wouldn't cover the expense. They reassured me they understood my financial difficulty and would help me.

For some reason, their help never came and I was close to bankruptcy and losing my home. In the meantime, their recommendation obviously hadn't worked. The committee lost interest in my situation. I believe they didn't know what else to recommend. This awkward situation was very painful for Julia and me. This church had been our lifeblood and a major part of our lives. For 14 years I had been a member and Julia had been a member for more than 20 years. Both of us grew bitter and resentful about the situation.

God graciously gave us insight about how to release our bitterness. If we planned to continue to walk in the freedom of God, we needed to forgive those committee members who didn't follow through on their promises. It wasn't easy, but we learned that we could choose to forgive. We needed to forgive from our hearts in obedience to God for our sake and for our own freedom. None of them considered our financial problems and feelings of resentment as anything they had caused. Perhaps these committee members didn't have a problem. They recommended what they thought was best for me and I believed they acted in love.

Regardless of their actions or motives, Julia and I were both hurt and angered by their actions. We needed to forgive them. God enabled us both to forgive, and He freed us from our anger and bad feelings. If we hadn't forgiven, we wouldn't have continued enjoying our freedom. One of the most common ways Satan robs us of freedom is through unforgiveness.

Freedom to Fail

I was also free to fail. My alcoholic past probably caused most people to consider me an expert at failure. There is a distinction between being free to fail and just being a failure. One of the largest barriers in my life was the fear of failure. I did everything I could *not* to fail, yet believed that failure was looming ahead.

In October 1988 when I returned to Birmingham from Lookout Mountain after discovering my freedom, I had to face the ongoing discipline proceedings of Presbytery. As we discussed in chapter 3, the assistant pastor, Stan, was a caring person. He was also chairman of the minister's committee. One of Stan's duties was to inform me that I would face some

....

Many of us live our lives trying to avoid failure. God's purpose, however, is to show us what a failure we are in our own resources.

....

discipline. I didn't want to hear anything about discipline from a church committee, but when he gave me the bad news, I had some unusual thoughts: *It looks as though I'm in for more disgrace and public humiliation. I don't want that, but it's OK. No matter what they do or think, I'm still a child of God and I'm in Christ. Nothing can change that.*

Ordinarily such a meeting would have devastated me, but I walked away experiencing an unusual joy and peace in my heart.

Many would consider me a colossal failure. God showed me that on my own and in the flesh I was born a failure. What do failures do? They fail. But that wasn't me anymore. My identity and my sense of worth no longer came from my performance and the opinion of others. My identity came from God and I was OK. God said I was His dearly loved child and in addition, I was a saint, Christ's friend, complete in Christ and God's workmanship. My life was hidden with Christ in God.

Many of us live our lives trying to avoid failure. God's purpose, however, is to show us what a failure we are in our own resources. We can then give up on our lives in the flesh and find our life in Christ. Let's be honest. You and I are going to fail again. No one lives a perfect life.

Recently a good friend told me about her "fear of failure." It was robbing this friend of her freedom in Christ. I told her she was free to fail. Her identity didn't depend on her performance. Every time I see her, she thanks me for releasing her from this unfounded fear.

A man in the Sunday School class I am currently teaching lamented how he couldn't make his Christian life work. He knew his identity in Christ, but it didn't work for him. As we talked, he related a series of problems about his attempts to succeed in business.

"Have you ever given up the right to succeed," I asked him, "so that you're free to fail?"

"Absolutely not!" he said emphatically. Despite his head knowledge about his identity in Christ, he sought his identity through success in business. He wasn't free to fail.

G. K. Chesterton said, "There is nothing that fails like success."[1] Why? Most people look at success as an impersonal and abstract concept instead of in terms of people and relationships. Relationships and people are the important part of success. Success at the expense of family and relationships is not success.

If you understand your identity in Christ, you know no setback or failure will separate you from Him. You become free to fail. You aren't really free to succeed until you are free to fail. By having this new perspective, you can enter life, relationships and ministry without worrying about the results. Colossians 3:23 says, "Whatever you do, work at it with all your heart, as working for the Lord, not for men" (NIV).

I had believed I was a failure in ministry. As I learned more about freedom in Christ, I understood my problem in ministry. I was trying to meet my needs for self-worth and self-acceptance through success in my ministry. Although I never vocalized it, it was "my" ministry and hooked to my identity. When the ministry didn't go my way, I viewed my ministry and myself as a failure.

I have met many pastors and Christian workers who are depressed and discouraged about their ministries. Not realizing their work and ministries belong to God, they have assumed ownership of their ministries. When we take possession of the ministry, we position ourselves for failure. Today I love my ministry, but I don't look to it as the basis for my identity or to meet my needs.

Freedom to Be Rejected

I was also free to be rejected. In a chance meeting and having great enthusiasm, I told my pastor about the new truths I learned. He expressed concern that this teaching didn't agree with the doctrines of our denomination. He arranged a meeting between him, Stan and me. I shared my story of how I gained freedom by listening to Bill Gillham's tapes "Victorious Christian Living."

This pastor reached over and picked up a copy of Gillham's book *Lifetime Guarantee*. It contained the same teaching as the tapes. Point by point, he explained how Gillham was off in his theology and as a result I had fallen into error. More than anyone else I knew, I respected this man as my mentor. If I could select someone to be a godly example and minister to emulate—it would be him. He had recommended me to the church where I received my pastorate and his endorsement carried a great deal of weight within the denomination.

Now as I sat with him, it came as a shock that his explanation didn't threaten or faze me one bit. I knew God had revealed this truth to me. My life was drastically altered and I lived in freedom and peace. Although I respected and loved this man, I wasn't shaken. For at least an hour, we discussed the major issues where we disagreed. The tone of the meeting was friendly and I knew both men had my best interests at heart. Our major disagreement was about identity.

"I don't think you can stay in the denomination, Mike, if you continue to hold to these unacceptable doctrines," Drew said.

As our meeting came to an end, I said, "Drew, it's amazing to me that for eight years, you and the church did everything you knew to help me with my problem. But you couldn't help me. Now I've found an answer and am walking in freedom and you tell me I have to leave the denomination? Something is wrong somewhere."

I agreed with him that I had changed my beliefs. Rather than stir up something contrary to the church, it would be best if I left the denomination. Although I had spent 17 years in this denomination, had been theologically trained and ordained and had many friends in it, leaving didn't concern me greatly. For me the change was a small price for my freedom.

After the meeting, Stan walked me to my car. "Don't do anything hasty," Stan said. "Presbytery doesn't meet for several months. Maybe you'll change your mind."

"Stan, I don't think I'll change my mind because what I believe is the truth that set me free," I said. "But maybe Drew will change his mind."

"Well, I don't know about that," Stan said.

"It's a possibility," I said. "I heard Dr. Charles Stanley say he stood up in his pulpit and apologized to his congregation at First Baptist Atlanta for teaching them what he had about who they are."

Drew didn't change his mind and I left the denomination. However, I left without any regrets or anger. Drew was right. I had changed my beliefs and needed to leave. I preferred to stay, but I learned that it was all right to be rejected. Along with the rest of the world, I want to be accepted and I don't enjoy rejection. Because I knew my identity was in Christ, the rejection wasn't devastating to me. When we discover who we are in Christ, we may face opposition in our churches, our marriages, our families, our jobs or our reputations. Thankfully none of these things can dislodge our secure positions "in Christ." Freedom always demands a price, but it will always be worth it.

"If we are faithless, he will remain faithful, for he cannot disown himself," (2 Tim. 2:13, *NIV*). I believe God is saying that no matter what happens or what we do, we are secure because we are in Christ and "he cannot disown himself." Romans 8:39 tells us that nothing "in all creation, will be able to separate us from the love of God that is in Christ Jesus" *(NIV)*.

New Freedom in Relationships

One of my greatest areas of freedom was in relationships. When I learned my true identity in Christ, I forgave myself and accepted myself just as I was. Some people struggle with forgiving themselves, but defeated Christians feel guilty and condemned. Scripture is clear, "Therefore, there is now no condemnation for those who are in Christ Jesus" (Rom. 8:1, *NIV*).

If people feel guilty, they haven't appropriated the forgiveness purchased for them at the Cross. A good way for them to experience this forgiveness is to accept God's forgiveness and let themselves off their own hook. All Christians understand their sins were placed on the Cross, but many live as though only their sins *before* becoming Christians were forgiven. I have heard Dr. Charles Stanley say that God isn't surprised when we sin because these sins have already been put on the Cross.

How did this new acceptance of self give me freedom in relationships? Because until I accepted myself just as I was, I couldn't accept others just the way they are. Through the years I have made a private study of this matter with the people I have counseled. Without exception, the most judgmental and condemning people are those who can't accept themselves. These Christians treat others with the same harshness and strict standards they place on themselves.

How can I possibly accept myself with the full knowledge of my past and what I have done? The Cross is the answer. If I only look at my past behavior, I can never accept myself. If I look at God's acceptance of me, however, I can accept myself. Until I received this acceptance, I was not able to walk in freedom and love others. I have found a new inner peace I couldn't have when I was always trying to measure up and fell short. Now I accept others just the way they are. As I chose to accept Julia, we experienced God's healing and restoration of our marriage. Unless we do this our marriages will have little chance of succeeding.

Earlier I mentioned writing to my three children to confess my legalistic and unaccepting behavior toward them. I resolved to accept them just the way they were—regardless. Not long afterward my daughter, Audrey, gave me an opportunity to put this principle into practice. She called me and said she was planning to move in with her boyfriend. I sat down and wrote a six-page letter. In my first four pages I told her how much I loved and accepted her no matter what she did or didn't do. Also I let her know I would always be there for her. Her actions or beliefs didn't affect my love and acceptance, which were given unconditionally. Then in my last two pages I wrote that I wouldn't be acting in love if I didn't confront her about her lifestyle choice. It was outside God's will and not the best thing for her. The results wouldn't be good.

Shortly after receiving my letter, Audrey called and said she loved me. She appreciated my concern for her and said she also let her boyfriend read my letter. I continued to reach out to them in love and acceptance. When they got married a couple of years later, Julia and I had a party for them when they visited us.

Two years ago when Audrey learned she was pregnant with her first child, she called from Los Angeles. She and her husband decided to raise their child around family who were Christians. They wanted to move to Atlanta. Could they move in with us for the time being? For six months they lived with us until Mark got a good job. One evening after dinner we sat around our table and Audrey said, "Dad, we came here and moved in with you because we knew you accepted us." That was music to my ears.

Since then I've seen my daughter grow in the Lord and become a godly woman, a wife of noble character. Audrey set aside her burning ambition to be an actress so she could be a mother for her little girl, Aryele. A few months ago she thanked me for the spiritual encouragement I had given her. She said she didn't know what she would do without me. If I never have another ministry in anyone's life, that alone would be enough.

Another blessing in the area of relationships is with Julia's son, Bradley, and his wife, Susan. We have the joy of being grandparents to three grandchildren, Kaitlin, Brad IV and William. In a city the size of Atlanta, we are fortunate to live

....

Neil Anderson says, "People don't care what you know until they know you care." You cannot have a ministry with people unless they know you accept them.

....

only about 15 minutes from all four grandchildren.

At a pastor's seminar I conducted a few years ago a youth pastor asked, "All this stuff about grace and acceptance is well and good, but how are we going to make these kids do right?" It's not up to us to make anybody do right. We can't make anybody do anything—that's a ministry of law. The law is a ministry of death and condemnation (see 2 Cor. 3:7-9).

As Neil Anderson says, "People don't care what you know until they know you care." You cannot have a ministry with people unless they know you accept them. Mother Teresa said being accepted is the greatest need we have. It frees us to understand that change isn't our responsibility. That is God's responsibility, and only He can change a person. If we don't understand this, we are headed for burnout. If we are parents or in some position of authority, discipline is often necessary, but our discipline should be directed at behavior, not at the person or the person's character.

The Freedom to Enjoy Life

Another unexpected result of my freedom was my freedom to

enjoy life. Have you looked around and noticed how many Christians seem to be killjoys? I was the world's worst. Throughout my Christian life I was busy trying to do right and get everybody else to do right. I couldn't enjoy life. Once I received a letter from an old friend in Birmingham. Years ago, we had participated in an early-morning Bible study. He said in the letter that he always had been impressed with my "serious and somber demeanor." That statement leaped off the page at me.

I immediately wrote back that my "serious and somber demeanor" was from my bondage and my legalistic lifestyle. Roger Ailes, who headed the advertising effort of George Bush's presidential campaign in 1988, wrote in his book *You Are the Message*, "Don't take yourself too seriously." That's good advice.

I first met Neil Anderson when I attended his conference in Birmingham, Alabama, in 1993. We had breakfast together and discussed the possibility of Julia and me joining the staff of Freedom in Christ Ministries. What impressed me the most was not his dynamic leadership, his incredible insights or his powerful presentation (although they are impressive), but his great sense of humor and love of life. Neil didn't take himself too seriously. That settled it for me. On our way home I told Julia, "I can work with a guy like that."

One of my first counselees who found her freedom was a young housewife. We could see the change in her face when she returned for her next appointment. When I told her about the visible change, she replied, "I know I'm different because my sense of humor is back and I'm not trying to change my husband anymore." Those are two undeniable pieces of evidence.

One of my heroes is Phil McLain. He was my supervisor during my counseling internship at Grace Ministries International in the summer of 1989. Later when I joined the staff in 1990, it was my privilege and pleasure to work for three years alongside Phil until his retirement. Phil was almost 65 when I began to work there, but I've never met anyone who has more zest for life than he does. He used to say, "If I can't have a little fun along the way, I'm not going." Phil had pastored churches in Minnesota, and every week he told at least one new (or old) Sven and Oly joke.

Neil says in *Victory over the Darkness* that when we have fun it's usually spontaneous and unplanned. Julia and I attended the World's Fair in Knoxville, Tennessee, in 1986. The crowds were incredible and we spent more time standing in line than viewing the exhibits. One hot, humid day, we and another couple sat down at a sidewalk cafe and enjoyed a cold drink. As we sat there we mentioned that this break was the most enjoyable part of our day. Just then, three young girls walked by. One carried her shoes in her hands and looked tired and weary. We heard her say to her friends, "Don't tell me I'm having fun. I know when I'm having fun and I'm *not* having fun." She matched our feelings exactly. On the drive back home we laughed about this girl's comment, and that's what I remember about the World's Fair.

Christians are some of the most uptight people. Why? Isn't God in control and isn't our future secure? Hasn't Satan been defeated and haven't we been given every spiritual blessing? Christians, of all people, should enjoy life and laugh at themselves.

Some of my greatest pleasures in life are simple—walking in the woods with my wife, sitting in front of a fire reading a good book, playing with my grandchildren, having lunch with a friend, praying with some close friends or just talking with friends about what God has done in our lives. In Christ, we are free to enjoy life.

While writing this particular chapter, I'm in the middle of the wooded mountains of Dahlonega, Georgia. My dear friends Charlie and Ann Cox allowed me to use their Prophet's Chamber (a garage apartment) for a quiet place to write. Before I finish this chapter I will take a break and enjoy a walk in the beautiful woods of north Georgia.

Freedom to Receive

Another truth I learned is freedom "to receive." In Christ, we no longer have to work to achieve freedom, but by faith we receive it from God. This puts an entirely different perspective on life.

When we moved to Atlanta in 1990, our desire was to secure a home loan and purchase a house. However, I had a poor credit record and an inconsistent record of employment. I had been with Grace Ministries for only one year and had raised my own support. We signed a "lease purchase" on a house and moved in, but we had to make a substantial down payment and then spend several thousand dollars to fix up the house. It wasn't the most prudent action, but we did it. At

....

"My greatest lesson in 57 years is that all my needs are met in Christ." I don't have to drive myself to be the greatest, have the best, or even to get my circumstances worked out to my advantage. If Christ is in me and I am in Him, what else could I possibly need?

....

the end of the year we applied for a loan. Julia and I sat in an office talking to the mortgage-loan people. They discovered a judgment had been filed against me seven years earlier and I knew nothing about it. The people who filed it had forgotten it, but it was still there.

"Mr. Quarles," the loan officer said, "there's no way you can get a loan. There's a judgment against you." To make matters worse, the judgment had been accumulating interest at 12 and a half percent a year. I had no earthly hope to pay it off.

I felt crushed. Now I couldn't get a loan and would lose all the money I had put into the house. We would have to move again. I walked out of the office in a state of shock. Julia turned and said, "There was a picture of a ship, the USS *Victory*, on the wall in that office. I kept looking at it and thinking, *Victory.*" *Yeah sure, some victory.* That was about the last thing on my mind. *What could I do to get a loan?* I was willing to do practically anything.

As I drove back to the office a verse came to mind, "But thanks be to God! He gives us the victory through our Lord Jesus Christ" (1 Cor. 15:57, *NIV*). Then in my mind I heard God say, "Mike, I have given you the victory. Who are you going to believe, Me or your circumstances?"

I thought in response, *OK, God, I'm going to believe You—You say that You have given me the victory so I receive it right now. Thank You for it.* Then I had a peace about the situation and never worried about it again.

A day later one of the mortgage-loan officers called me and said, "We would be willing to attempt a loan even with the judgment. All you need to do is write a letter of explanation about the judgment."

Without hesitation, I said, "I don't want to do that." I believed God wanted me to face my situation and trust Him for the funds. Later, an attorney friend helped me so I was able to pay off the judgment at a fraction of the original amount, without interest, and got it off my record.

We secured our loan and closed escrow when interest rates were the lowest in many years. I believe I experienced "victory" not when we signed the new loan, but when I believed God and received His promise. Even if we hadn't acquired the loan and had lost the house, God had given me the victory. Your situation may not look like victory. Although people tell you differently, God's Word is clear—He has given us the victory. It is up to us to believe and receive it.

Many people say to me when I counsel them, "Just tell me what to do and I'll do it." Most of us are good at formulas, but we aren't good at receiving. If God has given us everything for life and godliness, we need to learn to receive. Everyone searches for a simple formula or brief list, but it doesn't work that way. If people are looking for formulas, I encourage them to read the simple biblical formula in Romans 5:17 (*NIV*), "How much more will those who receive God's abundant provision of grace and of the gift of righteousness reign in life through the one man, Jesus Christ." Simply receive God's abundant provision of grace and the gift of righteousness!

Two years ago Audrey invited Julia and me over to celebrate my fifty-seventh birthday. During dinner she asked, "Dad, what's the greatest lesson you've learned in 57 years?" It didn't take long for me to answer.

I said, "My greatest lesson in 57 years is that all my needs are met in Christ." I don't have to drive myself to be the greatest, have the best, or even to get my circumstances worked out to my advantage. If Christ is in me and I am in Him, what else could I possibly need?

We don't learn this lesson from reading a book or listening to someone speak. Sometimes we have to endure a painful search before we learn that other things don't satisfy. It took more than 50 years for me to learn that lesson, but I wouldn't take anything for those experiences. It's the difference between rest and anxiety, peace and confusion, fulfillment and frustration.

Freedom Gave Me Rest

I believe the primary result of freedom is rest. I don't mean passivity, but rest from the struggles of life. If you live by faith, you'll still be active, but the strain and the striving will be removed. The responsibility to make things happen isn't yours, but God's. Hannah Whitall Smith says our responsibility is to trust and God's responsibility is to work. When the disciples came to Jesus and asked, "What shall we do, that we may work the works of God?" (John 6:28, *NKJV*), He answered, "This is the work of God, that you believe in Him whom He sent" (v. 29, *NKJV*).

Many Christian workers and pastors are facing spiritual burnout. Perhaps they are trying to carry a responsibility that isn't theirs. As someone pointed out, sheep aren't burden-bearing animals. Hebrews 4:10 says, "For anyone who enters God's rest also rests from his own work, just as God did from his" (*NIV*). Our choices to work prevent us from finding God's rest. Hebrews 3:19 sums it up, "So we see that they were not able to enter, because of their unbelief" (*NIV*).

Most people believe the way to find rest is to be in control, but this drive for control keeps us from finding rest. We need to realize that we aren't in control and don't have the ability for control. As Bill Gillham says, controlling things is God's job description. If you're trying to do God's job, you are going to be at cross purposes with Him. Each of us have out-of-control areas in our lives—such as children, health, finances, job, security or our future. Although we might have some input, we definitely aren't in control. Our good news is that God is in control and He "works for the good of those who love him, who have been called according to his purpose" (Rom 8:28, *NIV*).

Last year I got a personal reminder of this truth. My precious 16-month-old granddaughter, Aryele, was in intensive care at a hospital. She had several seizures and things didn't look good. Despite Aryele being in one of the best children's hospitals in the world, the doctors didn't know what was wrong. Her parents, grandparents, uncles and aunts would have done anything for her, but we were helpless. All we could do was cry out to God and confess our total dependence on Him. Audrey, her mother, said, "She's in God's hands." It was a good place to be.

Saturday she lay limp and listless, but by Monday afternoon, we took turns being a "designated chaser" to follow her around the hospital halls. That night she was released after a "miraculous" recovery. Our hope and trust was in God. As Ephesians 2:4-7 says, "But because of his great love for us, God, who is rich in mercy, made us alive with Christ even when we were dead in transgressions—it is by grace you have been saved. And God raised us up with Christ and seated us with him in the heavenly realms in Christ Jesus, in order that in the coming ages he might show the incomparable riches of his grace, expressed in his kindness to us in Christ Jesus" (*NIV*).

Sometimes my counselees are striving for control. I ask, "If you are in control, then who is not?" If we control or we think we are in control, then God is not. Ray Alton, a friend at Grace Ministries International, says, "The best way to lose your mind is to concentrate on not losing it." The best way to be out of control is to concentrate on being in control. We are free to settle this issue of control because we depend on a loving, heavenly Father. He can be trusted. The hymn "I Know Who Holds Tomorrow," by Ira Stanphill, says we don't understand many things about the future, but we know who holds the future and who holds our hands.

Some have said that if the only response is to believe, it's too easy. I would beg to differ. Believing isn't easy. To believe God works everything together for good when your granddaughter is lying lifeless in ICU after her fifth seizure doesn't come easy. Jairus faced this problem when he came to Jesus, "He fell at his feet and pleaded earnestly with him, 'My little daughter is dying. Please come and put your hands on her so that she will be healed and live.' So Jesus went with him....And a woman was there who had been subject to bleeding for twelve years....When she heard about Jesus, she...touched his cloak,...she was freed from her suffering" (Mark 5:22-25,27-29, *NIV*). Jesus was delayed while he told the woman, "Your faith has healed you" (v. 34, *NIV*). Then some men came from the house of Jairus, the synagogue ruler.

"'Your daughter is dead,'" they said. "'Why bother the teacher any more?'" (v. 35, *NIV*). Jairus could have taken these men at their word, returned home and made preparations to bury his daughter. But the next verse says, "Ignoring what they said, Jesus told the synagogue ruler, 'Don't be afraid; just believe'" (v. 36, *NIV*).

You and I face many situations in which we are told a situation is beyond help. To Jairus (and I'm sure to us) those appeared to be the facts. But the next verse says, "Ignoring what they said." If you and I are going to follow Jesus' instructions, "Don't be afraid; just believe," at times we have to ignore what others say. We'll have to ignore experts, professionals, information in newspapers or on TV, and even our own common sense when it runs contrary to Scripture.

No, it's not easy to believe God. Faith isn't exercised in a vacuum. Instead, faith is exercised in the hard-core everyday circumstances of life. At the conclusion of the story about Jairus, Jesus arrived at the house and people were crying and wailing loudly in mourning. Jesus asked why all the commotion, then told them the child wasn't dead, but asleep. "But they laughed at him. After he put them all out, he took the child's father and mother and the disciples who were with him, and went in where the child was. He took her by the hand and said to her,...'Little girl, I say to you, get up!'...Immediately the girl stood up and walked around" (vv. 40-42, *NIV*). He is in control and worthy to be trusted. We are free to rest in Christ.

Julia's Perspective

Editor's Note: While Mike found his freedom in Christ, Julia began to change her thinking as well. Here's her story from this same time period.

It Sounded Like Me

Mike learned that a friend had the Gillham videos and arranged to borrow them. I watched the videos with him to find out what this was about.

As I listened and watched, I couldn't get over the similarities between Bill Gillham's wife, Anabel, and myself. What Anabel called her "flesh patterns" fit my actions perfectly. She labeled herself a "performer" who lived on "performance-based acceptance." When she told about Bill trying to tear her down and destroy her with his tongue, I knew exactly what she was talking about! But they were teaching from a videotape titled *Victorious Christian Living*, filmed at First Baptist Atlanta in 1981. How could this be? Could God change us and restore us as He had them? I had to know more!

Bill and Anabel taught that once we become Christians, we are saints who sometimes sin. In the past, I called myself a saint but I still considered myself a forgiven sinner. As I listened, I slowly began to understand. Early in the mornings I started putting the tapes into my Walkman as I hiked the hills of our neighborhood before work. Whenever I drove my car, I listened to the tapes in the cassette player. I played another tape while I did housework. I couldn't get enough of the teaching! I found their insight refreshing and liberating. The good news gave me hope for us.

A similar joy flooded my heart when I became a Christian

22 years ago. The Gillhams were teaching from God's Word and it was truth. I had never heard the Bible taught like this before. I began to understand Mike's many years of bondage and I saw I was in bondage also. I had been responsible those years and had not given up. Now I understood that my perfectionism was based on "my flesh pattern" rather than on God's strength. All along, God had been trying to break my strong ways. Much of my Christian life I thought I relied on God. Instead I was being strong in myself. I looked to God for "help," but not in complete dependence. I learned that God was not interested in strengthening my flesh, even when it is "good" flesh. He wanted to give me His life in exchange for my old natural life in the flesh.

God's love and acceptance was overwhelming to me. In God's eyes, I was special and worthy of Mike's respect. Through these teaching messages I learned how I had never given up on handling our circumstances. I seemed to need to prove to God that I could take anything. I continually bounced back, strong, brave, gritting my teeth and bearing it, being overly responsible, and thinking I was trusting God. Throughout my Christian life I knew Jesus was in me. I had never known that I was "in Him." I learned that when Jesus died on the cross for my sins, I died with Him and didn't have to keep working to earn His love.

Ruth and Charlie came to our house and watched the videos with us. From the Gillhams we purchased a booklet to lead us in a discussion after each video. We invited other friends to watch the videos. Within a few months we gathered one group on Friday nights and another on Sunday nights. I watched the same video on Sunday and discovered teaching I didn't hear on Friday. It was a time of renewing my mind after more than 20 years of being told how to become righteous—instead of knowing I was righteous and accepted by God all along. I could do nothing to add to what Jesus did on the cross. I moved from "doing" Christianity to resting in Christ and being secure in Him.

Mike heard the Gillham tapes during the last week in October 1988. We spent November and December listening to tapes and watching the Gillham videos. Mike remembered a friend, Blake Rymer, had talked to him about this teaching several years earlier. Blake lived in Montgomery so Mike drove there and spent the day. Blake was now with a counseling ministry and used these truths in his counseling. He and his partner, Mike Darnell, were teaching a three-day conference the last weekend in January. They invited us to attend. We invited Ruth and Charlie to go with us.

We Hung On to Every Word
The conference began Thursday night and continued through Saturday afternoon. Mike and I hung on to every word of the teaching from Blake and Mike Darnell. It was good news to our ears! How had we missed this all along? We couldn't remember hearing Scripture taught this way before.

To add to the delight we experienced from the conference, we received a call Saturday night in the middle of the night. Bradley told us their baby was about to be born. We wanted to be there for this wonderful event, so we quickly drove to Atlanta. What rejoicing and praise when Kaitlin Prater Fulkerson arrived. Much to the doctors surprise, but not ours, she was normal and healthy.

Several years earlier my friend CeCe had told me she was praying Psalm 40 for Mike. Verses 1-5 say, "I waited patiently for the Lord; he turned to me and heard my cry. He lifted me out of the slimy pit, out of the mud and mire; he set my feet on a rock and gave me a firm place to stand. He put a new song in my mouth, a hymn of praise to our God. Many will see and fear and put their trust in the Lord. Blessed is the man who makes the Lord his trust, who does not look to the proud, to those who turn aside to false gods. Many, O Lord my God, are the wonders you have done. The things you planned for us no one can recount to you; were I to speak and tell of them, they would be too many to declare" *(NIV)*.

Then verse 11 says, "Do not withhold your mercy from me, O Lord; may your love and your truth always protect me" *(NIV)*. Truly God had answered this prayer.

Psalm 66:10-12 says, "For you, O God, tested us; you refined us like silver. You brought us into prison and laid burdens on our backs. You let men ride over our heads; we went through fire and water, but you brought us to a place of abundance" *(NIV)*. God brought us through these deep waters. Now we were in a place of spiritual abundance.

A Renewed Appreciation for Mike
As we learned this truth together, we rekindled a new appreciation for each other. The atmosphere at home continued to change. We were both excited about what we were learning. Mike was different. I'd never seen him have such peace and contentment. Our circumstances, as far as his job and our finances were concerned, were as bad as ever, but this underlying peace and trust gave us a rock on which to stand. Both of us were learning to rest and abide in Jesus.

Only God had kept us together through these years, and we were thankful. I learned that I did not need Mike to make me complete. He could never meet my needs for security and significance. All I needed was Jesus. Mike was a bonus. My dependence on him was broken and my security was totally in Christ. As I learned about my security in Christ, I began to blossom in my relationship with the Lord. I understood how much He loved me and accepted me. I didn't have to perform anymore for Him or for Mike or for anyone to gain His acceptance. He loved me just because I'm His. My performance, strength and resiliency didn't impress God. He was my Shepherd, not my critic and judge.

Through listening to the Gillhams, I learned how Satan had deceived me through lies. Thoughts would pop into my mind and I believed they were true—such things as: *he'll never change; you deserve this unhappy life; everyone looks down on you because of this; you've got to act like everything is all right; carry his responsibility; you've had it, your life will be like this forever; no one has any answers for you; God just has to keep you on your knees to keep you close to Him; you are not a very good Christian or you wouldn't have a marriage like this.*

Each of these statements was a lie, but I didn't know it at the time. They controlled my thinking most of the time. Satan is a deceiver and his only means to reach Christians is through their minds. As I gained this new insight, I gained the resulting freedom.

That summer Mike was accepted for a two-month internship at Grace Ministries International, an Exchanged Life Counseling office in Atlanta, Georgia. Our friend Blake Rymer had been trained at the same office. Mike thought the training would help him in his counseling with alcoholics.

For years I had prayed Jeremiah 29:11, "'I know the plans I have for you,' declares the Lord, 'plans to prosper you and not to harm you, plans to give you hope and a future'" *(NIV)*. I had no idea what God planned for us.

After that summer Grace Ministries invited Mike to join its staff as a counselor and the conference coordinator. This was almost too good to be true! To join a loving and supportive group of people; to know we were loved and accepted and respected by them; to move to Atlanta where my son and his wife and my grandbaby lived! My cup was overflowing!

Note
1. G. K. Chesterton, *Heretics* (London, England: Bodley Head, 1960), p. 13.

Strongholds of Addiction—The Lies That Keep Us in Bondage

Give beer to those who are perishing,
wine to those who are in anguish; let them
drink and forget their poverty and remember
their misery no more.
—Proverbs 31:6,7 *(NIV)*

What keeps us in bondage and what is behind it? How does Satan keep so many people, including Christians, in bondage? Jesus tells us, "Then you will know the truth, and the truth will set you free" (John 8:32, *NIV*). If truth sets us free, then the lies we believe keep us in bondage.

These lies originate from the "father of lies," our arch enemy, Satan. For those in bondage, it is their beliefs or mis-beliefs rather than their behaviors that hold them there. We are told, "Buy the truth and do not sell it" (Prov. 23:23, *NIV*).

Many, however, have sold the truth and bought Satan's lies. Satan is the master of deception.

Neil Anderson has said many times that if Satan can get you to believe a lie, he can control your life. Sadly, this is the plight of countless Christians. Psalm 4:2 says, "How long, O men, will you turn my glory into shame? How long will you love delusions and seek false gods?" *(NIV)*. How many Christians live in bondage because they love delusions and seek lies?

Neil teaches that "a true knowledge of God and our identity in Christ are the greatest determinants of our mental health."[1] Two of Satan's primary strategies are to present a false concept of God and a distorted understanding of our identity in Christ. If Satan can encourage you to believe either one of these lies, your life will be miserable and in bondage.

Every person grows up with a false concept of God. When we become Christians, we don't automatically believe the truth about our identity in Christ. Our minds have been programmed to believe certain things about ourselves. God doesn't push the CLEAR button when we become Christians. Through the years, I have counseled hundreds of Christians who believe the lie that they are sinners, alcoholics, addicts, anorexics, bulimics, homosexuals or...you insert the lie.

Most of us try to create the impression of strength instead of inadequacy or insecurity. I certainly didn't introduce myself in the past by saying, "Hi, I'm Mike Quarles. I'm guilty, insecure, inadequate and worthless." Yet deep down, I felt that way and believed it. Satan wants you to believe these lies about your identity. His plan is not to get you to drink alcohol, do drugs or be sexually immoral. He knows that if you believe a lie about who you are, the steps into a life-controlling bondage are easy. If you believe the truth about your identity in Christ, you'll be free from life-controlling bondages. A person who is free in Christ doesn't engage in addictive, self-destructive behavior.

These addictive behaviors are mental strongholds in your life. Second Corinthians 10:3-5 tells us that strongholds are arguments, pretensions and thoughts that oppose the knowledge of God and His truth. These lies we believe keep us in bondage. Ed Silvoso defines a stronghold as "a mindset impregnated with hopelessness, that causes us to accept as unchangeable, what is known to be against the will of God."[2]

On the following pages, I'll cover four strongholds that kept me in bondage. Almost without exception, when I counsel people who have addictive behaviors, they exhibit at least one of these strongholds in their lives and many have all four.

Four Strongholds of Addiction

Stronghold of Hopelessness

Every person in bondage feels hopeless. Scripture says, "Give beer to those who are perishing" (Prov. 31:6, *NIV*). For a long time I thought this passage was strange. Why would God encourage us to give others beer and wine? The *Brown, Driver, Briggs Hebrew Lexicon* defines "perishing" as "to wander away, to lose oneself, to perish, to be destroyed, to be undone, to be void of and have no way to flee." That's a good description of hopelessness. Those who have these feelings believe they have no hope of escape.

I lost hope when I struggled with my addiction and failed time after time. I was stuck in a vicious cycle of getting drunk followed by inevitable remorse and guilt. As I wallowed in self-pity and remorse, I thought, *It's hopeless; I'm a helpless, incurable alcoholic who is never going to change.* I had bought the lie. Satan used this lie to keep me in bondage for years.

It doesn't matter what behavior or addiction enslaves you, if you feel helpless, and your situation is hopeless, you will never change. Recently I talked with a successful Christian attorney. He said, "I've been this way for 40 years; it's hopeless, I'm never going to change." This man didn't have any addictive problems and was a well-respected Christian leader, an officer in his church and a Sunday School teacher. His problem? He thought he couldn't get his Christian life together and be the kind of husband, father and person he should be. Because of his hopeless feelings, he was severely depressed, was having anxiety attacks and was in danger of losing his position in his firm. His life was as miserable as any alcoholic or addict I've ever known.

"I'm a victim"—*a misbelief of hopelessness.* Inherent in hopelessness is the misbelief that "I'm a victim." Defeated Christians believe they are victims of circumstances, the past or their own bad characters. A great part of this misunderstanding occurs because Christians don't understand their identity in Christ and do not experience victory over the world, the flesh and the devil. Most Christians are jerked around daily by their circumstances, by others and by Satan; but Satan is a defeated foe and his only weapon against Christians is the lie!

Our victory in Christ is explained in Ephesians 2:6 *(NIV)*: "God raised us up with Christ and seated us with Him in the heavenly realms in Christ Jesus." Where are the heavenly realms? If we know where the heavenly realms are we'll never consider ourselves victims and be defeated again.

Ephesians 1:20,22 tells us the exact location of the heavenly realms. Ephesians 1:20 *(NIV)* says, "He raised him [Christ] from the dead and seated him at his right hand in the heavenly realms." The next verses describe exactly where they are: "Far above all rule and authority, power and dominion, and every title that can be given, not only in the present age but also in the one to come. And God placed all things under his feet and appointed him to be head over everything for the church" (vv. 21,22, *NIV*). The heavenly realms are a place of spiritual authority and because we are "in Christ," we are appointed over everything. I have heard Jack Taylor say, "Nothing under Christ's feet can be over your head, because you are in Christ and everything is under Christ's feet."

Christ was seated in the heavenly realms and we were seated with Him to live in victory. "How much more will those who receive God's abundant provision of grace and of the gift of righteousness reign in life through the one man, Jesus Christ?" (Rom. 5:17, *NIV*). Our destiny is to reign in Christ. The Greek word "reign" literally means to reign as kings. The first part of Proverbs 31 says that drinking alcohol isn't for those appointed to reign, "It is not for kings, O Lemuel—not for kings to drink wine, not for rulers to crave beer." (Prov. 31:4, *NIV*).

The day I understood that I wasn't fighting *for* victory, but coming *from* victory, it changed my life. Now as Christians, we can stand against Satan (see Eph. 6:11) because our victory has already been won: "Thanks be to God, who gives us the victory through our Lord Jesus Christ" (1 Cor. 15:57). We can stand against the "schemes" of Satan (see Eph. 6:11) because

....

God's truth applies to *everyone* regardless of differences such as the past, education, age, sex, color, appearance, character or IQ. At the cross of Christ, the ground is level.

....

the only means Satan has to defeat us is to get us to believe his lying schemes. Christians aren't victims: "We are more than conquerors through him who loved us" (Rom. 8:37, *NIV*).

Although your situation may not seem victorious, look victorious or feel victorious, we can hold on to God's promise: "God, who always leads us in triumphal procession in Christ and through us spreads everywhere the fragrance of the knowledge of him." (2 Cor. 2:14, *NIV*) Your beliefs determine the difference between victory and defeat—the lying schemes of Satan or the truth of God.

"I'm different"—another misbelief of hopelessness. Also inherent in the stronghold of hopelessness is the misbelief that "I'm different and my problem is different and I need a different answer." Throughout my growing up years, I believed I was different from most people. My parents continually exhorted me to be as good as my brother and sister were. I believed I was deficient in character and deep inside something was wrong. Many times I thought, *I wish I could be like that person and do the right, responsible thing, but I can't.* In the many AA meetings I attended, practically everyone believed his or her problem was different. This is one of the major attractions of AA. You discover that many other people are just like you. One of the major hurdles for my counselees is their attitude,

"Well this worked for you, but I don't believe it will work for me. I'm different and my problem is different."

God's truth applies to *everyone* regardless of differences such as the past, education, age, sex, color, appearance, character or IQ. At the cross of Christ, the ground is level. Because we believe we are different, we think the "victorious Christian life" won't work for us. As I take people through The Steps to Freedom, I ask them to tell me their negative thoughts. By far the most common statement is "this isn't going to work." If a person believes the Christian life won't work, freedom is not possible.

The same successful Christian attorney I mentioned earlier taught a Sunday School class about "Identity in Christ" and the "Victorious Christian Life." He has read more books about those subjects than anyone I know; *but* he is convinced it won't work for him. As long as he believes this lie, it won't work for him.

Our society has been sold a bill of goods that the problems of the alcoholic, addict, anorexic, bulimic, sex addict or homosexual are so different from each other that each needs some specialist to understand the problem. Granted, each of these addictions involves many different factors; but because the behavior is different, we erroneously believe each problem is unique and requires a different answer. Each of these behaviors are manifestations of the flesh and not the real root problem. Now some people will accuse me of being simplistic in my explanation. As Neil says, however, we suffer from the paralysis of analysis. If you were hopelessly lost in a maze, would you want a mazeologist to explain the intricacies of the maze? Or would you want someone to show you the way out?

Satan has convinced many people that their problems are unique and require a unique answer. My personal story is a classic example of this misunderstanding. I learned the "truth that sets you free" from Bill Gillham, a man who never had a problem with alcohol. He taught the truth. My ministry and burden from God is to set hurting people free from bondage. In my 25 years as a Christian, I've tried (and watched other Christians try) myriad things to be free. Only the truth can set us free. I have seen people who have a variety of life-controlling addictions discover freedom in Christ after appropriating these truths.

One lady I counseled and took through The Steps to Freedom has become a good friend to Julia and me. When we first met, however, she had absolutely no hope. When she sat in my office, she couldn't finish a sentence without crying. She had recently spent six months in a psychiatric ward and was for all practical purposes dysfunctional. After learning of her identity in Christ and going through the Steps to Freedom in Christ, I received a letter from her, and having her permission, I want to include part of it:

> Daily I'm learning to put on my armor and stand in the truth of God's Word. What a difference it has made! And a psychiatrist diagnosed me as mentally ill, with no hope of functioning in the real world. It seems like a bad dream. Praise God I no longer depend on anti-psychotics, anti-depressants or tranquilizers. Instead I'm clear minded, victorious, and healed from the repercussions of incest and child abuse. I'm free from suicidal depression, self-mutilation, dissociation and worm theology. I'm free from condemning voices and confusion.
>
> There is much to rejoice about! Today I feel like my life is one big kick in Satan's teeth! He has no power over me. Christ has totally set me free. Even during those times I don't "feel" particularly free, I know I am. Thank you for your devotion to sharing the Truth with others. I am one life that's remarkably changed.

Does it work? Yes, she has been enjoying her freedom for more than three years.

Of all people, Christians ought to be filled and overflowing with hope. *Vine's Expository Dictionary* defines the Greek word "hope" this way: "In the New Testament, a favorable and confident expectation." Because our hope is secure and definite, we can live in confidence. The New Testament uses four adjectives to describe hope: "good," "blessed," "better" and "living." God is called the "God of hope" (Rom. 15:13). We have an eternal hope because of "Christ in you, the hope of glory" (Col. 1:27), and "we have hope in Christ" (1 Cor. 15:19, *NIV*).

The Christian can "rejoice in the hope of the glory of God" (Rom. 5:2, *NIV*) because our "hope does not disappoint us" (v. 5, *NIV*). We don't receive hope as the world does, hoping things will work out. We receive hope by believing God's truth, then putting our trust in him: "May the God of hope fill you with all joy and peace as you trust in him, so that you may overflow with hope by the power of the Holy Spirit" (15:13, *NIV*).

A Christian shouldn't ever be without hope. We are in Christ and He is in us (see John 14:20). We are more than conquerors (see Rom. 8:37), have been given the victory (see 1 Cor. 15:57) and are always led in triumph in Christ (see 2 Cor. 2:14).

The Stronghold of Guilt

I have yet to meet a defeated Christian who didn't feel guilty. Without exception, alcoholics and addicts are mired and consumed with guilt. When I struggled in my bondage to alcoholism, I was laden with guilt. As my constant companion, guilt accused me, threatened me and reminded me of my miserable life as a Christian. My seminary degree and experience as an ordained minister and a former pastor only made matters worse.

No one can experience peace, freedom or joy when consumed with guilt. Satan uses this scheme to rob Christians of their freedom. A question in a survey of 500 people asked, "When you experience guilt, how do you feel?" Their answers were: punishment, depressed, sense of worthlessness and a loss of self-esteem. A person who feels guilty and doesn't choose God's remedy will be defeated.

Proverbs 31:6 *(NIV)* says, "Give...wine to those who are in anguish." The Hebrew word for anguish literally means "to make bitter, provoked, sorely grieved, vexed and discontented." People experiencing the bitterness of guilt often experience these emotions. A Christian psychiatrist has said that if people understood they were loved and forgiven, we could empty most of the mental institutions and prisons.

Wait a minute. Hasn't God done something about guilt? Wasn't freedom from guilt gained as a result of Christ's death

....

The stronghold of guilt involves a strange paradox. To be guilt free, you must be honest, admit your problem and confess your sin.

....

on the Cross? Yes, but sadly most Christians seem to have little understanding of the accomplishment of the Cross except the forgiveness of their sins and their eternal destiny in heaven. If people understood the accomplishments of the Cross, I believe it would solve their problems. Romans 8:1 tells us: "There is therefore now no condemnation for those who are in Christ Jesus."

Those who permit guilty feelings to rob them of their freedom let the past control them. They believe they are products of their pasts rather than products of the Cross. Alcoholics and addicts are prone to this cycle of drinking or drugging followed by remorse and guilt. It is repeated endlessly.

The stronghold of guilt involves a strange paradox. To be guilt free, you must be honest, admit your problem and confess your sin. One of the first major barriers for the alcoholic/addict is the admission of a problem. Most of us fear exposure. We'll go to great lengths to create the impression that we are OK; but we won't ask for help until the great wall of denial is broken. Alcoholism and addiction create out-of-control people; they then perform many unusual acts they wouldn't do if they weren't under the influence of alcohol/drugs. Therefore, they spend a lot of time covering their tracks and denying the obvious rather than admitting their problems.

Mike Stewart, the former director of Bethel Colony in North Carolina, said, "All alcoholics are liars; not all liars are alcoholics, but all alcoholics are liars." You can't live a life of denial and deception without lying. After I became a Christian, I prided myself on always telling the truth. Before becoming a Christian, I had created a completely fraudulent expense report for one whole year. As a new Christian, my tax return was reviewed. When I met with the IRS agent, I freely confessed my wrong actions. When I began struggling with alcoholism, however, I lied about almost anything. It became my way of life.

How do we face the awful truth about ourselves and our past? Only through the Cross. First we have to admit the problem. I have talked to alcoholics/addicts who have lost homes, families, possessions, reputation and health, yet are unwilling to admit a problem. They continue holding to the lie that they are really OK, yet they are the only ones who believe it. For guilt to be removed, the wrongdoing must be admitted.

The worst thing you can do for your loved one caught in alcoholism or addiction is to help the person continue in the deception that he or she is OK. Your best course of action is to speak the truth in love (see Eph. 4:15) and don't allow him or her to escape the consequences of wrong behavior. Alcoholics or addicts will not get help until they admit their problems.

Many Christians are caught in guilt—not just alcoholics and addicts. Why? Although Bible-believing Christians understand that Christ's death on the cross paid for their sins, past, present and future, sadly, not many live in this glorious truth. To determine if a person enjoys the benefits of living guilt free, I ask, "Do you accept yourself just the way you are?" Despite asking hundreds of Christians this question, only one or two have ever answered yes.

I then ask, "Does God accept you just the way you are?" Almost all of them will admit that God accepts them just the way they are—even if they don't feel as though He does. Then I ask, "What causes you not to accept yourself?" Again, practically everyone admits of thinking about past performances such as failures and wrongs. Sooner or later they admit God accepts them because of Christ's death on the cross, which paid for their sins.

If people can't accept themselves, it may be because they haven't appropriated the forgiveness provided at the Cross. Although Christians, they aren't walking in freedom. We are our own worst critics, and Satan accuses us day and night. We go to God in fear and confusion acting like sinners who can't be forgiven. We get upset when we fail miserably because deep down we believed we could do better.

Will you stop condemning yourself and receive the forgiveness provided through Christ's death on the cross? Until you do, you'll never experience freedom. I heard Jack Miller say at a conference, "The last judgment for the Christian was at the Cross." I almost jumped out of my chair! I wanted to stand up and shout, but I restrained myself. Romans 8:1 says, "There is therefore now no condemnation for those who are in Christ Jesus." Sin—past, present and future—has been eliminated. Romans 4:8 *(NIV)*, "Blessed is the man whose sin the Lord will never count against him."

Only those who are honest, admit their wrongs and confess their sins will ever be free. In his book *Freedom from the Performance Trap*[3], David Seamands tells of a man named Stypulkowski who was a fighter with the Polish underground resistance in World War II from 1939 to 1944. When the war ended, he was captured by the Russian army. Along with 15 other Poles, he was taken to Russia for trial before the war-crimes court. Before the trial, the men were rigorously interrogated to break them mentally, emotionally and spiritually. They wanted to destroy their integrity so these men would confess to anything. Fifteen of the 16 men broke under the grueling pressure. Only Stypulkowski did not break.

Stypulkowski was brutally questioned for 69 out of 70 nights during 141 interrogations. At one point, even his interrogator broke and had to be replaced. Again and again, his tormentors relentlessly examined his life—his work, marriage, family, children, sex life, church, community life and his concept of God. This treatment was followed by weeks of starvation, sleepless nights and calculated terrorizing. His best friends had signed confessions and now blamed him. His torturers told him his case was hopeless and advised him to plead guilty—otherwise face certain death. But Stypulkowski refused.

He had not been a traitor and could not confess to something that was not true. At the trial, he pleaded not guilty and largely because of Western observers there, he was freed. In a natural and unself-conscious way, he witnessed to his Christian faith. His faith was kept alive through regular prayer. His every loyalty was subordinated to his loyalty to Christ.

Stypulkowski endured because daily he presented himself to God and his accusers in absolute honesty. He knew he was accepted, loved of God, forgiven and cleansed. So when they accused him of some wrong, he freely admitted it, even welcomed it.

Repeatedly he humbly said, "I never felt it necessary to justify myself with excuses. When they showed me I was a coward, I already knew it. When they shook their finger at me with accusations of filthy, lewd feelings, I already knew that. When they showed me a reflection of myself with all my inadequacies, I said to them, 'But gentlemen, I am much worse than that. For you see, I had learned it was unnecessary to justify myself. One had already done that for me—Jesus Christ!'"

When we learn it's unnecessary to justify ourselves, we can begin to walk in freedom. Because of the Cross, we can find the courage to face the truth and experience God's liberating grace. The J. B. Phillips translation, *The New Testament in Modern English*, of Colossians 2:13-15 summarizes this truth: "He has forgiven you all your sins: He has utterly wiped out the written evidence of broken commandments which always hung over our heads, and has completely annulled it by nailing it to the cross. And then, having drawn the sting of all the powers and authorities ranged against us, he exposed them, shattered, empty and defeated, in his own triumphant victory!"

The Stronghold of Self-Help

Particularly in the United States, we are a people of self-starters, go-getters, hard chargers and high achievers. We carry these feelings into our relationships with God. We admire the movers and the shakers.

Several years ago, I talked to a pastor who was on a denominational committee that selected pastors for starting new churches. They were looking for a person who would be a self-starter, a go-getter, someone to make things happen— those were his exact words. Later, I talked about it with Julia. These qualifications matched an IBM salesman. There was no mention of spiritual qualifications, such as a relationship with the Lord. Incidentally, the man this committee selected to

Several hundred years ago, Martin Luther pointed out that nothing we do helps us spiritually. Only faith helps us—only what we believe.

begin a new church in that area developed all kinds of relationship problems with his supervising pastor and the sponsoring church.

Inherent in the stronghold of self-help is the misbelief that I can change myself. It's a commitment to the old cliché, "If it is going to be it is up to me." In Christianity, it's nothing but bootstrap religion and positive legalism. It's just another version of "God helps those who help themselves." For some strange reason, most people believe that if they can change their behaviors, they will be able to change as a person. This is simply untrue.

Alcoholics and addicts know they can enter a treatment center for any length of time and be fine while there and have little struggle. If their beliefs aren't changed, however, they leave and quickly return to their old habits. Only God can change a person. When Christians understand their identities in Christ, their behaviors will change. Most Christians are trying to be someone they already are and get something they already have. The truth is we are in Christ, dead to sin, freed from it, alive to God, victorious and righteous in Him. When we believe these truths, our behaviors will change.

One of the greatest deceptions is believing that if we do something spiritual, our lives will automatically change. Nothing could be further from the truth. Several hundred years ago, Martin Luther pointed out that nothing we do helps us spiritually. Only faith helps us—only what we believe. I believed that if I could spend enough time in prayer, read my Bible enough, memorize enough Scripture, it would change me; it didn't.

When we give up on ourselves, then we're ready to look to God and get some help. Several years ago, I was instrumental in convincing the court to release a young woman from jail so she could enter a Christian treatment center for her drug problem. She was from an affluent family, and her mother told me they had spent more than $250,000 on her treatment. Her life was turned around at the Christian treatment center, which was free of charge.

It is most difficult to let go of our own beliefs and devices. God only responds to faith, not our empty promises and futile strivings. Isaiah 50:11 (NIV) tells us what happens to those of us who try to work it out by ourselves: "But now, all you who light fires and provide yourselves with flaming torches, go, walk in the light of your fires and of the torches you have set ablaze. This is what you will receive from my hand: You will lie down in torment."

The prophet Jeremiah got to the heart of the issue, "My people have committed two sins: They have forsaken me, the spring of living water, and have dug their own cisterns, broken cisterns that cannot hold water" (Jer. 2:13, NIV). Anything done in your own energy is a broken cistern that won't help you—no matter how noble or spiritual.

The major reason for the anemic condition of today's Church is our lapse into positive legalism. If we can do enough of the right things, we believe all will be well. Paul addressed this in his letter to the Galatians. Paul is amazed and dumbfounded that the Galatians would return to their own pitiful efforts. Eugene Peterson's *The Message*[4] captures it vividly:

> You crazy Galatians! Did someone put a hex on you? Have you taken leave of your senses?

Something crazy has happened, for it's obvious that you no longer have the crucified Jesus in clear focus in your lives. His sacrifice on the Cross was certainly set before you clearly enough.

Let me put this question to you: How did your new life begin? Was it by working your heads off to please God? Or was it by responding to God's Message to you? Are you going to continue this craziness? For only crazy people would think they could complete by their own efforts what was begun by God. If you weren't smart enough or strong enough to begin it, how do you suppose you could perfect it? Did you go through this whole painful learning process for nothing? It is not yet a total loss, but it certainly will be if you keep this up!

Answer this question: Does the God who lavishly provides you with his own presence, his Holy Spirit, working things in your lives you could never do for yourselves, does he do these things because of your strenuous moral striving or because you trust him to do them in you? (Gal. 3:1-5).

Whenever people say, "Just tell me what to do and I will do it," I know they are not yet ready for God's help. These people still harbor the belief that they can personally do something to make it happen. Those who are ready for God's help know they can do nothing. The most difficult people to help are those who think they can do it, are willing to do it and are going to do it. We may have to step back and let these people give it their best shot. People must disabuse themselves of that notion before they can get help. The AA saying is true: "It takes what it takes." People need to reach the end of themselves and their resources.

Have you tried everything you know how to try—to the point of exhaustion? Great! You're a candidate to throw yourself totally on God's grace and find His answer. Proverbs 31:7 says, "Let them...remember their misery no more" *(NIV)*. The Hebrew word for misery literally means "to toil with irksome, wearing effort." The apostle Paul describes these kinds of people in Galatians 3 as those who are working in their own efforts, even if they believe they are doing it for God.

Today, few Christians understand that they are no longer responsible to the Law. They may acknowledge that truth, but it hasn't affected their lives. Many of them are still running on the performance-based acceptance treadmill. They are trying to prove to themselves, to God and to others that they can measure up to His standards. God, however, has said we can do nothing on our own; if we trust in the work of Christ on the cross and our position in Christ, then we will be worthy.

When it comes to self-help strongholds, I was the world's worst offender. In chapter 3, I detailed the variety of things I tried. This list was not exhaustive. For example, I created a detailed, hour-by-hour schedule for every hour of the day and tried to use it to keep me out of trouble. This schedule was one of my most disastrous and short-lived plans.

Almost every week or two I created another scheme. Countless times I ran to Julia or my minister or the assistant minister and told them about a wonderful, new spiritual plan to solve my problem. Within a week (and sometimes sooner) my plan was shattered in ruins. The greater my hopes rose, the harder I fell. Every fall validated my hopelessness and guilt and strengthened those strongholds.

When I was counseling with Grace Ministries, Bill Bufton, one of the counselors, asked me to talk with a counselee who struggled with alcoholism. I went to the session, but never got much of a chance. This counselee spent the whole time telling Bill, his wife and me about his plans to solve his problem. Although his wife may have been encouraged to hear these plans—such as get up early, read his Bible, pray and go to church—I explained that I had tried these plans and many more. It did not work for me, but he could not hear me. After the session, I told Bill, "I seriously doubt if he lasts a month." He didn't and the next time he got drunk, he landed in jail.

During my ministry to alcoholics and addicts in Birmingham, Alabama, one young woman created a unique solution. At one of our counseling sessions she said, "Because I always get drunk on either Friday or Saturday night, I have solved my problem. I'll start my "Sabbath" early by attending a messianic worship service on Friday night, then another one on Saturday night." I attempted to point out that she was setting herself up for a fall; but I didn't dampen her enthusiasm a bit and she didn't listen. What happened? She didn't last till Friday; instead she got drunk on Thursday—two days after telling me her plan.

Roy Hession puts this issue into focus in the following poem from his book *Be Filled Now*[5]:

> Nothing either great or small,
> Nothing Christian, no!
> Jesus did it, did it all,
> Long, long ago.
>
> Till to Jesus' work you cling,
> By a simple faith,
> Doing is a deadly thing,
> Doing ends in death.
>
> Cast your deadly doing down,
> Down at Jesus' feet,
> Stand in Him, in Him alone,
> Gloriously complete!

You and I don't have to shape up the old person in ourselves in an all-out spiritual boot camp. That isn't Christianity. It will only bring despair and grief. The stronghold of self-help is nothing but self-improvement. God doesn't want us to improve the flesh, as it is hostile to God (see Rom. 8:7), and the mind-set on it is death (see v. 6). "Those who belong to Christ Jesus have crucified the flesh with its passions and desires" (Gal. 5:24). Today's secular programs are designed to improve the flesh and to modify behavior. Unfortunately, many "Christian" programs do the same, but have a spiritual slant. I've heard Neil Anderson say it is nothing but Christian behaviorism, which is legalism.

Why is it so difficult to let someone else do it? Because then we have to admit we can't do it ourselves. And why is the Cross such an offense? Because the Cross says that the human's way failed. The Cross says we are so bad that God had to crucify us with Christ, raise up a new person and start over again. The Cross is meant only for people who fail; but that's the good news! Everyone tries something else—a new self-help book, a different program, a creative method or a support group. When we admit failure, God doesn't do a retread job on our old per-

....

We were created for a relationship with our Creator. Through Jesus Christ, God made this relationship possible and our lives are meaningless without Him. In our search for meaning and significance, we find self-worth and self-acceptance in relationships.

....

son. Galatians 2:20 can't be improved: "I have been crucified with Christ and I no longer live, but Christ lives in me. The life I live in the body, I live by faith in the Son of God, who loved me and gave himself for me" (*NIV*).

The Stronghold of Insecurity
I have never counseled an alcoholic or addict who did not struggle with insecurity. Today's family has never been more fragmented or threatened. Divorce rates skyrocket and more children are raised in single-parent homes than are raised in traditional family structures. To provide security for the children, the best thing a father can do is to love their mother. That love, combined with unconditional love and acceptance, can give a child a great deal of security. Unfortunately, few children receive such security.

Insecurity involves relationships. Who is the most insecure person? The most insecure person is someone who is alone, without friends or relatives or family. I ask my counselees, "What's your greatest fear?" More than all the others combined, they say the fear of being alone. Why? Because we were created to be in relationships and our lives are meaningless without them.

We were created for a relationship with our Creator. Through Jesus Christ, God made this relationship possible and our lives are meaningless without Him. In our search for meaning and significance, we find self-worth and self-acceptance in relationships. Proverbs 31:7 (NIV) says, "Let them drink and forget their poverty." The Hebrew word for poverty literally means "destitute, have lack, needy." *Webster's American Dictionary of the English Language*[6] defines destitute as "One who is without friends or comfort." Those without meaningful relationships are the most destitute and poverty stricken. They comprise the largest group of insecure people because of their lack of relationships.

What is your greatest need? It is to be loved and accepted. God made us that way; and God's design is for us to meet that need through a relationship with Him. As a song says, many people are "looking for love in all the wrong places." Despite your age, gender, health, nationality or wealth, you need love—you were made that way. Everyone needs love. That's why relationships are important.

In his book *Classic Christianity*, Bob George writes the following:

> A person has no identity apart from his relationship with someone or something else. That's why we will latch onto practically anything in our desperate need to discover who we are....There is only one way to discover your identity that cannot be shaken, one foundation that cannot be taken away from you, "I am a child of God." Now you might be a child of God who happens to be a businessman...or a mother...or an athlete. But the core source of your identity is your relationship with God as Father. Only in this way can you ever begin to discover true security.[7]

Although you have friends and may not be physically

alone, you still may have the stronghold of insecurity. Most do, and I did as well. Earlier, I told you about my home life as a child. My parents fought violently. As a young child at night, I lay down in my bed listening to them fight and wondered if one of them might kill the other. These seeds of insecurity were planted and began to grow. The prevailing philosophy during my youth was: "Children should be seen and not heard." My parents believed that philosophy and told us so many times.

I learned that it wasn't safe to express negative emotions. If someone told me how bad I was, I came home upset. Then my mother told me, "Sticks and stones will break your bones, but words can never harm you." Her words were not true, although I am sure she thought it was the best thing to say. Other times I was told, "Big boys don't cry."

If that didn't work, my dad said, "If you don't shut up, I'll give you something to cry about." Because big boys don't cry, I learned to stuff my emotions. I grew up being out of touch with my emotions and was unable to develop healthy relationships.

Insecure people search for someone of the opposite sex to respond to them. I desperately searched for love in all the wrong places. Whenever I found a woman who responded, it made me feel good—for a while. After this woman wised up and moved on, I needed to locate another one and my pattern was established. I became a womanizer. A womanizer is an insecure male who needs a woman to validate his masculinity. Usually my relationships didn't last long. The woman disappeared and I was driven to find another one. I was so driven that I would do whatever it took. I was so insecure that I couldn't consider the woman's needs and value her as a person. Womanizing isn't about sex. The same is true when a woman is promiscuous. I have counseled many promiscuous women, and not one of them pursued men for sexual reasons. One said, "I knew it was wrong and I hated it, but it was the only way I knew to get love."

The greater the insecurity, the more you develop insecure patterns. No one could get too close to me. At all costs, I avoided intimacy. Anyone who got too close might discover the real me and I could not let that happen. Not being vulnerable and open results in fewer chances of meaningful relationships. The stronghold of insecurity becomes more entrenched.

I was like a dog chasing a car—when I caught what I was chasing, I had absolutely no idea what to do with it. I could not receive love from anyone because I believed I was unacceptable and not worth loving. Throughout high school and college, I would diligently pursue a girl; then if she started responding, I would quickly lose interest. If she liked me, something must be wrong with her. My wife, Julia, accepted me and loved me unconditionally, but I could not receive it. How could she love me? *She must be faking it*, I thought.

The first years of our marriage I was insanely jealous and accused her of many ridiculous and untrue things. Julia was, as Proverbs 31:10 *(NIV)* says, "A wife of noble character...is worth far more than rubies." Today, I can honestly say I have "full confidence in her and [lack] nothing of value" (v. 11). For many years I was driven to prove that Julia didn't love me and she was going to leave. When she finally kicked me out of the house, I handled it better than I did her love.

Unworthy, unacceptable feelings are at the core of insecurity; but God has spoken clearly and acted decisively. He said that we are so worthy that He sent His one and only Son to die for our sins. Then we could have a relationship with Him.

When Christians learn their true identity in Christ, they will no longer be insecure. When we receive Christ, we receive Him as a person and we receive His life (see John 5:24). To have Christ is to have eternal life (see 1 John 5:12).

Anabel Gillham said, "Anything that comes your way must first come through the Father, then through Jesus, and when it gets to you it finds you filled with Jesus." Our security doesn't depend on performance. We are secure because we are "in Christ."

In Hebrews 13:5, God tells us of His commitment to us:

> For He [God] Himself has said, I will not in any way fail you nor give you up nor leave you without support. [I will] not, [I will] not, [I will] not in any

degree leave you helpless nor forsake nor let [you] down (relax My hold on you)! [Assuredly not!] *(AMP)*.

How much does God love us? Hundreds of verses in the Bible tell us of God's love. I want to point out just one: Jesus said, "As the Father has loved me, so have I loved you. Now remain in my love" (John 15:9, *NIV*). Christ loves you and me just as much as God loves Him. Today, most Christians seem obsessed with their lack of obedience. I believe the most disobeyed commandment is "remain in my love." If we would choose to remain in His love, I believe it would go a long way to clear up our problems. We have been united with Christ and are one with Him. We are "in Christ," and we can't be more secure than that.

You may be thinking, *I just don't feel it. I wish I could.* If you wait until you feel it, it will never happen. The following true story illustrates this point.

During World War II, Lieutenant General Jonathan Mayhew Wainwright was commander of the Allied Forces in the Philippines. Following a heroic resistance of enemy forces, he was forced to surrender Corregidor and the survivors of the Philippine campaign to the Japanese on May 6, 1942. For three years he suffered as a prisoner of war in a Manchurian camp. During his internment, he endured the incessant cruelties of malnutrition, physical and verbal abuse, and psychological mind games. Through it all he maintained his dignity as a human being and soldier. After the Japanese surrendered the war, his captors kept Wainwright and the other prisoners incarcerated—the war ended, but the bondage continued.

One day an Allied plane landed in a field near the prison. Through the fence that surrounded the compound, an airman informed the general of the Japanese surrender and the American victory. Wainwright immediately pulled his emaciated body to attention, turned and marched toward the command house, burst through the door, marched up to the camp's commanding officer and said, "My Commander-in-Chief has conquered your Commander-in-Chief. I am now in charge of this camp." In response to Wainwright's declaration, the officer took off his sword, laid it on the table and surrendered his command.[8]

Our Commander-in-Chief, the Lord Jesus Christ, has conquered Satan. I am certain that General Wainwright did not feel victorious and in charge, but he chose to believe the truth and act on it. Satan has deceived many Christians who still believe they are in bondage. As long as they believe it, their bondage will continue. Perhaps you are one of them. It is time for you to stand up and claim your rightful victory. Our war has been won—Satan is defeated. You are in Christ and are more than a conqueror!

Bondage is nothing but lies that comprise strongholds in your mind. Freedom is believing the truth that sets you free.

Julia's Perspective

Editor's Note: Freedom was a growing part of Julia's life as well. Here is her final reflection about her new lease on life and ministry with Mike.

During Mike's first year on staff with Grace Ministries International in Atlanta, Georgia, our house in Birmingham, Alabama, did not sell. He lived with another staff family while I stayed in Birmingham and continued working. I sold *other* houses—just not ours. Most weekends, Mike came home or I went to see him in Atlanta. We began some wonderful friendships with staff families. During that summer and fall of 1990, we were asked to house-sit for several families. We lived in about eight houses and got to know several areas of town. We joined a church and became involved with a home-fellowship group. Then I found a part-time secretarial job.

When others asked us about the problems because of our house not selling, I said, "We've had problems in the past. This is an inconvenience, not a problem." Finally we moved into our own home, and we have found that God continually sends people to stay with us in our home. Some are interns who are here for two months training at Grace Ministries, but most are family and friends passing through town for a few days. We are blessed to have this kind of lifestyle, and we don't take it for granted. We enjoy telling others about the miracles God has done in our lives and our marriage, and enjoy passing these truths on to others.

It has been a tremendous blessing in our lives to live near two of our children, Bradley and Audrey, and to be a vital part of their families. We have been blessed with three more grandchildren. Being a grandmother to Kaitlin, Brad IV and William Fulkerson, and to their cousin, Aryele Forte, is my greatest joy. To have the opportunity to love them and give them unconditional acceptance is an incredible blessing. It is an additional measure of God's grace to me.

For years, I prayed Proverbs 3:5,6 *(NKJV)*: "Trust in the Lord with all your heart, and lean not on your own understanding; In all your ways acknowledge Him, and He shall direct your paths." He is faithful to His word.

In early 1994, I was accepted for the exchanged life counseling training at Grace Ministries International. I wanted to counsel women by telling them the truths that had set me free. I had done some counseling in the past; my counseling, however, usually involved reciting a few verses that were nothing but bandages, and then telling the people to trust God. I was eager to learn an effective way to offer solid, biblical truth to hurting women.

One of the greatest truths I learned was that one of my biggest sins was unbelief—not believing how much God loved me and how much He accepted me. This affected my identity and security. I learned the reality of Lamentations 3:22,23—God's mercy is limitless; it goes beyond our need. We can never use up His mercy—it is new every morning. Great is His faithfulness.

Another big issue I had to cope with was unforgiveness. I had already forgiven Mike and other people for many things. I thought I had already handled it all; but I realized I had forgiven Mike for his actions, but not for how they made me feel. Ongoing consequences also lingered from the drinking years.

The need to forgive in this way was for my good—not his. It freed me from roots of deeply planted bitterness. It was painful, but necessary, and brought me to a new level of peace.

The training helped me learn how to talk with women who are stuck in the same situation I had experienced, and to show them from Scripture about their identity in Christ. Now I can teach women about the principle that they can't change someone or meet someone else's need for love and acceptance. God doesn't require that from anyone—only He can do it.

I enjoy helping women learn that only Christ can meet those needs—not their husbands, children, friends or jobs. I help women see that enabling others to continue in their sinful behaviors does not help anyone. Nor does God expect a woman to live in an abusive situation just because she is a Christian. What I learned in our miserable years can be used to help others.

I also learned the difference between a goal and a desire from Neil Anderson's ministry. My goal was for Mike to quit drinking and to be a godly husband. That seemed reasonable. If a goal involves someone else and that person's behavior, however, we are setting ourselves up for failure and disappointment. For Mike to quit drinking would have been a good "desire." When we have desires for our spouses and children, we can be prayer warriors instead of manipulators.

Currently I am privileged to be on the staff of Freedom in Christ Ministries along with Mike. It is a joy to counsel women in bondage and to help them find freedom. I am also Mike's administrative assistant.

To my continual amazement, I would rather hear Mike teach than anyone else. Each day, he lives out his teaching in front of me, so as I listen I can say "Amen." He is a gifted teacher and God enables me to learn from him. I enjoy accompanying him when he teaches and to pray for him and be an encouraging support to him.

Psalm 30:11,12 (NIV) says: "You turned my wailing into dancing; you removed my sackcloth and clothed me with joy, that my heart may sing to you and not be silent. O Lord my God, I will give you thanks forever." Great is Thy faithfulness.

Notes

1. Neil Anderson, *The Steps to Freedom in Christ* (La Habra, Calif.: Freedom in Christ Ministries, 1993), p. 1.
2. Ed Silvoso, *Free to Reach Our City Workbook* (San Jose, Calif.: Harvest Evangelism, n. d).
3. David Seamands, *Freedom from the Performance Trap* (Wheaton, Ill.: Victor Books, 1988), pp. 121-123.
4. Eugene H. Peterson, *The Message: The New Testament in Contemporary English* (Colorado Springs: NavPress, 1993), p. 465.
5. Roy Hession, *Be Filled Now* (Fort Washington, Pa.: Christian Literature Crusade, n.d.), pp. 26, 27.
6. *Noah Webster's First Edition of an American Dictionary of the English Language*, 1828 edition (San Francisco: Foundation for American Christian Education, 1967).
7. Bob George, *Classic Christianity* (Eugene, Oreg.: Harvest House, 1989), pp. 83,84.
8. Don McMinn, *Spiritual Strongholds* (Oklahoma City: NCM Press, 1993).

Strongholds of Addiction—
The Lies That Keep Us in Bondage

Stronghold	Description	The Lie	The Truth
Hopeless	Loss of self-esteem No purpose or direction Total loss of hope that things will ever change Sense of inadequacy	*I am a victim and helpless I will never change —it's hopeless I am different and so is my problem, so it won't work for me*	I am a victor in Christ I am the righteousness of God in Christ The truth sets you free regardless of the problem or person
Guilt	Depressed and bitter Discontented and grieved Sense of worthlessness Denial and dishonesty	*I deserve to be punished and condemned I cannot face the awful truth about myself I am a product of my past*	There is no judgment in Christ In Christ I am a new creation I am a product of the Cross
Self-Help	Behavior oriented Judgmental Weary and tired Trying to earn acceptance through performance	*If it is going to be it is up to me God helps those who help themselves If I change my behavior, it will change me as a person*	Only God can change me God helps those who give up and trust Him If I change my beliefs, it will change my behavior
Insecurity	Worried and anxious Feels forsaken and without support Absence of meaningful relationships Unable to receive love and avoids intimacy	*I am unworthy to be loved and accepted I need someone to validate me as a person I need someone or something to be secure*	I am loved and accepted by God I am one with Christ. He is in me and I am in Christ I am eternally secure in Christ who will never forsake me

Part Two

....

Overcomers in Christ

The Making of an Addiction

One of my seminary students walked into my office and slowly closed the door. "I'm checking out of seminary," he said. He stood nervously in front of me waiting for my response. His eyes never left the floor. Not everybody finishes seminary, so this wasn't out of the ordinary. He was a capable student, however, he had a tendency to miss more classes than he should have.

"Why are you leaving?" I asked. His fidgeting worsened. He finally responded, "I guess I'm an alcoholic."

A moment of awkward silence passed before I asked, "So why are you dropping out?" I think he was a little surprised by my response. Most people struggling with addictive behaviors are deathly afraid that one day they will be found out. They expect the hammer to fall when their behavior is exposed. We had a long talk that afternoon, and together we began to construct a plan for his recovery. Fortunately he had a caring pastor whom I knew would work with us to help him get free from his addiction to alcohol.

Two years later when he walked across the platform to receive his diploma, I experienced one of the more meaningful graduations of my career as a seminary prof. He had been sober for two years. I suppose it is a little unusual for a seminary student to be hooked on alcohol. It is not unusual, however, to find alcoholism in our churches or in Christian leadership. That is why Mike and Julia's story is so critical. The "Christian religion" of many may not work, but Christ does. I know an effective associate pastor who finally checked himself into a chemical dependency unit. He claimed his drinking problem was recent in origin. He blamed it on current problems within his church. Not true! No adult becomes an alcoholic in such a short time.

Approximately 15 million people in the United States are alcoholics. An estimated 25 percent of them are teenagers. One in 10 of all social drinkers is an alcoholic. Incredibly, the ratio is 1 in 3 for those who attend church. Christians tend to be more secretive about their drinking, which explains the ratio difference between Christians and non-Christians. Unfortunately, secrecy is counterproductive to the Christian walk and recovery in Christ.

Why do people drink and how do some become chemically addicted? This chapter offers a brief psychological as well as a sociological explanation. The remaining chapters will give biblical answers for chemical as well as sexual bondage. My firm conviction is that Christ is the answer and truth will set us free. My conclusions will be summarized in an "Overcomers Covenant in Christ" (see appendix B). Why then do people drink or take drugs? I'm sure a million reasons exist, but they would probably fall into one of three general categories: to appease peer pressure, to escape life's pressures and to stop the pain.

Party Time

When I was an engineering student, my wife and I were having dinner with an Air Force captain and his wife. The captain's wife complained that her cocktail before dinner was too weak and too small. "It didn't even give me a buzz," she said. She, like many others, "needs" a drink to reduce her inhibitions. Many can't have fun without being a little tipsy to dull their consciences and to forget their problems and responsibilities. After all, "It's Miller time!" Most drinkers or alcoholics don't necessarily care to get drunk. Some manage their consumption by setting limits beforehand. Others don't seem to know when to stop.

Social drinkers simply respond to peer pressure. I spoke at a Friday night gathering for "Parents Without Partners." My parenting message was sandwiched between the happy hour and the dance. My wife and I conversed with a single mother who had a cigarette in one hand and a drink in the other. As we talked, the cigarette burned itself out and the ice cubes melted in her drink. Anyone could tell that she neither smoked nor drank on any other occasion. So why was she doing it now? Peer pressure. It's the social thing to do!

Some settings intimidate people into doing what everyone else is doing. You might ask, "If they don't want to do it, why are they there?" Probably because each of us has a need to be accepted and to have some sense of belonging. For example, Mike's first experience with alcohol enabled him to relate and feel more accepted.

Many business men and women are confronted with compromising situations. They battle mental thoughts such as:

> *I don't really want to drink, but if I don't, I might lose the business. I better go along with their luncheon plans and cocktail party.*
> *If I don't go along with what they are doing, they may think I won't play ball with them.*
> *This is not the time to make some moral stand.*
> *They may take offense if I turn up my nose at their drinking habits.*

A successful corporate officer told me that his unlimited expense card made any vice he wanted including an "escort" available to him. No questions were asked. Business people in this position begin to think:

> *Who would know? The company expects me to enjoy a few perks and write it off as a business expense. After all, I work hard. I'm not near the one I love, so why not love the one I'm near. Everyone else does. Don't they?*

Our ability to stand against peer pressure and to resist the temptation to throw off our inhibitions is dependent on how secure we are and how our basic needs are being met. This is probably the primary reason young people drink or take drugs. They don't want to be the odd man out or the nerd or the party pooper! Not many of them are secure enough in

....

Rules without relationships lead to rebellion.

....

their identities to stand alone. Less secure people can stand against peer pressure—if they have another group to accept them and to provide a sense of belonging for them.

The psychological basis for temptation is legitimate needs. The question is: Are these needs going to be met in Christ who promised to meet all our needs "according to His riches in glory" (Phil. 4:19)? Or, are we going to succumb to the temptation to turn to counterfeit attempts by the world, the flesh and the devil to meet our needs? Paul admonished, "Let our people also learn to engage in good deeds to meet pressing needs, that they may not be unfruitful" (Titus 3:14).

The first puff on a cigarette and the first taste of beer or hard liquor is never a good experience. So why do people proceed with something their natural tastes and their own bodies reject? Most are driven to fulfill inner needs for acceptance and belonging. Many will compromise their own convictions. Teenagers will ignore their parent's warnings to gain acceptance and to avoid feeling alone.

Some people act out of rebellion to authority. They drink alone to show that they will not be pushed around or told what to do. They deliberately join offensive groups. These youngsters usually come from dysfunctional homes, or legalistic religious settings. Rules without relationships lead to rebellion. Their first tastes of the vices are repugnant. Yet they continue to indulge, and they insist they don't want our love or acceptance. Oh yes they do! But they refuse to accept our rigid standards or abide by our wishes without first receiving our love and acceptance. Initial attempts to overcome their rebellious attitudes with unconditional love and acceptance will often be rebuffed with hostile rejection. We have to "out love" them without compromising what we believe.

Escaping the Pressures of Life

The second possible reason people drink is to escape the pressures of life. Happy hour beckons those whose hearts cry out for relief.

- Work is unbearable.
- Nobody understands me.
- My boss is an unreasonable jerk.
- I didn't have one sale today, and my bills are piling up.
- Maybe I could get my work done if they would just get off my back.
- They laid off another bunch! Am I next?
- I'll stop off at the club on my way home to have a drink with the boys.
- It will help me get the pressures of work off my mind and allow me to relax.
- Just one drink. Well, make it two.
- How about one for the road?

The pressures of life can feel overwhelming. However, running away from them or abdicating our responsibilities will only make our problems worse. Paul said, "We also exult in our tribulations, knowing that tribulation brings about perseverance; and perseverance, proven character; and proven character, hope; and hope does not disappoint, because the love of God has been poured out within our hearts through the Holy Spirit who was given to us" (Rom. 5:3-5). I want to establish hope for people. But too many people think:

My job is hopeless! Solution? Change jobs!
My marriage is hopeless! Solution? Change spouses!
My situation is hopeless! Solution? Change the situation!

We may legitimately need to change jobs or remove ourselves from oppressive situations at times. Usually, however, we cannot do so without abdicating our responsibilities. What then should we do? In most cases, we should "hang in there." We should decide to grow up. Our hope lies in our proven character, not in changing the circumstances of our lives or drowning out the consequences with drugs and alcohol. Paul said in Philippians 4:11-13:

> Not that I speak from want; for I have learned to be content in whatever circumstances I am. I know how to get along with humble means, and I also know how to live in prosperity; in any and every circumstance I have learned the secret of being filled and going hungry, both of having abundance and suffering need. I can do all things through Him who strengthens me.

I believe we can learn to live by the grace of God in spite of our circumstances. Unfortunately some choose to believe their "hope" lies in altering their circumstances. These people become possessive controllers. Those who live around them become co-dependents to survive. Even the sickest manipulators cannot control every circumstance of life, so they drink to cover their anguish. They are angry, bitter people.

Others who are overcome by their circumstances feel totally helpless. They drown their sorrows in booze. They have never learned how to cope with the responsibilities of life. One tragic result of alcoholism and drug addiction is that people who escape through these substances do not learn how to grow from the trials and tribulations of life. The addict's growth in character and emotional development is arrested.

We are supposed to "cast all [our] anxiety upon Him [Christ], because He cares for [us]" (1 Pet. 5:7). Christ has our best interests at heart. Drug dealers and bartenders could not care less about us. Their businesses are better served if we keep using and drinking. A bad fix and a drunken patron are bad for business, so dealers or bartenders will attempt to prevent us from destroying ourselves only when our destruction may incriminate them. The "cure" their chemicals offer is only temporary. When the effects wear off, their victims still have to face the same world with the same responsibilities they sought to escape. Each successive trip to the dealer or bar worsens the circumstances.

The Bar

The Saloon is called a bar...
It is more than that by far!
It's a bar to heaven, a door to hell,
Whoever named it, named it well.
A bar to manliness and wealth;
A door to want and broken health.
A bar to honor, pride and fame;
A door to grief, and sin and shame.
A bar to hope, a bar to prayer;
A door to darkness and despair.
A bar to an honored, useful life;
A door to brawling, senseless strife.
A bar to all that's true and brave;
A door to every drunkard's grave.
A bar to joys that home imparts;
A door to tears and aching hearts.
A bar to heaven, a door to hell;
whoever named it, named it well.

Anonymous

Stop the Pain

If you have experienced a banging toothache, you know the only thought in your mind is to stop the pain. You don't want to debate politics, discuss life or do anything that wouldn't help you to eliminate the pain. I believe this is the third reason people turn to chemicals.

Many people become addicted to prescription drugs because their pain is unbearable. Responsible doctors will not

·····

Learning to cope with pain is a critical part of growing up.

·····

prescribe dosages that cause chemical addiction. Some patients, therefore, look for additional sources to prescribe more medications. I have heard about people who have three or more medical sources who call in their prescriptions to several different drug stores. Others add alcohol to their prescriptions. Society has erected safeguards for our protection, but people find numerous ways to beat the system.

Our hearts ache for those who are in great pain because of injury or illness. Pain, however, is not the enemy we believe it is. Dr. Paul Brand and Philip Yancey wrote an incredibly insightful book, *Pain, The Gift Nobody Wants*. They correctly explain that physical pain is a gift from God. If we could not feel pain, we would be hopeless masks of scars. Not that pain killers are never necessary, but I believe we are a pill-happy society. Every little pain is unacceptable and must be immediately eliminated at any cost. This kind of thinking can potentially destroy us. Everyone has to live with a certain amount of pain. No pain, no gain! Learning to cope with pain is a critical part of growing up.

The physical pains we feel are not always the worst kinds of pain. The emotional pain of failure, rejection, loss of a loved one, etc., can be more devastating than anything physical. Years ago I counseled a husband who was one of the most exasperating men I have ever known. His job wasn't working out, and neither was his marriage. He was even having a bad experience at church. I have never seen a man so flat on his back who continued to spit at everybody. He believed his boss, his wife and even his pastor were all screwed up, but he wasn't! Although he seemed to connect with me, he stopped our occasional talks.

Several months after the last time I saw him, I received a telephone call from him late one night. To my surprise he had just been released from jail. I did not know he had been arrested. His wife had left him, and his family wanted nothing to do with him, so I was the first person he called. He said, "This is the first time I have been off drugs in 10 years." I was surprised. Neither his wife nor I knew he had been on drugs. A small drug dealing business at work had paid for his secret habit. His call caused me to believe he was more open than he had been before. I asked, "Knowing that you were losing your wife, your job and your church, why did you continue to use drugs?" His answer was unforgettable.

He explained, "That was the only time I ever felt good about myself."

Regardless of why people choose to drink or take drugs, each person with an addiction has at least two of the following three conditions. First, their basic needs are not being met in legitimate ways. Second, they have not learned how to cope with life's problems. Third, they can't seem to resolve their personal or spiritual conflicts in responsible ways. The chemicals they become addicted to will not meet their needs, enable them to cope or resolve their conflicts. Their addictions only make matters worse. Nobody plans to become addicted. Nobody likes being addicted. And everyone is sure it will *never* happen to them. So how does it happen?

The Addiction Cycle

Each person travels a private path to addiction, but the downward spiraling cycles are all remarkably similar. Please refer to the chart that follows as I discuss the addiction cycle. People are mentally, emotionally and relationally at the "baseline experience" when they first begin to use or drink. Most party people probably have a pretty good baseline experience. They are merely looking for a good time, and want to join in the celebration. The first drink, puff or snort causes an immediate onset of chemical reaction in their bodies. They feel a certain rush. Alcohol and drugs don't step on the accelerator, they release the brake. Inhibitions are overcome, and feelings of euphoria flood the mind. Getting high can be momentarily fun.

The baseline experience is different for those who are searching for a temporary reprieve from the pressures of life. They are usually a bundle of nerves or depressed about their circumstances. They are looking for a high to lift their spirits or calm their nerves. Melancholy people just want to drown their sorrows. Drinking helps them mellow out. It works! Within a matter of minutes they feel better. The same is true for those who want to stop the pain. They can't wait for the rush to take effect, so they will feel better.

Unfortunately the effects wear off. The morning after is an unpleasant reality. They wake up feeling just a little lower than their baseline experiences. They suffer with a gripping headache. The person in the mirror looks slightly unfamiliar. Work or school, and all the pressures and responsibilities of life come rushing back. A twinge of guilt, shame or fear takes root, depending upon their moral and social consciences. Some experience a complete violation of everything they have been taught and believed. It was a bad experience, and they would never again put themselves in such a compromising position. For the party animal, however, it was a great experience. They can hardly wait to do it again. Party animals live from weekend to weekend, from party to party. They live for the euphoria. They get a rush just thinking about it.

Steps to Addiction

The first step toward addiction is habit. Alcohol and drugs become the means to having a good time or coping with life. A habit is a knee-jerk response. This is how is happens: You feel pain, so you reach for the pills. You feel down, so you do something to pick yourself up. You feel stressed out, so you do

The Addiction Cycle

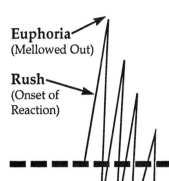

Euphoria
(Mellowed Out)

Rush
(Onset of
Reaction)

Addiction:
1. Habituation
2. Dependency
3. Tolerance
4. Withdrawal

Baseline Experience

Guilt
Fear
Shame

Grandiose, Aggressive
Behavior

Efforts to Control Fail
Repeatedly

Tries Geographical Escapes

Family and Friends
Avoided

Loss of Ordinary
Willpower

Tremors and Early
Morning Drinks

Decrease in Ability to Stop
Drinking

Onset of Lengthy
Intoxication

Moral Deterioration

Impaired Thinking

Drinking with Inferiors

Unable to Initiate Actions

Obsession with Drinking

All Alibis Exhausted

Occasional Drinking

Increase in Tolerance

Memory Blackouts

Excuses Increase

Surreptitious Drinking

Increased Dependency

Persistent Remorse

Promises Fail

Loss of Interest

Work, Money Troubles

Resentments
Pile Up

Neglect of Food

Physical
Deterioration

Irrational Fears

Obsessions

Physical Illness

Complete Defeat

Death or
Recovery

something to calm yourself down. It worked before, so it will work again. You have trained yourself to depend upon chemicals to pick yourself up, to stop the pain, to soothe your nerves and to feel good. You really can't have a good time or feel good without it. Occasional drinking has become a habit, a means of emotional support and a crutch to lean on. When the effects wear off, the guilt, fear and shame become more and more pronounced. Each successive use moves you further and further away from your original baseline experience.

When addicts are on a high, they feel like the king of the hill. They are filled with grandiose ideas, and often become aggressive in their behavior. On the downside, they begin to experience memory blackouts, and they repeatedly fail when they try to regain control of their lives. They think:

How did I get home last night?

What happened?

I better get a grip on myself, I'm starting to lose control!

Guilt feelings about their behavior cause them to drink surreptitiously. They leave familiar surroundings and go where they are unknown. They can't bear the shame.

These people just want to reach the elusive initial high and euphoria again. Unfortunately, it takes more and more alcohol or a greater fix to reach the original high. Every user develops a tolerance for their drug of choice. They may start with two beers, but eventually it takes a case. Then they decide that beer is too slow so they need a chaser to speed up the process. At first marijuana is fine, but ultimately they move into cocaine. No matter how many drugs they consume, addicts never experience the original euphoria. As the lows get lower, so do the potential highs. Before long they only hope to get back to their baseline experiences. But that experience also begins to elude them.

Their loss of willpower robs them of their abilities to live responsible lives at home and eventually at work. Severe financial problems develop as they struggle to support their habits. Many white-collar workers are able to support their habits and hide behind their public masquerades for years, but their families suffer tremendous hardships. The poor steal and become pushers to support their addictions.

Whether poor or white-collar, their morality deteriorates. They have no sense of self-worth or self-respect. They perceive themselves as disgusting. They don't eat well and they don't take care of themselves. Consequently, their physical health becomes a factor. People who suffer with chemical addictions also withdraw from social contacts. They don't want their weaknesses to be seen or known, and they fear being publicly humiliated or exposed. They become paranoid about people looking at them or talking about them. They have no mental peace. Condemning inner voices haunt them day and night:

You're disgusting.
Why don't you just check out, you're no good for anything.
Your family would be better off without you.

The only way to silence the voices is to continue drinking.

Solomon's description of the one who lingers too long over wine ends with, "They struck me, but I did not become ill; They beat me, but I did not know it. When shall I awake? I will seek another drink" (Prov. 23:35). A sure sign of alcoholism for some people, is waking up in the morning with a desire to drink. However, many people who are like Mike, never reach that point. Some party on weekends and drink socially for years without that happening. When the body begins to experience tremors that can only be calmed with another drink, help is necessary. How can people know when they are addicted to alcohol? Johns Hopkins University Hospital, Baltimore Maryland uses the following test questions to help their patients decide:

	Yes	No
1. Do you lose time from work due to drinking?	___	___
2. Is drinking making your home life unhappy?	___	___
3. Do you drink because you are shy with other people?	___	___
4. Is drinking affecting your reputation?	___	___
5. Have you ever felt remorse after drinking?	___	___
6. Have you gotten into financial difficulties because of drinking?	___	___

	Yes	No

7. Do you turn to lower companions and an inferior environment when drinking? ___ ___
8. Does drinking make you careless of your family's welfare? ___ ___
9. Has your ambition decreased since drinking? ___ ___
10. Do you crave a drink at a definite time daily? ___ ___
11. Do you want a drink the next morning? ___ ___
12. Does drinking cause you to have difficulty in sleeping? ___ ___
13. Has your efficiency decreased since drinking? ___ ___
14. Is drinking jeopardizing your job or business? ___ ___
15. Do you drink to escape from worries or trouble? ___ ___
16. Do you drink alone? ___ ___
17. Have you ever had a complete loss of memory as a result of drinking? ___ ___
18. Has your physician ever treated you for drinking? ___ ___
19. Do you drink to build up your self-confidence? ___ ___
20. Have you ever been to a hospital or institution on account of drinking? ___ ___

According to Johns Hopkins University Hospital, if you have answered yes to any one of the questions, it is a definite warning that you may be an alcoholic. If you have answered yes to any two, you probably are an alcoholic. If you have answered yes to three or more, you are definitely an alcoholic.

Admit You Have a Problem
My first experience with an alcoholic recovery program was eye opening. I was sitting with a group of people who were identifying themselves as being co-addicts or co-alcoholics and co-dependents. They were participating in the program to help their friends or family members. They were asked to write out their life stories, then share them with the group. One couple attended to help their daughter, who was a classic party animal. This young woman could outdrink anybody. She had initially taken pride in her tolerance for alco-

hol, but now she couldn't stop. Sharing her own personal story was a painful experience for the mother, but she got through it. She was more than willing to do anything necessary to help her daughter. The father had a terrible time sharing his life story. It was short, factual and superficial. He obviously had never been able to share his inner self. The others were not going to let him get away with his cover-up. They began to question him mercilessly. I was a little upset. I

....

The first step the addict must take in recovery is to admit he or she has a problem.

....

sat there thinking, *Come on! Give the guy a break. He's here for his daughter. Back off a little!*

After tearing down his story, they pursued his present life. "Do you ever drink?" they asked.

"A little I suppose—a beer now and then," he answered.

"How many beers?" they inquired.

"I suppose I occasionally have a few at home."

"How many is a few? How many nights a week do you have a few?" they relentlessly questioned.

As he struggled to answer, his wife suddenly burst into tears. Years of frustration and embarrassment spilled out as the untold part of the story unfolded.

I am thankful I kept my mouth shut during their inquisition. He probably would have conned me, but he couldn't fool them. Within half an hour, they had uncovered a drinking habit that had been established for years.

The first step the addict must take in recovery is to admit he or she has a problem. They must start speaking the truth. As long as people believe they can hide their addictions, or live with their addictions, they will continue in their addictions.

A widely held belief used to be that people could not be helped until they hit bottom. Not until they lost their jobs, their health and their families would they finally admit they had a problem. Only then would they either seek the help they so desperately needed or head for skid row to die.

Professional groups now practice something called "intervention." This approach requires experienced help, because family members are often too judgmental and condemning, or too busy covering up and pretending, to employ it themselves. Intervention coordinators gather all the principal people in the alcoholic's life—including his or her employer—for a well-orchestrated confrontation. The group often rehearses the intervention several times without the alcoholic's knowledge. The confrontation is scheduled for a time when the alcoholic is sober. Each person present then relates what the alcoholic's addiction is doing to them personally, as well as how they see it affecting the alcoholic. The alcoholic is then given an opportunity to seek treatment. The ability to speak the truth and maintain tough love is vital to a successful intervention. Alcoholics need to comprehend that their downward spirals will eventually destroy not only themselves, but also every meaningful thing in their lives.

Recovery from the Addiction Cycle
How do people recover from this cycle of addiction? First, we need to understand that these people do not have drug or alcohol problems. They have life problems. Simply getting them to abstain would leave most of them miserable. Their self-images are down in the mud. They suffer with low self-esteem. They don't know who they are. They have not learned how to live responsible lives, or how to overcome trials and temptations. When their addictive substances are withheld from them, they no longer have a way to cope. That is why many traditional secular treatment programs have such dismal lasting results.

Second, they don't just have personal problems, they have family and community problems. Their addictions have affected every person who has had any meaningful relationship with them. Relationships need to be restored, and wrongs need to be made right. Our generation has discovered that the whole family needs help.

Third, their problems are not just rooted in physical disease. Their problems are physical, mental, emotional and spiritual. The latter is usually overlooked in most treatment programs. I believe it is the most critical factor in treatment. Sobriety is the wrong goal. It deals with only a small dimension of reality. We have to help people understand their freedom in Christ and show them how Christ can meet their most critical and personal needs. Jesus is not just some higher power whom we acknowledge while working a program. Programs don't save people, nor can they set people free—only Jesus can do that.

Co-Dependent No More

The downward spiral of addiction is similar to a whirlwind that gathers up victims in its path and hurls them out of the way. The primary victims are the family members. The spouse is the first to be affected.

When I was pastoring a church, a faithful attendee and worker in the church made an appointment to see me. I hardly knew her husband because he seldom accompanied her to church. I assumed he just wasn't interested in spiritual things. His wife had often requested prayer for his salvation, but she never shared the family secret. Twenty years of silence were broken that afternoon. His alcoholism had destroyed their family and their marriage. She could no longer live with it. I felt sick hearing she had waited so long to share her problem. For 20 years she had been the classic enabler. If he couldn't make it to work because of his drinking, she covered for him. If he passed out drunk on the front lawn, she would somehow get him in the house, clean him up and put him to bed. The children were trained to do the same. They had to protect the family name, and make sure the chief breadwinner didn't lose his job. Lying and covering up became their means of survival. Many family members live under the constant threat of abuse if they don't play along; and even if they do, they may still suffer mental, emotional and physical abuse. The shame they bear keeps them locked in silence.

Family members need help as much as addicts do. They have learned to cope and survive by lying and covering up. The fear of retaliation keeps their mouths shut. Their self-images are shattered by the circumstances within their homes. They refuse to lose their last shreds of dignity by blowing the whistle. They fear people will blame them for breaking up the

....

Discipline is proof of our love, not a violation of it.

....

family, and this actually happens in some abuse cases. The biblical mandates of "speaking the truth in love" (Eph. 4:15), and "walk[ing] in the light" (1 John 1:7) are abandoned for self-preservation. Instead, the opposite happens—self destruction. They live in bondage to their own lies and bitterness. I asked the lady in my church why she was lying and covering up for her husband. She said, "I was too embarrassed to tell anyone. I was also afraid he would leave me if I didn't do what I was told."

I advised her, "As long as you continue to lie and cover up for him, you are enabling him to remain a drunk."

When someone is barreling down the wrong road, the last thing you should do is to enable the process. You are not helping, you are hurting that person, and hurting yourself by violating the Word of God. You can never help addicts or the abusers by enabling them to continue in their irresponsible behavior. It will only get worse for both of you. It will also undermine the most important relationship you have—your relationship with God. If you cover up, you are participating with the father of lies, the prince of darkness.

I say turn them in to their bosses, their churches and even the police if necessary. I do not say that because I don't care for them, but because I *do* care for them. Their actions scream like those of misbehaving little children, "Doesn't anybody care enough about me to stop me from destroying myself?"

Discipline is proof of our love, not a violation of it. Remember, for the addict, the fear of being exposed is far worse than the actual consequences of being exposed. In the same way, the consequences for continuing to cover up the addiction through inaction are far worse than taking a stand for the sake of everyone else involved.

Talk to your addicted spouse or child first. Assure that person of your love. Explain that because you love him or her, you are no longer going to tolerate his or her substance abuse. Let the person know that you will do whatever it takes to help him or her get free from the addiction. Most addicts will probably deny they have a problem.

Tell your addicted loved one that you will no longer lie or cover up for him or her. Let the person know that you are going to seek help for yourself. Next make an appointment with your pastor. You need moral support and spiritual advice. Find a Christian-based ministry that supports spouses and children of alcoholics. Seek professional help to schedule an intervention. You must do something constructive for yourself. Julia finally took a stand, and most readers were probably thinking, *What took you so long?*

One word of caution: Every Christian is co-dependent in a positive sense. We are commanded to love one another, which means we are subject to one another's needs. This is not wrong, it is Christlike. However, Christlike love must be tough when the situation calls for it. When others dictate how and when we are to love them, it is wrong. They are controlling us by their sicknesses.

We are not subject to another person's wants or addictions. When we cover up their addictions, their bondage becomes our bondage. The Spirit of God enables us to have self-control. That same Holy Spirit will lead us into all truth, and the truth will set us free. Nobody on planet Earth can keep us from being the person God wants us to be. Both the addict and the co-addict need to find freedom in Christ. That is what the remainder of this book is all about.

Our Greatest Needs

Woe to those who rise early in the morning that
they may pursue strong drink; Who stay up late
in the evening that wine may inflame them!
—Isaiah 5:11

For those who sleep do their sleeping at night,
and those who get drunk get drunk at night. But
since we are of the day, let us be sober, having
put on the breastplate of faith and love, and as a
helmet, the hope of salvation.
—1 Thessalonians 5:7,8

I was invited to speak to the interns and then to the counseling staff at a rescue mission. The interns were men fresh off
the street who had made some commitment to Christ. As I
walked into the meeting room, they stood up and applauded.
I looked around to see if Billy Graham was following me. I
was relieved to learn they were applauding my message and

not me. I did not know they had been watching my video series, "Resolving Personal and Spiritual Conflicts." The message that got through to them was this: "You are not a derelict, you are not a bum, you are not a drunkard, you are not a pervert, you are not an alcoholic, you are not a drug addict, and you are not a pimp—you are a child of God." Knowing that wonderful truth and everything it implies provides the only real answer and lasting hope they need to overcome bondage.

It Started at Creation

To understand how and why this is true, we must first look at the bigger picture. Let's start with the original Creation:

> God said, "Let Us make man in Our image, according to Our likeness; and let them rule over the fish of the sea and over the birds of the sky and over the cattle and over all the earth" (Gen. 1:26).
>
> Then the Lord God formed man of dust from the ground, and breathed into his nostrils the breath of life; and man became a living being (2:7).
>
> The Lord God said, "It is not good for the man to be alone; I will make him a helper suitable for him" (v. 18).
>
> The man and his wife were both naked and were not ashamed (v. 25).

Sounds good! God created humans in His own image. He breathed life into a hunk of clay and Adam became spiritually and physically alive. However, something was missing. It was not good for Adam to be alone, and no animal form of life could fulfill his need. So God created a suitable helpmate for him (see vv. 21-23). Together they were "naked and were not ashamed (v. 25). Their bodies had no dirty parts. The sexual relationship between husband and wife was not separated from an intimate relationship with God. There was no sin, nothing to hide, therefore, no reason to cover up.

Adam and Eve's purpose and responsibility was to rule over

the rest of God's creation. God placed them in the "Garden of Eden to cultivate it and keep it" (v. 15). By being fruitful and multiplying, they could fill the earth. As long as they remained in a dependent relationship with God, Adam and Eve were given tremendous freedom. They had a perfect life, and they could have lived forever in the presence of God. There was no need to search for significance nor strive for acceptance, because they had a divine purpose. They were totally secure in the presence of God. They also had a sense of belonging to God and to each other. God provided for their every need.

The ability to think and make choices was inherent in Creation, because Adam and Eve were created in the image of God. It is apparent from Scripture that evil was in the universe (see Isa. 14:12-14; Ezek. 28:11-19). The Lord, therefore, commanded Adam and Eve not to eat from the tree of the knowledge of good and evil (see Gen. 2:17). He explained that if they ate the fruit, they would die. Satan was not going to silently sit by and let God's plan to rid the universe of evil go uncontested. So he questioned and twisted the Word of God and tempted Eve (see 3:4-6). Satan used the same three channels that exist today: "the lust of the flesh and the lust of the eyes and the boastful pride of life" (1 John 2:16). Deceived by the craftiness of Satan, Adam and Eve made a choice, thus declaring their own independence. They died!

They did not die physically, they died spiritually, although physical death would also be a consequence of sin (see Rom. 5:12). The effect was immediate. All the inherent personal attributes of Creation (spiritual life, identity, acceptance, security, significance) were gone, and each became a glaring need.

Adam was overcome with shame and guilt. He covered his nakedness, and hid from God. But the Lord immediately took the initiative by confronting Adam.

"'Where are you?'"

"And he [Adam] said, 'I heard the sound of Thee in the garden, and I was afraid because I was naked; so I hid myself.'"

"And He said, 'Who told you that you were naked? Have you eaten from the tree of which I commanded you not to eat?'"

"And the man said, 'The woman whom Thou [You] gavest to be with me, she gave me from the tree, and I ate'" (Gen. 3:9-

12). The Lord knew the answers before He asked Adam the questions. So why did He ask? He wanted Adam to immediately become accountable for his actions.

Adam responded by blaming Eve and suggesting maybe even God had something to do with his downfall. He thought, *After all God, You were the one who created this woman for me.* Ever since Adam's first sin, we have resorted to defensive patterns of projecting blame for our own downfalls. Every addict must first get through his or her own denial of the problem before he or she can begin to address it.

Precedence was established for the degradation of humanity in the Creation and Fall of Adam and Eve. The gospel offers the only hope for a solution. When Adam and Eve lost their relationship with God, they were immediately overcome with fear and guilt. The first emotion expressed by fallen humanity was fear. Adam confessed, "I was afraid because I was naked, so I hid myself" (3:10). Fear of being exposed drives many away from the light that reveals their sin. They run from the light or discredit its source because they do not understand God's unconditional love and acceptance. Satan raises up thoughts "against the knowledge of God" (2 Cor. 10:5), and a deceived humanity mocks His very existence. Unable to achieve God's eternal standards for morality, the fallen are left alone to deal with their fears, guilt and shame.

Every descendant of Adam and Eve is born into this world physically alive, but spiritually dead (see Eph. 2:1). They are helpless to do anything about it, and hopeless without God. No person living independently from God can live a holy life nor withstand the conviction of His perfect light. "Everyone who does evil hates the light, and will not come into the light for fear that his deeds will be exposed. But whoever lives by the truth comes into the light, so that it may be seen plainly that what he has done has been done through God" (John 3:20,21, *NIV*).

Face the Truth

Face the truth! This is the first step toward recovery for anyone in bondage. Many people have told me they want to get out of bondage because they are tired of living a lie. The more evident a bondage is to others, the more likely they are to acknowledge their problems. We will privately and inwardly feel guilty before a Holy God, but shame is only sensed as the bondage becomes known to others. Some people can be torn up on the inside while outwardly appearing to have it all together. They fear having their inner worlds exposed. I suspect they don't admit to their problems because they can't

....
Secret sin on earth is open
scandal in heaven.
....

face the shame. That is why intervention is so effective. It catapults them over that hurdle in one setting with all the principal people they are trying to hide it from.

I used to require my seminary students to attend and report on an Alcoholics Anonymous (AA) meeting. They all shared their disappointment with the smoking and the blue language. Almost every student, however, said in effect, "I wish I could get the people in my church to be as honest as those people were!" People in AA meetings have already been exposed. They no longer have to hide anything. AA meetings provide a place where they feel accepted for who they are, warts and all. Some members continue to carry on their facades outside of the group; therefore, some AA meetings are closed to visitors. Shame is an issue. They don't want others to know, or they have a reputation to protect, so they want to remain anonymous. The guilt and pain of living a lie are far more devastating to people than the shame of being exposed. Many are relieved when they are caught or confronted. Because the sham is finally over, they often decide to get some help.

Many people in our churches have not been exposed. They are not necessarily struggling with drugs or alcohol, but they have problems they don't want to share with others. They hide their troubled marriages or rebellious children. Usually these people won't seek help until their spouses walk out or their children are expelled, jailed or become runaways. They strive to protect their reputations at the church, so they seek help outside the church. This is the ugly side of pride. Pride robs themselves and their families of help during times of need.

The Lord does not let us get away with our prideful cover-ups. "For nothing is hidden, except to be revealed; nor has anything been secret, but that it should come to light" (Mark 4:22). Secret sin on earth is open scandal in heaven. "If we walk in the light as He Himself is in the light, we have fellowship with one another, and the blood of Jesus His Son cleanses us from all sin" (1 John 1:7). Walking in the light is not moral perfection. The next verse says, "If we say that we have no sin, we are deceiving ourselves, and the truth is not in us" (v. 8). Walking in the light is a continuous form of confession. It is living in conscious moral agreement with God, and honestly relating to others. Paul admonishes us, "laying aside falsehood, speak truth, each one of you, with his neighbor, for we are members of one another"(Eph. 4:25).

Don't Live a Lie
The Lord loves us too much to allow us to walk in darkness and live a lie. He knows the lies will eventually destroy us. Our heavenly Father gives us a lot of slack to come to this conclusion by ourselves. Eventually, however, He will expose us for our own good and for the good of others who are being negatively affected by our "secret" sins. "God is opposed to the proud, but gives grace to the humble" (Jas. 4:6). We cannot be right with God and not be real. If necessary, God will arrange the events of our lives to force us to be real, so we can be right with Him.

To live a lie is to play right into the hands of the devil. He is the father of lies and the prince of darkness. Truth is not an enemy, it is always a liberating friend. No matter how painful it is initially to face the truth, the consequences will always be infinitely better than the consequences of living a lie. "Humble yourselves, therefore, under the mighty hand of

God, that He may exalt you at the proper time" (1 Pet. 5:6). We can play the hypocrisy game for a season, but eventually it will take its toll on us. The effects of drugs might not show for a couple of years, and alcohol can be covered up for many years. Sexual addictions, however, can remain a private nightmare for a much longer period of time.

Chemical Addiction and the Connection to Sexual Bondage

Many chemically addicted people are also in some form of sexual bondage. The percentage is very high. These people will seek treatment for their chemical addictions, but probably won't share their struggles with lust, pornography or homosexuality. They reason, *Why suffer the shame if I don't have to tell them?* As with other addictions, people struggling with sexual bondage need help long before they are caught. Most will share how they were sexually abused, because there is less shame in that—it wasn't their fault—but few know how to resolve their sexual bondage. Consequently, they may achieve a degree of sobriety in a recovery program, but still remain in sexual bondage. I am going to make several comments about sexual freedom throughout the remainder of this book, because it overlaps freedom from chemical addiction. A more comprehensive answer to sexual bondage can be found in my book *A Way of Escape* (Harvest House).

The Fall had another devastating effect upon Adam and Eve. They were "darkened in their understanding, excluded from the life of God" (Eph. 4:18). When Adam tried to hide from God, he revealed his misunderstanding about God's character. How do you hide from an omnipresent God? The Lord did not create humans to live independently from Him. This is evidenced in the natural person's inability to understand the things of God. "The man without the Spirit does not accept the things that come from the Spirit of God, for they are foolishness to him, and he cannot understand them, because they are spiritually discerned" (1 Cor. 2:14, *NIV*).

What a dilemma! Satan had usurped the role of God's people and become the rebel holder of earthly authority. Satan even tempted Jesus by showing and offering Him the kingdoms of the world. Satan offered to give Jesus the earthly authority if He would bow down and worship him. "I will give you all their authority and splendor, for it has been given to me, and I can give it to anyone I want to" (Luke 4:6, *NIV*). Jesus never corrected Satan's claim and even referred to Satan as the "ruler [prince] of this world" (see John 12:31; 14:30; 16:11). Paul called him, "the prince of the power of the air, of the spirit that is now working in the sons of disobedience" (Eph. 2:2). Consequently, "the whole world is under the control of the evil one" (1 John 5:19, *NIV*).

But God's plan of redemption was under way immediately after the Fall. The Lord cursed the snake and foretold the downfall of Satan, "Cursed are you above all the livestock and all the wild animals! You will crawl on your belly and you will eat dust all the days of your life. And I will put enmity between you and the woman, and between your offspring and hers; he will crush your head, and you will strike his heel" (Gen. 3:14,15, *NIV*). "He" (a person from the woman's seed, namely Christ) will deal a death blow to Satan's head at the Cross, while "you" (Satan) will strike Christ's heel. Some commentators suggest that the root word for strike *(shuph)* implies "to lie in wait for." This definition suggests a prolonged conflict with an element of expectancy.

This cosmic battle is the backdrop for the drama that unfolds in the pages of Scripture and continues into our present day. There will be enmity between the spiritual descendants of Satan and those who are in the family of God. We are either "children of God" (John 1:12) or "sons of disobedience" in whom the evil one is now working (Eph. 2:2). We are either in the "domain of darkness" or "the kingdom of His beloved Son" (Col. 1:13).

The Old Testament ends on a sour note. The New Testament begins with the Lord's chosen people in political bondage to Rome and spiritual bondage to an apostate Sanhedrin. The glory has departed from the nation of Israel, but the seed of Abraham is about to make His entrance. "The Word became flesh and made his dwelling among us. We have seen his glory, the glory of the One and Only, who came from the Father, full of grace and truth" (John 1:14, *NIV*). The blessing of Abraham was about to be extended to all nations of the world.

Throughout the Old Testament nothing had happened to change the basic nature of fallen humanity. "The intent of man's heart is evil from his youth" (Gen. 8:21). Jeremiah says,

....

The law actually has the capacity to stimulate the desire to do what it is trying to prohibit.

....

"The heart is deceitful above all things and beyond cure" (17:9, *NIV*). The law had done nothing to change this. "For if a law had been given that could impart life, then righteousness would certainly have come by the law. But the Scripture declares that the whole world is a prisoner of sin" (Gal. 3:21,22, *NIV*). Telling people that what they are doing is wrong does not give them the power to stop doing it. The law is powerless to give life.

Even more discouraging is the statement by Paul that "the sinful passions, which were aroused by the Law, were at work in the members of our body" (Rom. 7:5). The law actually has the capacity to stimulate the desire to do what it is trying to prohibit. If you don't think that is true, try telling your children they can go "here," but they can't go "there." The moment you say that, where do they want to go? They want to go "there." They probably did not even want to go "there" until you said they couldn't! I do not know why the forbidden fruit is more desirable, but it certainly seems to be. Much of Romans 7 and Galatians 3 is written to correct the wrong conclusion that the law is sinful. Laying down the law will not resolve the sinful passions. The core problem is not the behavior, but the basic nature of mankind.

I read an incredibly honest and insightful story on the front page of the *Los Angeles Times* a few years ago. A lady had been commissioned by the state of California to teach sex education in the public schools. According to the state's theory, if children knew the dangers of promiscuity, they would practice safe sex, or even better, abstain from sex until they were married. As she reflected upon what she was hoping to accomplish, the teacher was convicted of her own problem with obesity. Because of her weight, she had read many books on nutrition, exercise and diet. She had accumulated enough head knowledge to give lectures on those subjects as well. But her knowledge did not give her the power to stop having a second piece of pie. Here was an educated person promoting a program for children that was not even working for herself as an adult. Her discovery was the same as Mike's. Mike Quarles was finally able to admit as a pastor that what he was preaching wasn't even working for him. Doubling his efforts had only increased his frustration. He wanted to believe that Christ was the answer, but he didn't know how. So he quit the ministry.

The Pharisees were the moral perfectionists (legalists) of their day. But Jesus said, "For I tell you that unless your righteousness surpasses that of the Pharisees and the teachers of the law, you will certainly not enter the kingdom of heaven" (Matt. 5:20, *NIV*). The Sermon on the Mount confronts the issue of genuine righteousness, which is determined by the condition of the heart. For instance, "You have heard that it was said, 'Do not commit adultery.' But I tell you that anyone who looks at a woman lustfully has already committed adultery with her in his heart" (vv. 27,28, *NIV*). He did not commit adultery when he looked. The looking was just evidence that adultery had already been committed in his heart.

The text continues, "If your right eye causes you to sin, gouge it out...and if your right hand causes you to sin, cut it off and throw it away" (vv. 29,30, *NIV*). Does your eye or hand cause you to sin? No! If we kept cutting off body parts to keep ourselves from sinning, we would become to be nothing more than bloodied torsos rolling down the street. Many see this passage as an admonition to take whatever drastic means are necessary to stop sinning, thus emphasizing the hideousness of sin.

In actuality, it would be better to be dismembered than to

spend eternity apart from Christ, however, that is not His point. Taking cold showers to put out the fires of passion and walking blindfolded to avoid sunbathers at the beach are solutions that may bring temporary relief, but they do not deal with the condition of the heart. Such behavior would be necessary if the only option we had was to live under the law.

Trying to live a righteous life externally when we are not righteous internally will only result in being "whitewashed tombs, which look beautiful on the outside but on the inside are full of dead men's bones and everything unclean" (23:27, *NIV*). What goes into a man is not what defiles him, he is defiled by what comes out of him. "For from within, out of men's hearts, come evil thoughts, sexual immorality, theft, murder, adultery, greed, malice, deceit, lewdness, envy, slander, arrogance and folly. All these evils come from inside and make a man 'unclean'" (Mark 7:20-23, *NIV*). Paul wrote:

> For as many as are of the works of the Law, are under a curse; for it is written, "Cursed is everyone who does not abide by all things written in the book of the law, to perform them." Now that no one is justified by the Law before God is evident; for, "The righteous man shall live by faith." However, the Law is not of faith; on the contrary, "He who practices them shall live by them." Christ redeemed us from the curse of the Law, having become a curse for us—for it is written, "Cursed is everyone who hangs on a tree"—in order that in Christ Jesus the blessing of Abraham might come to the Gentiles, so that we might receive the promise of the Spirit through faith (Gal. 3:10-14).

The Law Is Powerless to Give Life

We don't understand this passage or the full purpose of the gospel; therefore, we fall back under the law. We operate according to laws or principles that mandate our obedience. The buzz words are, "Just say no," or "Work the program, it works." We commit ourselves to a program or to an institution and attempt to follow its principles and advice. We voluntarily agree to be accountable to sponsors or counselors who are committed to helping us. Some of us do manage to obtain a degree of sobriety with the help of these external constraints, the support of others and sheer willpower. However, because an internal and eternal change have not been effected, most fall back into their old habits when the external constraints and support are removed.

The law is powerless to give life. Because the law actually stimulates the desire to do what it prohibits, those who try to live under it are cursed. If we try to fulfill the law or the expectations of others by willpower and human effort alone, we will become driven people who never obtain that for which we strive. The law is a taskmaster or a tutor intended by God "to lead us to Christ" (v. 24). When we are alive in Christ, "[we] can do all things through Him [Christ] who strengthens [us]" (Phil. 4:13).

"Not that we are adequate in ourselves to consider anything as coming from ourselves, but our adequacy is from God, who also made us adequate as servants of a new covenant, not of the letter [law], but of the Spirit; for the letter [law] kills, but the Spirit gives life" (2 Cor. 3:5,6). Most recovery programs promote a law/principle concept requiring us to respond in obedience. The new covenant we have in Christ is a spiritual life concept that requires us to repent, come alive in Christ and walk by faith according to what God says is true in the power of the Holy Spirit. When we walk in God's truth, then we "will not carry out the desire of the flesh" (Gal. 5:16).

"The reason the Son of God appeared was to destroy the devil's work. No one who is born of God will continue to sin, because God's seed remains in him" (1 John 3:8,9, *NIV*). No two verses in the Bible capture more succinctly what must happen if we are to live a righteous life in Christ. Our basic nature has to change and we need a means for overcoming the evil one. We "were by nature children of wrath" (Eph. 2:3). "You were formerly darkness, but now you are light in the Lord; walk as children of light" (5:8). Only God can change who we are. Our responsibility is to believe the truth that will set us free and direct our steps for responsible living.

We were born "dead in [our] trespasses and sins" (2:1). That does not mean we were stillborn. It means we were born physically alive, but spiritually dead, separated from God. Jesus came to give us life. Jesus restored the same life that Adam and Eve lost when they sinned. Jesus said, "I came that they might have life, and might have it abundantly" (John 10:10). I used to believe that verse referred to our physical lives, meaning that Jesus was going to make them better. I now realize He was talking about our spiritual lives. He was saying that our souls are in union with God. To be spiritually alive means that we are "in Christ." Jesus said, "I am the resurrection, and the life; he who believes in Me shall live [spiritually] even if he dies [physically]" (11:25).

Half a Gospel
I believe we in America are laboring under half a gospel. We have presented Jesus as the Messiah who came to die for our sins so we will get to go to heaven. What's wrong with that? First, it gives the impression that eternal life is something we get when we die, which isn't true. "He who has the Son has life; he who does not have the Son of God does not have life" (1 John 5:12, *NIV*). Every child of God is alive in Christ *right now.* "For He has rescued us from the dominion of darkness and brought us into the kingdom of the Son he loves, in whom we have redemption, the forgiveness of sins" (Col. 1:13,14, *NIV*).

Second, it is only half the gospel. If you wanted to save a dead person, what would you do? Give him life? He would only die again. You would have to do two things. First, you would have to cure the disease that caused him to die—"the wages of sin is death" (Rom. 6:23). So Jesus went to the Cross to die for our sins. Is that all? Absolutely not! He was resurrected so that we may have life. Now finish the verse: "but the free gift of God is eternal life in Christ Jesus our Lord" (6:23). The fact that we are "in Christ" is our only hope. It is "Christ in you, the hope of glory" (Col. 1:27). Our position in Christ is what guarantees our victory over sin. (The next chapter will cover that subject.)

Because we are in Christ, we have the spirit of God within us. We must learn how to live our lives in total dependence upon God. Before we were in Christ, we depended on our parents, our government, ourselves, our doctors or counselors and our drugs to help us survive; and we can continue to do so after salvation. We must realize, however, that this choice as well as every other temptation is an attempt by the evil one to get us to live our lives independently from God. The deceiver is so subtle. He gets us to put all our confidence in our programs, strategies, others and even ourselves. Paul had incredible self-confidence until Christ struck him down. Then he was able to say, "We are the true circumcision, who worship in the Spirit of God and glory in Christ Jesus and put no confidence in the flesh" (Phil. 3:3). Apart from Christ, we are not handicapped. Apart from Christ, we are not limited in what we can do. Apart from Christ, we can do *nothing* (see John 15:5).

Second, because we are in Christ, we have the assurance that He will meet all our needs (see Phil. 4:19). Trying to break the bondages of alcohol, drugs, or sex without fulfilling our essential needs will only prove counterproductive in the long run. We should never attempt to understand the problems of alcohol, drugs and sex as separate issues unrelated to the rest of our lives. Like any other single problem we have, these are only a part of a greater whole. In *Living Free in Christ* (Regal Books), I explain how Christ meets our critical needs or "being" needs, i.e., life, identity, acceptance, security and significance. Let me encourage you to read out loud the subtitles of the chart as follows:

Who I Am in Christ

I Am Accepted in Christ:

John 1:12	I am God's child
John 15:15	I am Christ's friend
Romans 5:1	I have been justified
1 Corinthians 6:17	I am united with the Lord and one with Him in spirit
1 Corinthians 6:20	I have been bought with a price—I belong to God

1 Corinthians 12:27	I am a member of Christ's body
Ephesians 1:1	I am a saint
Ephesians 1:5	I have been adopted as God's child
Ephesians 2:18	I have direct access to God through the Holy Spirit
Colossians 1:14	I have been redeemed and forgiven of all my sins
Colossians 2:10	I am complete in Christ

I Am Secure in Christ:

Romans 8:1,2	I am free from condemnation
Romans 8:28	I am assured that all things work together for good
Romans 8:33,34	I am free from any condemning charges against me
Romans 8:35	I cannot be separated from the love of God
2 Corinthians 1:21	I have been established, anointed, and sealed by God
Colossians 3:3	I am hidden with Christ in God
Philippians 1:6	I am confident that the good work that God has begun in me will be perfected
Philippians 3:20	I am a citizen of heaven
2 Timothy 1:7	I have not been given a spirit of fear, but of power, love and a sound mind
Hebrews 4:16	I can find grace and mercy in time of need
1 John 5:18	I am born of God and the evil one cannot touch me

I Am Significant in Christ:

Matthew 5:13,14	I am the salt and light of the earth
John 15:1,5	I am a branch of the true vine, a channel of His life

John 15:16	I have been chosen and appointed to bear fruit
Acts 1:8	I am a personal witness of Christ
1 Corinthians 3:16	I am God's temple
2 Corinthians 5:17-20	I am a minister of reconciliation
2 Corinthians 6:1	I am God's coworker
Ephesians 2:6	I am seated with Christ in the heavenly realm
Ephesians 2:10	I am God's workmanship
Ephesians 3:12	I may approach God with freedom and confidence
Philippians 4:13	I can do all things through Christ who strengthens me

Taken from *Living Free in Christ* by Neil Anderson. © 1993, Regal Books.

You might be tempted to say, "If I believed that I would be prideful." Not true! But if you don't believe it, you are defeated. These clear statements from Scripture are not true because of what we have done. They are true because of what Christ has done for us. The only way we can appropriate these scriptural truths is by faith. The problem is not that every child of God doesn't share in His rich inheritance, nor that we lack the power to live victoriously in Christ; the problem is that we just don't see it. That is why Paul prayed in Eph. 1:18,19, "I pray also that the eyes of your heart may be enlightened in order that you may know the hope to which he has called you, the riches of his glorious inheritance in the saints, and his incomparably great power for us who believe" (*NIV*).

The lay leader of a recovery ministry in a church where I was speaking confessed, "I came to this conference with a gun in my mouth. If I hadn't found my freedom in Christ, I would have pulled the trigger." This dear man had been sober for several years, but he was not free. His leadership position made it even more difficult for him to admit that he still had problems. He told me, "I had no idea who I was as a child of God!"

Neither do most other people who are struggling with bondage. People in bondage have no understanding or assurance of who they are in Christ or what it means to be a child of God. This common denominator is shared by every person I have helped to find freedom in Christ. This is especially true for those living in bondage to alcohol and drugs. Before they seek help, their self-perception is extremely negative. The accuser of the brethren is having a field day with them. Those in treatment

....

We are not sinners in the hands of an angry God; we are saints who sin in the hands of a loving God.

....

stand and identify themselves at every AA and Al-Anon meeting by saying, "Hi, I'm Fred, and I'm an alcoholic or addict or co-addict, etc." They make this statement because people cannot be helped, unless they admit they have problems.

I agree that they must face the truth and admit their problems, but I don't agree that Christians are alcoholics or addicts. I believe they are children of God who struggle with alcohol, drugs and sex. We are not sinners in the hands of an angry God; we are saints who sin in the hands of a loving God.

Great Love from the Father

This is not a play on words or a minor point of theology, nor is it an attempt to dodge the sin issue. I believe rehearsing a weekly failure identity is counterproductive to the Holy Spirit's affirmation: "The Spirit Himself bears witness with our spirit that we are children of God" (Rom. 8:16). Dear Christian reader, who are you according to the following passages?

> But as many as received Him, to them He gave the right to become children of God, even to those who believe in His name (John 1:12).
>
> To the church of God which is at Corinth, to

those who have been sanctified in Christ Jesus, saints by calling, with all who in every place call upon the name of our Lord Jesus Christ, their Lord and ours (1 Cor. 1:2).

For you are all sons of God through faith in Christ Jesus....And because you are sons, God has sent forth the Spirit of His Son into our hearts, crying, Abba Father! (Gal. 3:26; 4:6).

You are a chosen race, a royal priesthood, a holy nation, a people for God's own possession, that you may proclaim the excellencies of Him who has

....

It is not what we do that determines who we are; it is who we are and how we perceive ourselves that determines what we do.

....

called you out of darkness into His marvelous light; for you once were not a people, but now you are the people of God; you had not received mercy, but now you have received mercy (1 Pet. 2:9,10).

See how great a love the Father has bestowed upon us, that we should be called children of God; and such we are. For this reason the world does not know us, because it did not know Him. Beloved, now we are children of God, and it has not appeared as yet what we shall be. We know that, when He appears, we shall be like Him, because we shall see Him just as He is. And everyone who has this hope fixed on Him purifies himself, just as He is pure (1 John 3:1-3).

This last verse reveals the critical reason we should know our true identity in Christ. People cannot consistently behave in a manner inconsistent with their self-perceptions. If we consider ourselves losers, and call ourselves alcoholics, these pronouncements can become self-fulfilling prophecies. It is not what we do that determines who we are; it is who we are and how we perceive ourselves that determines what we do.

Our performance-based culture promotes the tendency to identify ourselves by the things we do. So we are carpenters, plumbers and engineers. But what happens if we lose our jobs? Do we lose our identities? We have done the same thing with sin. If we sin, we must be sinners. If we burp, are we burpers? If we sneeze, are we sneezers? According to the Bible, we are saints who burp, sneeze and sometimes choose to sin. If we are sinners, how can we ever hope to do anything other than commit acts of sin? John writes, "If we say that we have no sin, we are deceiving ourselves, and the truth is not in us" (1:8). We have sin and we need to admit it, but we are not sin. "Having" sin and "being" sin are two totally different issues. Why do we insist on calling Christians sinners, and then expect them to act like saints?

We don't call a person "cancer" because he or she has cancer or some other physical disease. A person does not stand up in a cancer ward and say, "Hi, I'm Fred, and I am cancerous." He could appropriately say, "Hi, I'm Fred, and I have cancer." The person has a problem, but he or she is not the problem. The person could, however, choose actions such as smoking that would increase the susceptibility of cancer in his or her life.

Christians have problems, but they are not the problems. If they were the problems, the problems could not be resolved. We would have to get rid of Christians to get rid of the problems Christians have. Believers can also create problems for themselves by living in denial and by not assuming their responsibilities to live righteous lives. A Christian can appropriately say, "Hi, I'm Fred, a child of God. Right now I am struggling with sin. I know that I can resolve this issue and live free in Christ because I am 'dead to sin, but alive to God in Christ Jesus'" (Rom. 6:11).

Some Concerns About Secular Twelve Step Programs

Why do we Christians identify those who are addicted to chemicals by their bondages? I think we have borrowed this practice from the secular world. They cannot say they are children of God because they are not. I believe they would be better off, however, if they would say, "Hi, I'm Fred, and I have a major problem with alcohol."

The Twelve Step program practiced worldwide originated as a Christian program clearly identifying the higher power as the God of the Bible. Christians were finding freedom in Christ through genuine repentance and faith in God. Because of the program's effectiveness, other religious groups and those who would not put their faith in God wanted to use it. They thought the *program* was setting people free. It wasn't. God set them free—not an unknown higher power.

The non-Christian world adopted the Twelve Step program and secularized it. As a result, many people were taught to live more responsible lives. Some achieved sobriety from sheer willpower and the help of a supportive group, but they were not free in Christ.

Most Christian recovery ministries have tried to reclaim the 12 Steps as the primary means for recovery. They have identified the "higher power" as Christ and added Scriptures to each step, but they are still *working the program*. I appreciate their efforts, and I do not want to criticize my brothers and sisters in Christ, but I have two major concerns. One is with the program itself.

I do not believe the 12 Steps are wrong if each step is clearly understood from a Christian perspective. On the other hand, I don't believe the steps are complete. I have already identified the problem I see with the public pronouncement of a failure identity, but there are other concerns. The program includes a step to ask for forgiveness, which is very necessary. But the program does not emphasize the need to forgive others, which is the most important step to freedom in Christ. These concerns can be easily corrected by responsible Christians. The most serious oversight, however, is the absence of any biblical understanding of the spiritual battle in which all of these people are engaged.

My second major concern is the orientation of the program. Christian counseling is not a technique we learn or a program to follow. Christian counseling is an encounter with God. He is the wonderful counselor. He alone can grant repentance that leads to a knowledge of truth that sets people free (see 2 Tim. 2:24-26). Truth sets people free, not programs, strategies or human effort. Jesus is "the way, and the truth, and the life" (John 14:6). Accepting this requires a completely different orientation to the Christian care of those who are hurting and in bondage. I share this approach in *Helping Others Find Freedom In Christ* (Regal Books). People throughout the world are making the joyful discovery that Jesus is the Bondage Breaker. We are merely the Lord's privileged bondservants whom He works through to make it happen.

To illustrate my concern another way, let us look at John 15:8, "By this is My Father glorified, that you bear much fruit, and so prove to be My disciples." Some look at this passage and conclude that we have to bear fruit. No we don't! We must abide in Christ. If we abide in Christ, we will bear fruit. Bearing fruit is just giving evidence to the fact that we are abiding in Christ. Many Christian programs are trying to bear fruit without abiding in Christ. Programs don't bear fruit. I deeply believe that if Christ is in it, any program will work. If Christ isn't in it, then no program will work. But I do believe that if Christ is in it, a good program will bear more fruit than a bad program.

James 4:7 is the simple answer to what we are saying, "Submit therefore to God. Resist the devil and he will flee from you." If you try to resist the devil without first submitting to God, you will have a dog fight. This is the classic error of most deliverance ministries. You can submit to God and not resist the devil and stay in bondage. Unfortunately, most recovery ministries are not doing either. Submitting to God gives us the right to live like children of God. This is a winnable war if we (1) know who we are, (2) comprehend the tremendous position we have in Christ and (3) understand the nature of the spiritual battle we are all in. These concepts will be discussed in the next two chapters.

Please do not misinterpret what I am saying. I do not want to undermine the Twelve Step recovery ministry. I certainly don't want to take away the only program available to most hurting Christians. I do want to provide a resource to churches and Christian ministries that has a very practical and comprehensive theology of freedom in Christ. Truth sets people free, and God's Word is the truth.

The Assurance of Victory over Sin

How long will you make yourself drunk?
Put away your wine from you.
—1 Samuel 1:14

And do not get drunk with wine, for that is
dissipation, but be filled with the Spirit.
—Ephesians 5:18

Several years ago I spoke at a secular university about Christian morality in marriage and family. The class was predominantly attended by young women. One young man, however, purposely pulled his chair off into a corner to protest my being there. Occasionally, he would interrupt with a vulgar noise. A young lady asked me what Christians believe about masturbation. Before I could answer he piped up, "Well, I masturbate every day."

"Congratulations," I said. "Can you stop?" I didn't hear

from him again until after the class dismissed and everybody else had left.

Finally he spoke up, "Why would I want to stop?"

"That's not what I asked you," I replied. "I asked if you *could* stop. What you think is freedom really isn't freedom at all—it's just sexual bondage."

....

The ultimate question is not "Do you have the right to drink, take drugs or fornicate?" The real question is, "Can you stop?"

....

The world's definition of freedom is being able to do your own thing—to exercise your independence by being a free moral agent. "No rules! No regulations! No restrictions! You can do whatever you want to do. If you want to have a drink, you have a drink. "Make your own choices," say the libertarians. Everybody created in the image of God has that right. The greatest human power we possess is the power to choose. We can choose to pray or not pray, to think or not think, to learn or not learn. The choice is ours, and no one can take it away from us. Freedom, however, does not lie solely in the exercise of choices. It lies in the consequences of our choices.

I suppose I am free to tell a lie, but wouldn't I be in bondage to that choice? I would have to remember who I told the lie to and what I told them. I am also free to rob a bank, but wouldn't I be in bondage to that act for the rest of my life? I would always be looking over my shoulder wondering if I would be caught. You can choose to get drunk, sleep with a harlot and take dope, but you will have to live with the consequences of those acts. The so-called "free sex" that emerged during the '60s has led to rampant sexual bondage in the '90s, not to mention the sickness and death of many. That is not freedom, it is license, and it can only lead to bondage. The ultimate question is not "Do you have the right to drink, take drugs or fornicate?" The real question is, "Can you stop?"

When we act as our own gods, we are in bondage to our own flesh. We sell ourselves into the slave market of sin. Jesus purchased us from the kingdom of darkness; and in one sense, He saved us from ourselves. "Or do you not know that your body is a temple of the Holy Spirit who is in you, whom you have from God, and that you are not your own? For you have been bought with a price: therefore glorify God in your body" (1 Cor. 6:19,20). We are no longer slaves to sin, but bondservants of the Lord Jesus Christ. When we become believers in Christ, we are able to make choices that allow us to live in the freedom Christ purchased for us at the Cross.

Benefits of Freedom

The most practical, immediate benefit of being a child of God is freedom. Living as a servant of sin is bondage. Living as a bondservant of Christ is freedom in three ways.

First, we are free from the law. Galatians 5:1 says, "It was for freedom that Christ set us free....Do not be subject again to a yoke of slavery." The legalistic person who is driven by the law will feel cursed and condemned all his life. Those who live by the Spirit have life and liberty. "Now the Lord is the Spirit; and where the Spirit of the Lord is, there is liberty" (2 Cor. 3:17).

Second, we are free from our pasts. "Because you are sons, God sent the Spirit of His Son into our hearts, the Spirit who calls out, 'Abba, Father.' So you are no longer a slave, but a son; and since you are a son, God has made you also an heir. Formerly, when you did not know God, you were slaves to those who by nature are not gods" (Gal. 4:6-8, *NIV*). As children of God, we are no longer products of our pasts; we are primarily products of Christ's work on the cross. We have a new heritage; we are heirs of God. Let me share an analogy:

Freeing the Slaves[1]
Slavery in the United States was abolished by the Thirteenth Amendment on December 18th, 1865. How many slaves were there on December 19th? In reality, none, but many still lived

like slaves. Many did, because they never learned the truth. Others knew and even believed that they were free, but chose to live as they had been taught.

Several plantation owners were devastated by the Emancipation Proclamation. "We're ruined! Slavery has been abolished. We've lost the battle to keep our slaves." But their chief spokesman slyly responded, "Not necessarily, as long as these people think they're still slaves, the Emancipation Proclamation will have no practical effect. We don't have a legal right over them anymore, but many of them don't know it. Keep your slaves from learning the truth, and your control over them will not even be challenged."

One cotton farmer asked "But, what if the news spreads?"

"Don't panic. We have another bullet in our gun. We may not be able to keep them from hearing the news, but we can still keep them from understanding it. They don't call me the 'father of lies' for nothing. We still have the potential to deceive the whole world. Just tell them that they misunderstood the Thirteenth Amendment. Tell them that they are *going to be free*, not that they are free already. The truth they heard is just positional truth, not actual truth. Someday they may receive the benefits, but not now."

"But they'll expect me to say that. They won't believe me."

"Then pick out a few persuasive ones who are convinced they are still slaves and let them do the talking for you. Remember, most of these free people were born as slaves and have been their whole lives. All we have to do is to deceive them so they still *think* like slaves. As long as they continue to do what slaves do, it will not be hard to convince them that they must still be slaves. They will maintain their slave identities because of the things they do. The moment they try to profess that they are no longer slaves, just whisper in their ear, 'How can you even think you are no longer a slave when you are still doing things that slaves do?' After all, we have the capacity to accuse the brethren day and night."

Years later, many have still not heard the wonderful news that they have been freed. Quite naturally they continue to live the way they have always lived. Some have heard the good news, but evaluated it by what they are presently doing and feeling. They reason, "I'm still living in bondage, doing the same things I have always done. My experience tells me that I must not be free. I'm feeling the same way I was before the Proclamation, so it must not be true. After all, your feelings always tell the truth." So they continue to live according to how they feel, not wanting to be hypocrites!

One former slave hears the good news, and receives it with great joy. He checks out the validity of the Proclamation, and discovers that the highest of all authorities has originated the decree. Not only that, but it personally cost the authority a tremendous price which He willingly paid so the former slave could be free. His life is transformed. He correctly reasons that it would be hypocritical to believe his feelings, and not believe the truth. Determined to live by what he knows to be true, his experiences begin to change rather dramatically. He realizes that his old master has no authority over him and does not need to be obeyed. He gladly serves the one who set him free.

Third, we are "freed from sin" (Rom. 6:7).

A student asked, "Are you telling me that I don't have to sin?"

"Where did you get the idea that you have to sin?" I asked. John wrote, "My dear children, I write this to you so that you will not sin. But if anybody does sin, we have one who speaks to the Father in our defense—Jesus Christ, the Righteous One" (1 John 2:1, *NIV*). Obviously Christian maturity is a factor in our ability to stand against temptation. But what an incredible sense of defeat we would have if we believed that we had to sin while at the same time being commanded by God not to sin. "For you were once darkness, but now you are light in the Lord. Live as children of light (for the fruit of the light consists in all goodness, righteousness and truth)" (Eph. 5:8,9, *NIV*).

People living in bondage are caught in a web of faulty thinking: "God, you made me this way and now you condemn me for it!"

"The Christian life is impossible," they say. And when they fail, they proclaim, "I'm only human!"

Those who struggle with chemical and sexual addictions lead this parade of despair. They constantly entertain thoughts such as:

*I'm different from others. Christianity works for others,
but it doesn't work for me.*
    Maybe I'm not a Christian.
    God doesn't love me. How could He? I'm such a failure.
    *I'm just a miserable sinner with no hope of ever break-
ing the chains of alcoholism.*

What a pack of lies! They are still living like slaves because
they are still thinking like slaves. We need to examine the
Christian Emancipation Proclamation found in Romans 6:1-11.

The Only Proper Response—Obey It

Before we look at this liberating text about our identity and
position in Christ, let me clarify some simple principles of
Bible interpretation. The only proper response to a commandment in the Bible is to obey it. The only proper response to a
scriptural truth is to believe it. The only proper response to a
biblical promise is to claim it. The concept is simple, but it can
get twisted. This is especially true of Romans 6:1-11:

> What shall we say then? Are we to continue in sin
> that grace may increase? May it never be! How
> shall we who died to sin still live in it? Or do you
> not know that all of us who have been baptized into
> Christ Jesus have been baptized into His death?
> Therefore we have been buried with Him through
> baptism into death, in order that as Christ was
> raised from the dead through the glory of the
> Father, so we too might walk in newness of life. For
> if we have become united with Him in the likeness
> of His death, certainly we shall be also in the like-
> ness of His resurrection, knowing this, that our old
> self was crucified with Him, that our body of sin
> might be done away with, that we should no longer
> be slaves to sin; for he who has died is freed from
> sin. Now if we have died with Christ, we believe
> that we shall also live with Him, knowing that

Christ, having been raised from the dead, is never
to die again; death no longer is master over Him.
For the death that He died, He died to sin, once for
all; but the life that He lives, He lives to God. Even
so consider yourselves to be dead to sin, but alive to
God in Christ Jesus.

Many have a tendency to read this section and ask, "How
do I do that?" Romans 6:1-11 is not something we can do. It is
only something we can believe, but believing the truth will set
us free.

The New Testament Greek language is very precise in its
application of verbs. A verb is past, present or future tense,
and describes either a continuous action or a point in time.
But, we do not have to know the Greek language to appreciate what the Word of God is saying. Although the English
translations reveal this fairly well, I will attempt to further
clarify the truth of this text. Let me encourage you to pray,
asking the Holy Spirit—who is the Spirit of truth—to protect
your mind and to enable you to understand the truth of this
text. Now let's look at Romans 6:1-11—the basis for our hope
to be free from sin.

What shall we say then? Shall we go on sinning that
grace might increase? By no means! We died to sin;
how can we live in it any longer? (v. 1, *NIV*).

You may be tempted to ask, "How do I do that? How do I
die to sin?" The answer is, you can't! Why not? Because you
have already died to sin.

"We died to sin" is past tense. You cannot do what has
already been done. You might be saying, "But I don't feel
dead to sin, and frankly I am still sinning." Remember, it is
not what you do that determines who you are. You will have
to set your feelings aside for a few verses. It is what you *believe*
that is going to set you free, not what you feel. God's Word is
true whether you and I choose to believe it or not. Believing
the Word of God does not make it true. His Word is true,
therefore I believe it.

A pastor shared with me that he had struggled for 22 years in his Christian experience. "It's been one trial after another, and I think I know what my problem is. I have been reading Colossians 3:3, 'For you died, and your life is now hidden with Christ in God' (*NIV*). That's the key isn't it?"

I assured him I thought it was.

Then he asked, "How do I do that?"

I was surprised by his question, so I asked him to look at the passage again.

He read it again, "For you died and your life is hidden with Christ in God." Again, he asked, "I know I somehow need to die with Christ, but how do I do that?"

For 22 years this dear man had been desperately trying to become something he already is (i.e., dead to sin). So have many other Christians—especially those living in bondage.

Every Believer with Christ

Paul's argument in Romans 6:1-11 is twofold. First, we cannot identify with the death and burial of Christ, and not also be identified with His resurrection and ascension. We will live in defeat if we believe only half the gospel. We are also seated with Christ in the heavenlies (see Eph. 2:6). From this position we have the authority and power to live the Christian life. Jesus did not just die for our sins, He came to give us life; therefore, every child of God is spiritually alive "in Christ." Paul clearly identifies every believer with Christ:

In His death	Rom. 6:3,6; Gal. 2:20; Col. 3:1-3
In His burial	Rom. 6:4
In His resurrection	Rom. 6:5,8,11
In His ascension	Eph. 2:6
In His life	Rom. 5:10,11
In His power	Eph. 1:19,20
In His inheritance	Rom. 8:16,17; Eph. 1:11,12

The second half of Paul's argument is that death no longer has any power over us, therefore, neither does sin. We will see how and why this is true when we examine these verses. Returning to his first argument, let's continue with Romans 6:

> Or don't you know that all of us who were baptized into Christ Jesus were baptized into his death (v. 3, *NIV*)?

Are you still wondering, "How do I do that?" The answer is the same: You can't! Why not? Because you already have been baptized into Christ Jesus.[2] It is futile to seek something the Bible affirms we already have. "For we were all baptized by one Spirit into one body" (1 Cor. 12:13, *NIV*). "We were" is past tense.

Let's continue with Romans 6:

> In order that, just as Christ was raised from the dead through the glory of the Father, we too may live a new life. If we have been united with him like this in his death, we will certainly also be united with him in his resurrection (vv. 4,5, *NIV*).

Have we been united with Him? Absolutely! The syntax and verb form is described as a first-class conditional clause by those who study the original languages. It can literally be read this way: For if we have become united with Him in the likeness of His death *and we have*, certainly; we shall also become united with Him in the likeness of His resurrection.

We celebrate the Resurrection on Easter, not just the death on Good Friday. It is the resurrected life of Christ that God has given to us. Using the *New International Version*, notice how Paul develops this in Romans 5:8-11:

> But God demonstrates his own love for us in this: While we were still sinners, Christ died for us (v. 8).

Isn't that great, Christian? God loves you! But is that all there is to the gospel? No! Read on:

> Since we have now been justified by his blood, how

much more, shall we be saved from God's wrath
through him (v. 9)!

Isn't that great, Christian? You're not going to hell! But is
that the whole gospel? No! Read on:

> For if, when we were God's enemies, we were rec-
> onciled to him through the death of his Son, how
> *much more,* having been reconciled, shall we be
> saved through his life (v. 10, emphasis mine)!

Isn't that great, Christian? You have been saved by His life,
and eternal life is not something you get when you physically die. You are alive in Christ right now. But is that the whole
gospel? No! Read on:

> *Not only is this so,* but we also rejoice in God
> through our Lord Jesus Christ, through whom we
> have now received reconciliation (v. 11, emphasis
> mine).

This reconciliation assures us that our souls are in union
with God. This is what it means to be spiritually alive. If we
are spiritually alive in Christ, we have every reason to believe
there will be a positive result. Romans 5:17 shares what it is:

> For if, by the trespass of the one man, death reigned
> through that one man, how much more will those
> who receive God's abundant provision of grace and
> of the gift of righteousness reign in life through the
> one man, Jesus Christ (*NIV*).

Returning to Romans 6:6:

> For we know that our old self was crucified with
> him (*NIV*).

Simply Believe It
Are you still asking, "How do I do that?" This isn't something

you can do. This is only something you can know. The only proper response to this marvelous truth is to believe it. This is a question of knowledge, not experience. The text does not say, "For we must do," it says, "For we know." Many people are desperately trying to put the old self (old man) to death, but they can't do it. Why? Because he is already dead! You cannot do for yourself what God can and has already done for you.

Many fail in their Christian experience, so they begin to incorrectly reason: *What experience must I have for this to be true?* They will never get there! The only experience that has to happen for this verse to be true happened nearly 2,000 years ago on the Cross. The only way we can enter into that experience today is by faith. We can't save ourselves, and we can't overcome the penalty of death nor the power of sin by human effort. Only God can do that for us, and He did.

As I was explaining this during a conference, a man raised his hand and said, "Hey, wait a minute. I've been a Christian for 13 years. How come nobody ever told me this before?" Maybe nobody shared with him or maybe he wasn't listening. Some have asserted that this is just positional truth, implying there is little or no present-day benefit for being in Christ. What a tragic conclusion. In our industrialized "how to" Western world, we try to make this true by our experiences. We can't. No matter how we feel or how we fail in our Christian experiences, we must choose to believe the truth, then walk accordingly by faith. When we do, the truth of this passage manifests in our experiences. Trying to make it true by our experience will only lead to defeat. We are saved, not by how we behave, but by choosing to believe the truth of God's Word.

I don't do the things I do with the hope that God may someday accept me. I am accepted in the beloved; that is why I do the things I do. I don't labor in the vineyard with the hope that God may someday love me; God loves me, therefore, I labor in the vineyard. Remember, it is not what we do that determines who we are, it is who we are and what we believe that determines what we do.

We Walk by Faith
Let's look again at Romans 6:6:

For we know that our old self was crucified with him
so that the body of sin might be done away with, that
we should no longer be slaves to sin (*NIV*).

The latter part of the verse refers to our physical bodies. We
will explore this topic later. First, we must know that our
entire walk with God is by faith. We are not only saved by

....

If you only believe what you feel, you will never live a victorious life.

....

faith, but we also walk by faith. Paul considered thinking oth-
erwise a deceptive trick of the devil and foolish: "You foolish
Galatians! Who has bewitched you?...Did you receive the
Spirit by observing the law, or by believing what you heard?
Are you so foolish? After beginning with the Spirit, are you
now trying to attain your goal by human effort" (Gal. 3:1-3,
NIV)? We are still suffering from this Galatian heresy.

Paul wrote in Romans 6:

Anyone who has died has been freed from sin
(v. 7, *NIV*).

Have you died with Christ? Then you are freed from sin.
I'm sure you must be thinking, "I don't feel free from sin." If
you only believe what you feel, you will never live a victorious life. In all honesty, I wake up many mornings feeling alive
to sin and dead to Christ. But that's just the way I feel. If I
believed what I felt and walked accordingly throughout the
day, what kind of a day do you think I would have? It would
be a pretty bad day!

I have learned to say as I arise in the morning: "Thank you,
Lord, for another day. I deserved eternal damnation, but You
gave me eternal life. I now ask You to fill me with Your Holy
Spirit, and I choose to walk by faith regardless of how I feel. I

realize I will face many temptations today, but I choose to take every thought captive to the obedience of Christ and to think upon that which is true and right."

On more than one occasion, the Lord has said, "Be it done to you according to how you believe." There is no greater sin than the sin of unbelief. "Everything that does not come from faith is sin" (14:23, *NIV*). If we choose to believe a lie, we will live a lie; but if we choose to believe the truth, we will live a victorious life by faith in the same way that we were saved.

What would happen if you got up in the morning and based on your feelings, you said, "I'm an alcoholic who is hopelessly addicted to alcohol. I need to have a drink to cope with life." What would you do next?

Death Has No Mastery
Romans 6:8,9 tells us:

> Now if we died with Christ, we believe that we will also live with him. For we know that since Christ was raised from the dead, he cannot die again; death no longer has mastery over him (*NIV*).

Question: Does death have mastery over you? Absolutely not!

> "Death has been swallowed up in victory. Where, O death, is your victory? Where O death, is your sting?" The sting of death is sin, and the power of sin is the law. But thanks be to God! He gives us the victory through our Lord Jesus Christ (1 Cor. 15:54-57, *NIV*).

Paul argued that if death has no mastery over you, then neither does sin. Let's continue with Romans 6:10:

> The death he died, he died to sin once for all; but the life he lives, he lives to God (*NIV*).

This was accomplished when, "God made him who had no sin to be sin for us, so that *IN HIM* we might become the righteousness of God (2 Cor. 5:21, *NIV*, emphasis mine).

When Jesus went to the Cross, all the sins of the world were on Him. When they nailed those spikes into His hands and feet, all the sins of the world were upon Him. But when He was resurrected, there weren't any sins on Him. As He sits at

....

Death is the end of a relationship, not the end of existence.

....

the right hand of the Father; there aren't any sins on Him. He triumphed over sin and death. "He died to sin once for all" (Rom. 6:10, *NIV*)

Many accept the truth that Christ has died for the sins we have *already* committed, but what if we sin again in the future? When Christ died once for all our sins, how many of our sins were then future? All, of course!

How should we respond to this truth? Paul explained in verse 11, "In the same way, count yourselves dead to sin but alive to God *IN CHRIST JESUS*" (*NIV*, emphasis mine). We do not make ourselves dead to sin by considering ourselves so. We consider ourselves dead to sin because God says it is already so.

Years ago I was trying to minister to a number of people who struggled with this passage. The old King James translation reads:

Reckon ye also yourselves to be dead indeed unto sin.

I explained that if they thought it was the reckoning that made them dead to sin, they would reckon themselves into a wreck! We can't make ourselves dead to sin, only God can do that.

Paul was saying that we have to keep on choosing to believe by faith what God says is true even though all our feelings are screaming the opposite. The verb "consider" is present tense. In other words, we must continually believe the truth. This is parallel to abiding in Christ (see John 15:1-8), which is basically the same as walking by the Spirit (see Gal. 5:16). Then we will not be deceived or carry out the desires of the flesh.

Death is the end of a relationship, not the end of existence. Throughout the Bible, life means to be in union with, and death means to be separated from. When Adam sinned, he died spiritually. He did not pass out of existence. In fact he remained physically alive for more than 900 years. His soul, however, was separated from God. When we are born again, we are spiritually alive. Our souls are in union with God. We are alive in Christ. The prepositional phrase "in Christ," or "in Him," is repeated again and again throughout the New Testament.

Has sin passed out of existence because we have died to it? No! Has the power of sin died? No! It is still strong and still appealing. But when sin makes its appeal, we have the power to say no to it. Our relationship with sin ended when the Lord "rescued us from the dominion of darkness and brought us into the kingdom of the Son he loves" (Col. 1:13, *NIV*). Paul explained how this is possible in Romans 8:1,2:

> Therefore, there is now no condemnation for those who are in Christ Jesus, because through Christ Jesus the law of the Spirit of life set me free from the law of sin and death (*NIV*).

Question: Is the law of sin and death still operative?

Yes, because it is a law. We cannot do away with a law, but we can overcome an existing law with a greater law—the "law of the Spirit of life." For instance, can we as mere mortals fly by our own power? No, because the law of gravity will keep us bound to the earth. But we can fly if we unite ourselves with a power greater than gravity. As long as we remain in the airplane and operate according to that power, we will be able to fly. But if we step out of the airplane, we will find that the law of gravity is still in effect. Down we go!

The law of sin and of death is still here, still operative, still powerful and still making its appeal. But we do not have to submit to it. As long as we "walk [live] by the Spirit...[we] will not carry out the desire of the flesh" (Gal. 5:16). We must "be strong in the Lord, and in the strength of His might" (Eph. 6:10). The moment we stop being dependent upon the Lord and choose to walk by the flesh, we will crash and burn. The moment we think we can stand on our own, we are setting ourselves up for a fall. "Pride goes before destruction, a haughty spirit before a fall" (Prov. 16:18, *NIV*).

All temptation is an attempt by the devil to get us to live our lives independently from God. "So, if you think you are standing firm, be careful that you don't fall! No temptation has seized you except what is common to man. And God is faithful; he will not let you be tempted beyond what you can bear. But when you are tempted, he will also provide a way out so that you can stand up under it" (1 Cor. 10:12,13, *NIV*). If we succumb to his temptation or become deceived by the father of lies, we can repent from our ways, renounce the lies and return to our loving Father who has forgiven us and will cleanse us (see 1 John 1:9).

If you are still struggling with alcohol, sex or drugs, you are probably thinking, *All this sounds good and I want to believe it, but I am still struggling.* You probably are because "pleasures" are waging war in your members (see Jas. 4:1); and there is a battle going on for your mind. Understanding the battle and how to win it is the subject of the next two chapters.

Notes
1. Neil T. Anderson, *Living Free in Christ* (Ventura Calif., Regal Books: 1993), pp. 56-58, adapted.
2. The ordinance of water baptism is typically understood to be the symbolic representation of what has already been done. Augustine called it a visible form of an invisible grace. It is a public identification with the death, burial and resurrection of the Lord Jesus Christ. Those who practice infant baptism, however, understand the ordinance to be symbolic of the Holy Spirit coming upon Christ. They would then sprinkle water on the head as opposed to immersing the body. Both look to Scripture for the basis of their practice, and both see it as an identification with Christ. The passage we are looking at, however, refers to our spiritual baptism into Christ which is symbolized through the external ordinance practiced by our churches.

The Battle for the Body

For while they be folden together as thorns,
and while they are drunken as drunkards,
they shall be devoured as stubble fully dry.
—Nahum 1:10, (KJV).

I urge you therefore, brethren, by the mercies
of God, to present your bodies a living and
holy sacrifice, acceptable to God, which is
your spiritual service of worship.
—Romans 12:1

Various Purposes for a Car

Suppose we flew an aborigine from the outback of Australia to Detroit, Michigan. There we showed him a brand-new Lincoln just off the assembly line. The battery gives it a spark of life, but the gas tank is empty. We ask the aborigine, "What do you think the purpose is for the automobile?" He has never seen or heard of a car before. He only knows it is the prettiest object he has ever seen.

His original thought might be, *The purpose must be found in its appearance.* He sits in the leather seats that move up and down; and decides maybe its purpose is to provide comfort. Somebody switches on the stereo with quadraphonic sound. Now he thinks its real purpose is to make music. When he honks the horn, the aborigine is even more convinced that this is a noise machine. Suddenly someone else turns on the lights. He wonders if the purpose of this machine is to provide light.

An automobile has only one real purpose—to provide transportation. But a car can never fulfill its purpose without gasoline. When we don't know our real purpose for being here, we try to look good, seek man-made comforts, make a lot of noise and create our own light.

Then one day, we admit something is missing. The world suggests, "Something is wrong with your car." So we try harder. Our added efforts don't work. Finally we admit we need some help. Well-meaning people come alongside to offer their assistance. One group who believes something is still wrong with our cars strives to fix them for us.

Another group does not want to hurt our feelings by suggesting that our cars are no good. They use the nonthreatening approach. They see that our purpose for living has been misguided, so they attempt to help us get back on track by teaching us how to push our cars.

Still another group rescues cars that have been traveling on the wrong track for a long time. They have a towing service. They pull us out of the muck we are in, then help us wash our cars.

Many people are on the wrong tracks. Their self-imposed purposes for being here have been world-centered or self-centered, but trying to change them won't be enough. Unless their cars are filled with gasoline, they will never fulfill their created purpose.

Suppose a mule starts running in the wrong direction. Problems and difficulties begin to pile up. The mule won't admit he is wrong so he runs harder. He starts to eat the wrong oats and drink contaminated water. His sick running mates show him where to find even worse oats and even more contaminated water. Finally, he falls over in utter defeat and exhaustion. You could grab that old mule by the tail and turn him around in the road, but he would still lie there. You could hose him off until he appeared to be clean, but he would still lie there. Somebody needs to give that mule a blood transfusion and fill him up with good oats so he can have the energy to get up and start walking in the right direction.

Our Purpose on the Earth

Our purpose is to glorify God in our bodies (see 1 Cor. 6:20). The glory of God is a manifestation of His presence. "By this is My Father glorified, that you bear much fruit, and so prove to be My disciples" (John 15:8). We can only do this if we abide in Christ. We cannot do for ourselves what Christ has already done for us. But we can choose to repent for our self-centered ways, choose the right way, start living by faith according to what God says is true and receive the very life of Christ within us. He alone is "the way, and the truth, and the life" (14:6).

In the previous chapter, we looked at (1) what God has done for us, (2) how we must accept His work as truth and (3) how we must live accordingly by faith. What follows in this chapter will not be effective in our lives, unless we first believe what Paul taught in Romans 6:1-11. *Truth* sets us free. Believing the truth is what must precede and determine responsible behavior.

Whose responsibility—ours or God's?

Let's continue with Romans 6:12 to find the answer:

"Therefore do not let sin reign in your mortal body so that you obey its evil desires" (*NIV*). We can fully trust Him to be our life, the only infallible resource who will meet all our needs.

Question: Whose responsibility is it not to allow sin to reign in our mortal bodies? Clearly it is our own personal responsibility. I have never believed, nor taught, nor allowed any person I was working with to have a "devil-made-me-do-it" attitude. We are responsible for our own attitudes and actions. What must we do to prevent sin from reigning in our mortal bodies? Paul provided the answer in verse 13:

"Do not offer the parts of your body to sin, as instruments of wickedness, but rather offer yourselves to God, as those

....

We are not to use our bodies in ways that would serve sin.

....

who have been brought from death to life; and offer the parts of your body to him as instruments of righteousness" (*NIV*).

One Negative Action and Two Positive Ones

Notice we must take only one negative, but two positive actions. Let's look at the negative action first. We are *not* to use our bodies in ways that would serve sin. If we do, we allow sin to reign (rule) in our physical bodies. We are, however, to (1) offer ourselves to God and (2) to offer our bodies to Him. We are told to consciously present ourselves to God, because we belong to Him. Then we are to present our bodies to God. Why does Paul separate "ourselves" from our bodies?

"Ourselves" is who we essentially are. Our culture promotes the belief that our identities are derived from the things we do. We tend to identify one another by our physical bodies. As natural people, this is our *only* means of identification. However, as children of God, we have new identities.

"Therefore from now on we recognize no man according to the flesh" (2 Cor. 5:16). Paul acknowledged that we are "longing to be clothed with our dwelling from heaven" (v. 2). As long as we are still in these tents (meaning our physical bodies), we groan because we do not want to be unclothed.

I don't know about your tent, but my tent pegs are coming up, the seams are getting frayed and the zipper doesn't work very well anymore. My "car" is not as good as it was when it rolled off the assembly line! My hope, however, does not rest in the eternal preservation of my outer man. It is founded in the knowledge that "though our outer man is decaying, yet our inner man is being renewed day by day" (4:16).

Someday we are going to jettison our old earth suits. Then we will be absent from our bodies and present with the Lord (see 5:8). As long as we are on planet Earth, however, we need our physical bodies. Paul said, "The body that is sown is perishable, it is raised imperishable; it is sown in dishonor, it is raised in glory; it is sown in weakness, it is raised in power; it is sown a natural body, it is raised a spiritual body" (1 Cor. 15:42-44, *NIV*). Our inner man will live forever with our heavenly Father, but our bodies won't. "Flesh and blood cannot inherit the kingdom of God" (v. 50, *NIV*).

That which is mortal is also corruptible. Are our physical bodies evil? No, they are amoral or neutral. So what are we to do about the neutral disposition of our bodies? We are told to present them as instruments of righteousness. "Present" means "to put at the disposal of." An instrument can be anything the Lord has entrusted to us. The Lord is commanding us to be good stewards of our bodies and to use them only as instruments of righteousness.

For Sexual Bondage
Let's apply this line of reasoning to sexual bondage and read what Paul said in 1 Corinthians:

> The body is not meant for sexual immorality, but for the Lord, and the Lord for the body. By his power God raised the Lord from the dead, and he will raise us also. Do you not know that your bodies are members of Christ himself? Shall I then take the members of Christ and unite them with a prostitute? Never! Do you not know that he who unites himself with a prostitute is one with her in body? For it is said, "The two shall become one flesh." But he who unites himself with the Lord is one with him in spirit.
>
> Flee from sexual immorality. All other sins a man commits are outside his body, but he who sins sexu-

ally sins against his own body. Do you not know that your body is a temple of the Holy Spirit, who is in you, whom you have received from God? You are not your own; you were bought at a price. Therefore honor God with your body (6:13-20, *NIV*).

This passage teaches that we have more than a spiritual union with God. Our "bodies are members of Christ himself" (v. 15). Romans 8:11 says, "If the Spirit of him who raised Jesus from the dead is living in you, he who raised Christ from the dead will also give life to your mortal bodies through his Spirit, who lives in you" (*NIV*). Our bodies are actually temples of God, because His spirit dwells in us. If we use our bodies for sexual immorality, we defile the temples of God.

The Moral Outrage at Sex Outside of Marriage
It is hard for us to fully appreciate the moral outrage of uniting a member of Christ with a prostitute! It would be tantamount to Antiochus Epiphanes slaughtering a pig on the altar after declaring Mosaic ceremonies illegal, then erecting a statue of Zeus in the holy place of The temple. Can you imagine how God's people must have felt when that happened in the second century before Christ? Many were martyred as they attempted to stop him from defiling the Temple. As a Christian, aren't you offended when people suggest that Jesus was sexually intimate with Mary Magdalene? I am! It offends me when people suggest that Jesus masturbated or was a drunkard.

I believe Jesus was fully God and also fully man. I believe He was sexually a man and was tempted in the same way that we are tempted. But Christ never sinned. His earthly body was not meant for sexual immorality—neither is ours. If our eyes were fully open to the reality of the spiritual world and we completely understood the consequences of sinning against our own bodies, we would "flee from sexual immorality" (v. 18, *NIV*).

Can you think of a way to commit a sexual sin without using your body as an instrument of unrighteousness? A lot of kinky stuff takes place in the world, but I can't think of a single act. If we commit sexual sins, we allow sin to reign in our mortal bodies! Will we still be united with the Lord? Yes, because He will never leave us nor forsake us. We don't lose

....

We don't lose our salvation, but we certainly do lose a degree of freedom.

....

our salvation, but we certainly do lose a degree of freedom.

"For you were called to freedom, brethren; only do not turn your freedom into an opportunity for the flesh, but through love serve one another" (Gal. 5:13). What happens when a child of God (who is united with the Lord and one spirit with Him) also unites with a prostitute and becomes one with her in body? The Bible says they become one flesh. Somehow they are bonded together.

How many times have you heard about a nice Christian girl getting sexually involved with an immoral man, then continuing in a sick relationship with him for two to three years? Her friends try to tell her, "He's no good for you." Mom and Dad abhor the idea of this man becoming a future son-in-law. They beg her to leave. Yet the girl won't listen to them, so they pray she will someday come to her senses. Unfortunately, even when he treats her badly, she won't leave him. Why not? Because they have bonded. They have become one flesh.

Break Sexual Bonding with Complete Repentance
We have learned through much experience, that sexual bonding can be broken with complete repentance. We start the process by instructing people to pray. We ask the Lord to mentally reveal every sexual use of their bodies as instruments of unrighteousness. Some openly share one or two sexual experiences when we first begin to pray with them. But when they sincerely pray that prayer, we hear all of their other sexual experiences, even those they had no intention of sharing. We

don't do this because we want to hear about their sexual escapades. Frankly, I personally don't want to hear, but I will listen for their sakes because I really do want to see them free in Christ.

As the Lord brings every sexual sin into the minds of those who want to repent, we direct them to renounce the use of their bodies with (each name) and ask the Lord to break their bond with each individual. Next we have them commit their bodies to God, reserving the sexual use of their bodies only for their spouses.

Is this process biblical? We are urged "by the mercies of God" to take these steps (Rom. 12:1). Repentance means we turn away from something wrong and turn to something right. It is not enough to acknowledge the lie, we must choose the truth. To renounce or admit that something is wrong amounts to only the first half of repentance. We must announce or choose what is right to make it complete. Paul instructed us not to use our bodies as instruments of unrighteousness, but He didn't end there. He also enjoined us to commit ourselves and our bodies as instruments of righteousness.

Years of helping people find their freedom in Christ have revealed several generalities. First, if people have had "unholy" sex, they do not seem to enjoy "holy" sex. I have counseled many wives who loathe being touched. In difficult cases, they are actually repulsed by the idea until they break the bondage that has come from sex outside of God's will. Incredibly, their feelings toward their spouses change almost immediately.

Sex Before Marriage—Lack of Fulfillment After Marriage
We have also noticed that promiscuity before marriage leads to a lack of fulfillment after marriage. The fun and excitement of sex outside of God's will leaves people in bondage. If sex was performed with the woman's consent, the bondage only increases as the couple attempt to satisfy their lust. If sex was not performed with her consent (I mean she went along with it, but she didn't really want to), she shuts down and remains in bondage to her past until it is resolved. The couple lacks the freedom to enter into a mutual expression of love and trust.

They break this bondage only when they (1) renounce previous sexual uses of their bodies, (2) commit themselves and their bodies to God as living sacrifices and (3) reserve the sexual use of their bodies solely for their spouses. Repentance is then complete, and they are free to responsibly relate to God and others.

In rape and incest cases, the abusers have used the victims' bodies as instruments of unrighteousness. Tragically, these two people have become one flesh. When a sick person defiles a temple against the will of one who is trying to use it to glorify God, I want to scream, "Not fair!" It's not fair! It's sick, but we live in a sick world. This is no different than Antiochus defiling the temple against the will of those who died trying

....

If we are living wrong, the answer is not to stop living, the answer is to start living right.

....

to save it. The good news is that we can be free from such violations. We can renounce these uses of our bodies, "submit therefore to God [and] resist the devil" (Jas. 4:7). Then we can and must forgive those who have abused us.

The Connection Between Sex and Alcohol
Some may consider it strange to lump sexual bondage and alcoholism together. Rarely, however, do we find a liquor store that does not sell pornography. A deep need for acceptance drives many to the counterfeit world of illicit sex and/or alcoholism. In addition, alcohol and drugs dull the conscience impairing sexual judgment. This leads to many regrettable sexual escapades.

Chemical addiction is also a violation of the temple of God. We are instructed, "Do not get drunk with wine, for that is dissipation, but be filled with the Spirit" (Eph. 5:18). The problem with drunkenness is found in what it produces. Dissipation (*asotia*) means debauchery or dissoluteness. The Bible cites the "wild living" of the prodigal son as an example of this (see Luke 15:11-32). He lived wildly, extravagantly squandering his money and indulging his physical appetites. "When he came to his senses" (Luke 15:17), he returned home.

Notice that Paul's alternative to not getting drunk was not abstinence (Eph. 5:18). If we pour the wrong fuel into the gas tank, the answer is not merely to stop pouring. The complete answer is to stop pouring in the wrong fuel that ruins the engine, then start pouring in the right fuel.

If we are living wrong, the answer is not to stop living, the answer is to start living right. The worst treatment for alcohol and drug abuse is perpetuated by those who proudly advertise no counseling. They hospitalize people for short periods of time, then substitute their addictive substances with other drugs that cause them to vomit whenever they drink alcohol. Incredible! They haven't solved anything.

Perspective with the Bigger Picture

To put this into context, we must examine the bigger picture starting with the Old Testament. The sin offering was a blood offering. The blood was drained from the carcass, then the carcass was taken out and disposed of. Only the blood was sacrificed for the sin offering.

Question: Who is our sin offering? The Lord Jesus Christ, of course. "Without shedding of blood there is no forgiveness" (Heb. 9:22). After He shed His blood for us on the cross, His body was taken down and buried. But not for long, praise the Lord.

The Old Testament sacrificial system also required a burnt offering. In Hebrew "burnt" literally means "that which ascends." The burnt offering, unlike the sin offering, was totally consumed on the altar—blood, carcass and all.

Question: Who is the burnt offering? We are!

Paul wrote, "Therefore, I urge you, brothers, in view of God's mercy, to offer your bodies as living sacrifices, holy and pleasing to God—this is your spiritual act of worship" (Rom. 12:1, *NIV*). It is great to know your sins are forgiven—Christ did that for you. But if you want to live victoriously in Christ, then you must present yourself to God and your body as an instrument of righteousness. You need to be filled with the Holy Spirit. He is the right fuel for the engine.

Hezekiah sought God. As a result, a tremendous revival occurred during his reign (see 2 Chron. 29). First, he cleaned out the temple and prepared it for worship by purifying it. What a beautiful picture of repentance. Then he consecrated the priests. Because the New Testament teaches a priesthood of believers, Paul said, "Present yourselves to God" (Rom. 12:1). After that Hezekiah ordered the blood offering. Nothing externally noticeable happened, but their sins were forgiven. Then, "Hezekiah gave the order to sacrifice the burnt offering on the altar. As the offering began, singing to the Lord began also" (2 Chron. 29:27, *NIV*). Did you know that God ordered music to be sung in the temple day and night? Four thousand musicians were set aside for that purpose. When the burnt offering was presented the music began.

Now read Ephesians 5:18: "Do not get drunk on wine, which leads to debauchery. Instead, be filled with the Spirit" (*NIV*). In other words, don't defile the temple of God with wine. That would be debauchery, instead let the Spirit of God rule in your hearts. Guess what happens if God rules in your heart? You will, "Speak to one another with psalms, hymns and spiritual songs. Sing and make music in your heart to the Lord, always giving thanks to God the Father for everything" (vv. 19,20, *NIV*). The music begins in the temple when we yield ourselves to God, and are filled with the Holy Spirit.

I can't imagine Christians not wanting to sing and make melody in their hearts to the Lord; yet many do not seem to have a song in their hearts. If there is a song, it might sound more like a funeral dirge!

Many people sing when they are drunk, but not to the Lord. What would it be like if we used our bodies as instruments of unrighteousness and allowed sin to reign in our mortal bodies? Paul describes it clearly in Romans 7:15-25. Let me extract and modify a section of my book *The Bondage Breaker*, and apply it to those who are caught in the sin-confess-sin-confess and sin again cycle of chemical and sexual addiction:

Dan: Neil, I can't keep going on like this. I get so discouraged. I go out and get drunk, and wake up with a banging headache. I promise myself I will never do it again. Sometimes I am able to go a week and even a couple of weeks—then I fall again. I feel like such a failure. I have tried to hide it from my wife, but I can't even do that anymore. I have confessed it to the Lord a thousand times, but nothing seems to help. He has to be absolutely disgusted with me. There is one more thing that I just have to share with someone, and I can't share it with my wife. I can't even face God with it. I know you are going to think I'm a real scumbag.

Neil: Dan, I don't care what you share with me. It isn't going to make a difference in how I see you. I know you are a child of God, and I love you like a brother.

Dan: It's pornography! I got hooked on it a long time ago. I can't even look at a woman without thinking of sex. The temptation is overwhelming. I can't seem to get victory no matter what I do. I don't want to live like this! It is ruining my marriage.

Neil: Dan, let's look at a passage of Scripture that seems to describe what you are experiencing. Romans 7:15 reads: "For that which I am doing, I do not understand; for I am not practicing what I would like to do, but I am doing the very thing I hate." Would you say this describes your life?

Dan: Exactly! I really do desire to do what God says is right, and I hate being in bondage to alcohol and lust. I don't know which one is worse. I get drunk and wake up in some woman's bedroom. Or I sneak down at night and call one of those sex hotlines. It is as though I step through a door and I can't turn around until I'm drunk or I've mastur-bated, or worse. I don't want to cheat on my wife. I know it's wrong and I feel disgusted with myself afterwards.

Neil: You would probably identify with verse 16 as well: "But if I do the very thing I do not wish to do, I agree with the law, confessing that it is good." Dan, how many personalities are mentioned in this verse?

Dan: There is only one person, and it is clearly "I."

Neil: It is very defeating when we know what we want to do, but for some reason we can't do it. How have you tried to resolve this in your own mind?

Dan: Sometimes I wonder if I'm even a Christian. It seems to work for others, but not for me. I some-times question if the Christian life is even possible or if God is really here.

Neil: You aren't alone, Dan. Many Christians believe that they are different from others, and most think they are the only ones who struggle with these issues. If you and God were the only players in this scenario, it would stand to reason that you would question your salvation or the exis-tence of God. Look at verse 17: "So now, no longer am I the one doing it, but sin which indwells me." Now how many players are there?

Dan: Apparently there are two, but I don't understand.

Neil: Let's read verse 18 to see if we can make some sense out of it: "For I know that nothing good dwells in me, that is, in my flesh; for the wishing is present in me, but the doing of the good is not."

Dan: I learned that verse a long time ago. It has been easy to accept the fact that I am no good. I'm no good for myself and I'm no good for my wife. We would both be better off if I weren't here.

Neil: That's not true, because that is not what the verse says. In fact, it says the opposite. *Whatever it is that is dwelling in you* is not *you*. If I had a wood splinter in my finger, it would be "nothing good" dwelling in me. But the "nothing good" isn't me; it's the splinter. It is also important to note that this "nothing good" is not even my flesh, but it is dwelling in my flesh.[1] If we see only ourselves in this struggle, it will be hopeless to live righteously. These passages are going to great lengths to tell us that there is a second party involved in our struggle whose nature is evil and different from ours.

You see, Dan, when you and I were born, we were born under the *penalty* of sin. And we know that Satan and his emissaries are always working to keep us under that penalty. When God saved us, Satan lost that battle, but he didn't curl up his tail or pull in his fangs. He is now committed to keep us under the power of sin. In 1 John 2:12-14, John wrote to little children because their sins are forgiven. In other words they have overcome the penalty of sin. He wrote to young men because they have overcome the evil one. In other words they have overcome the power of sin.

The passage we are looking at also says that this evil is going to work through the flesh, which remained with us after our salvation. It is our responsibility to crucify the flesh, and it is also our responsibility to resist the devil. Let's continue in the passage to see if we can learn more about how the battle is being waged: "For the good that I wish, I do not do; but I practice the very evil that I do not wish. But if I am doing the very thing I do not wish, I am no longer the one doing it, but sin which dwells in me. I find then the principle that evil is present in me, the one who wishes to do good" (Rom. 7:19-21).

Dan: Sure, it is clearly evil and sin. But isn't it just my own sin? When I sin, I feel guilty.

Neil: There is no question that you and I sin, but we are not "sin" as such. Evil is present in us, but we are not evil per se. This does not excuse us from sinning, because Paul wrote earlier that it is our responsibility not to let sin reign in our mortal bodies (see Rom. 6:12). John said, "If we say that we have no sin, we are deceiving ourselves, and the truth is not in us" (1 John 1:8). We must admit that we have sinned, but "having" sin and "being" sin are two totally different issues. When you came under conviction about your addictions, what did you do?

Dan: I confessed it to God.

Neil: Dan, confession literally means to agree with God. It is the same thing as walking in the light or living in moral agreement with Him about our present condition. We must do this if we are going to live in harmony with our heavenly Father, but confession doesn't go far enough. Confession is the first step to repentance. The man Paul wrote about agreed with God that what he was doing was wrong, but that didn't resolve his problem. You have confessed your sin to God, but you are probably still in bondage. It has to be very frustrating for you. The battle for your mind must be incredible. You probably entertain a lot of condemning thoughts as well as struggling with lustful thoughts. Have you ever felt so defeated that you just want to strike out at someone or yourself?

Dan: Almost every day! And the battle for my

mind is overwhelming. That is probably why I get drunk, to drown out those thoughts. I never seem to have any mental rest.

Neil: But when you have sobered up, do you again entertain thoughts that are in line with who you really are as a child of God?

Dan: Always, and then I feel incredibly convicted. That is what makes it so hard. I know what I am doing is wrong. I hate it. I get this incredible passion for wine and women. I just have to have it. Then when I get my fill of it, I can't stand it. I hate it because of the hold it has on me. Then the next day I love it again. Or I should say, I lust it again.

Neil: Verse 22 of Romans 7 explains why: "For I joyfully concur with the law of God in the inner man." When we act out of character with who we really are, the Holy Spirit immediately brings conviction because of our union with God. Out of frustration and failure we think or say things like, "I'm not going back to church any more. Christianity doesn't work. It was God who made me this way. Now all I do is feel condemned all the time. God promised to provide a way of escape. Well, where is it? I haven't found it!" Then our true nature begins to express itself. "I know what I'm doing is wrong, and I know the Bible says God loves me, but I am so frustrated by my continuing failure."

Dan: Someone told me once, that this passage was talking about a non-Christian.

Neil: I know some good people who take that position, but it doesn't make sense to me. Does a natural man joyfully concur with the law of God in the inner man? Does an unbeliever agree with the law of God and confess that it is good? I don't think so! In fact, they speak out rather strongly against it. Some even hate us Christians for upholding such a moral standard. Now look at verse 23 which describes the nature of this battle with sin: "But I see a different law in the members of my body, waging war against the law of my mind, and making me a prisoner of the law of sin which is in my members." According to this passage, Dan, where is the battle being fought?

Dan: The battle appears to be in the mind.

Neil: That's precisely where the battle rages. Now if Satan can get you to think you are the only one in the battle, you will get down on yourself or God when you sin which is counterproductive to resolving the problem. Let me put it this way. Suppose you opened a door that you were told not to open, and a dog came through the door and wrapped his teeth around your leg. Would you beat on yourself or would you beat on the dog?

Dan: I suppose I would beat on the dog.

Neil: Of course you would. On the other side of the door, a dog is tempting you with thoughts like, *Come on, open the door, everybody else is doing it. You will get away with it. You know you want a drink.* So you open the door, and a dog comes in and grabs hold of your leg. You feel the pain of conviction and the sting of sin. The dog switches from being the tempter to being the accuser. Your mind is pounded with accusations, *You opened the door, you opened the door!* So you cry out, "God forgive me." Guess what God does? He forgives you. But the dog is still there! You have submitted to God, but you haven't resisted the devil.

People put themselves through all kinds of physical abuse to overcome their addictions. Some go overboard on physical exercise, and run for hours a day. Many take the path of self-destruction. I have seen young ladies purge themselves or take laxatives to defecate for the same reason that others cut themselves. They are trying to purge themselves of evil. Paul says, "These are matters which have, to be sure, the appearance of wisdom in self-made religion and self-abasement and severe treatment of the body, but are of no value against fleshly indulgence" (Col. 2:23).

People get tired of beating on themselves, so they walk away from God under a cloud of defeat and condemnation. Paul expressed this feeling in Romans 7:24: "Wretched man that I am! Who will set me free from the body of this death?" He did not say "wicked man that I am," he said "miserable man that I am."

This man is not free. His attempts to do the right thing are met in moral failure. There is nobody more miserable than someone who knows what is right, and wants to do what is right, but can't.

Dan: That's me. Miserable! And I don't see any way out of it. Death seems like my only option. At times I just want to cut off my head to silence the voices.

Neil: Wait a minute, Dan, there is victory. Jesus will set you free. Look at verse 25: "Thanks be to God through Jesus Christ our Lord! So then, on the one hand I myself with my mind am serving the law of God, but on the other, with my flesh the law of sin." Let's return to the dog illustration. Why wasn't just crying out to God enough?

Dan: Well, like you said, the dog was still there. I guess I would have to chase the dog away.

Neil: You would also have to close the door.

Concerning your alcohol and sexual sins, what have you done to resolve it?

Dan: Like I said, I confessed it to God and asked His forgiveness.

Neil: As you have already discovered, that didn't quite resolve it. First, I want you to know that you are already forgiven. Christ died once for all of your sins. He is not going to do it again. You were right in confessing it to God, because you do need to own up to the fact that you opened the door when you knew it was wrong. Second, to ensure that every door is closed, you need to ask the Lord to reveal every unrighteous use of your body. That includes being drunk with wine. As the Lord brings them to your mind, renounce every sexual use of your body that is immoral and the unrighteous use of your body that resulted in drunkenness. Your body belongs to God and it is not to be used unrighteously. Then present your body to God as a living sacrifice and reserve the sexual use of your body for your spouse only. Finally, "resist the devil and he will flee from you" (Jas. 4:7).

Dan: I think I'm getting the picture. But, every sexual use of my body? That would take a long time! Even if it took a couple of hours, I guess it would be a lot easier than living in bondage for the rest of my life. Would I have to renounce every time I got drunk? I've been condemning myself for my inability to live the Christian life. I can also see why I have been questioning my salvation. I see that Paul was frustrated about his failure, but he didn't get down on himself. He accepted his responsibility. More important, he expressed confidence by turning to God because the Lord Jesus Christ would enable him to live above sin.

Neil: You're on the right track. When you honestly ask the Lord to reveal every use of your body as an instrument of unrighteousness, trust Him to bring to your mind what you need to renounce. He is the One who grants repentance. Condemning yourself won't help because "there is therefore now no condemnation for those who are in Christ Jesus" (Rom. 8:1). We don't want to assist the devil in his role as the accuser. Most people who are in bondage question their salvation. I have counseled hundreds who have shared their doubts with me about God and themselves. Ironically, the fact that they are sick about their sin and want to get out of it is one of the strongest assurances of their salvation. Non-Christians don't have convictions.

There is one more important thing you need to know. No one particular sin is isolated from the rest of reality. To get complete freedom, let me encourage you to go through all the "Steps to Freedom" (see appendix A). You also need to understand the battle that is going on for your mind. Satan is a defeated foe, but if he can get you to believe a lie, he can control your life. So let's try to understand this battle that is going on for our minds.[2]

Notes
1. The *New International Version* of the Bible translates *sarxn* (flesh) as the sin or old nature. In any translation the "nothing good" is not the flesh or sin nature, but is operating in the sin nature.
2. Neil T. Anderson, *The Bondage Breaker* (Eugene, Oreg.: Harvest House Publishers, 1990), pp. 48-52.

The Battle for the Mind

*If a man walking after wind and falsehood had
told lies and said, "I will speak out to you concerning wine and liquor," He would be
spokesman to this people.*
—Micah 2:11

*And do not be conformed to this world, but be
transformed by the renewing of your mind, that
you may prove what the will of God is, that
which is good and acceptable and perfect.*
—Romans 12:2

My friend checked himself into a hospital advertising a
Christian chemical dependency unit. He brought his Bible to
the first group meeting he attended and was told by the spiritual advisor, "You won't need that here." He later learned
that the so-called "spiritual" advisor was living a homosexual lifestyle, as were all the other "counselors" in the program!

Micah would observe and write today as he did then, "He would be spokesman to this people."

When we lower God to a higher power to accommodate a person in bondage, we attempt to create God in our image. If we do not commit to absolute truth, false prophets, teachers and deceiving spirits will have a field day with our minds. A pastor attending my "Resolving Personal and Spiritual Conflicts" conference shared with me that many of his church attendees were struggling with alcohol. They had already met with him to organize a ministry for those who wanted to overcome their addictions. They insisted the catch phrase on the front of their brochure say, "Are you tired of listening to those voices?"

The Voices that Battle for Our Minds

What are those voices, and how can we win this battle for our minds? I will try to answer these questions in this chapter. Let's put the rest of the puzzle together.

In previous chapters, I have made strong biblical statements such as:

- The old self (man) is dead, and the new self (man) is alive.
- We've been transferred out of the kingdom of darkness into the kingdom of God's beloved son.
- We are no longer in Adam, we are in Christ.
- We are now children of God.
- We are no longer dead in our trespasses and sins, we are now alive in Christ.

You would probably like to believe these statements because they are taught in the Bible, but have you ever wondered: *If that is true, why don't I feel any different, and why am I still struggling with the same issues I had before I became a Christian?*

Allow me to explain why we have trouble appropriating the right foundation of truth for our lives in Christ. First, we will look at the big picture, then follow it with an illustration.

The Fall (of Adam) caused us all to be born physically alive, but spiritually dead in our trespasses and sins (see Eph. 2:1). At birth we have neither the presence of God in our lives nor the knowledge of God's ways. During our early formative years, we learn how to live our lives independently from God. We have no choice. Then one day we hear the gospel and decide to invite Jesus into our lives. We are born again. We are brand new creations in Christ, but everything previously programmed into our memory banks is still there. Nobody pushed the clear button! Unfortunately, these tremendous computers we call our minds are not equipped with an erase feature. That is why Paul said, "Do not conform any longer to the pattern of this world, but be transformed by the renewing of your mind. Then you will be able to test and approve what God's will is—his good, pleasing and perfect will" (Rom. 12:2, *NIV*).

Physical and Spiritual Change—Born Again

A greater transformation took place when we were born again spiritually than will take place when we physically die. We are now both physically as well as spiritually alive if we are born again.

When we die physically, we will jettison our old earth suits and receive resurrected bodies. Until then we have to do something with our physical bodies, which is what we discussed in the previous chapter. Paul urges us to present our bodies to God as a living sacrifice, and not to use them as instruments of unrighteousness (see v. 1, *NIV*). The next verse says we must reprogram our minds, because they were programmed to live independently from God (see v. 2, *NIV*). The two most critical issues that confront us as believers are to (1) do something about the disposition of our physical bodies and (2) reprogram our minds to the truth of God's Word.

New Captain—Old Man
Now let me illustrate. When I was in the United States Navy, it was customary to refer to the captain of our ship as the "old

man." The first captain I had was a lousy "old man." He belittled his officers, and drank excessively with the senior enlisted men.

I had to learn how to cope and defend myself under his authority to survive on board that ship. One day he was transferred. He was gone forever, and I no longer had any relationship with him. I wasn't under his authority anymore. We got a new "old man," and he was a good one. But how do you think I continued to live on board that ship? I lived the way I was trained under the former "old man" until I got to know the new captain. I slowly began to realize that my old means of coping were no longer necessary. I had to learn a new way to live under the authority of my new captain.

We are no longer under the authority of the god of this world, because our relationship with him has been severed. We are children of God. Our greatest priority is to get to know this new captain of our souls. That is why Paul wrote, "I consider everything a loss compared to the surpassing greatness of knowing Christ Jesus my Lord" (Phil. 3:8, *NIV*).

Every Resource We Need

Like a computer, our brains have recorded every experience we have ever had. These impressions have a lasting impact on our physical bodies. I have seen adults recoil in physical pain as they get in touch with childhood memories of abuse, because strongholds were raised up in their minds against the knowledge of God. These strongholds have affected their temperaments. It takes time to renew their minds, and to replace the lies they have believed with the truth of God's Word.

The Good News (gospel) is that we have every resource we need to break the strongholds. The Lord has sent us the Holy Spirit, who is the "Spirit of truth" (John 14:17), and "He will guide [us] into all the truth" (16:13). Because we are one with God, "We have the mind of Christ" (1 Cor. 2:16, *NIV*). We have superior weapons to win the battle for our minds. Paul said, "For though we live in the world, we do not wage war as the world does. The weapons we fight with are not the weapons of the world. On the contrary, they have divine power to demolish strongholds. We demolish arguments and every pretension that sets itself up against the knowledge of God, and we take captive every thought to make it obedient to Christ" (2 Cor. 10:3-5, *NIV*). Paul is not talking about defensive armor, he is talking about battering ram weaponry that tears down strongholds raised up against the knowledge of God.

How Strongholds Are Erected

How are these strongholds erected in our minds? A basic agreement exists among all developmental theorists that our attitudes are primarily assimilated from the environment we are raised in. The major programming of our minds took place during our early childhoods in two ways.

First, through prevailing experiences such as the families we were raised in, the churches we did or did not attend, the neighborhoods where we grew up, the communities where we lived, the friends that we did or did not have, etc. Every experience had an effect upon the development of our minds and our world views.

The environment, however, is not the only factor that determines how we develop. Two children can be raised in the same home, have the same parents, eat the same food, have the same friends, go to the same church and respond differently. We are not just products of our environments, because every individual can and does interpret the world they live in differently. In addition, God uniquely created each of us in our mother's womb and has known us from the foundations of the world (see Eph. 2:10). Jacob and Essau came from the same womb, but they were totally different people.

In addition to prevailing experiences, the second greatest contributor to the development of strongholds is traumatic experiences. For instance, you may have been raped when you were a child; your mom and dad could have divorced; or somebody could have died. These experiences are not assimilated into our minds over time, rather they are burned into our minds because of their intensity. All of these experiences have been stored in our memory banks. Remember, we do not have a "clear" button in our mental computers.

As we struggle to reprogram our minds, we are also confronted daily with a world system that is not godly. Paul warned us, "Do not conform any longer to the pattern of this world" (Rom. 12:2, *NIV*). Obviously even as Christians, we can continue to allow the world to effect our minds. That is

Temptation begins with a "seed" thought in our minds.

why Paul also warned, "See to it that no one takes you captive through hollow and deceptive philosophy, which depends on human tradition and the basic principles of this world rather than on Christ" (Col. 2:8, *NIV*).

Because we live in this world, we will continually face the reality of temptation. It is not a sin to be tempted. If it were, then the worst sinner who ever lived would be Christ, because He "has been tempted in every way, just as we are—yet was without sin" (Heb. 4:15, *NIV*). And Satan knows exactly which button to push! He knows our weaknesses and our family histories.

What tempts you may not tempt me at all. For instance, when was the last time you were tempted to turn a rock into bread? That temptation was unique to Christ. It was Satan's attempt to get Jesus to use His divine attributes independently from the Father. He faced the temptation by quoting a passage from Deuteronomy. "It is written, 'Man does not live on bread alone, but on every word that comes from the mouth of God'" (Matt. 4:4, *NIV*). Every temptation is an attempt by Satan to get us to live our lives independently from God; to walk according to the flesh rather than according to the Spirit (see Gal. 5:16-23).

Temptation begins with a "seed" thought in our minds. We

can't stop living in this world so we must learn how to stand against constant temptation. Because alcohol is socially acceptable and sex is used to sell everything from beer to cars, we will be constantly bombarded. Many people don't even have to be confronted with the external world. Their memory banks are so crammed with junk that they could fantasize for years without having to leave their homes. That is why sexual strongholds are so difficult to break. Once they are formulated in the mind, the mental impressions are available for instant recall.

Take the Original Thought Captive
God has provided a "way of escape." He requires that we take the original thought captive to the obedience of Christ. If we allow tempting thoughts to ruminate in our minds, we will eventually take a path that leads to destruction.

For instance, suppose a man is struggling with alcohol. One night his wife asks him to go to the store for some milk. When he gets in his car, he briefly wrestles mentally with his selection of stores. He decides upon a local convenience store that is more convenient to sell liquor than anything else. It also has a display of pornography. He did not have to choose that particular store. He could have purchased the milk at a grocery store where the atmosphere would have been much more wholesome and less of a temptation.

The battle for his mind was already lost, however, the moment he started driving to the wrong store. Before he even left the garage, all kinds of rationalizing thoughts crossed his mind. For example, *If you don't want me to buy any booze or look at the pornography, Lord, have my pastor be at the store buying milk or cause a wreck in the intersection, etc.* Because a wreck did not occur and the pastor was not there, he tells himself it must be okay to buy a bottle of booze and take a look at the pornography. The mind has an incredible propensity to rationalize, but the rationalizations are not long lasting. Before this man even leaves the store, guilt and shame overwhelm him. The choice to take the way of escape must be made before he gets into his car. It is a rare person who can turn the car around once the plan has been set in motion. Why?

To Escape Temptations

Scripture refers to the outer man and the inner man (see 2 Cor. 4:16). The outer man is our physical body that relates to the world. Our brains are a part of the outer man. Our minds are a part of the inner man. Our brains and our minds are fundamentally different. Our brains are meat! When we physically die, they will return to dust. We will be absent from the body, but we will not be mindless.

God created the outer man to correlate with the inner man. The correlation between the mind and the brain is obvious. The brain functions much like a digital computer. Every neuron operates like a little switch that turns on and off. Each has many inputs (*dendrites*) and only one output that channels the neurotransmitters to other dendrites. The computer hardware is made up of millions of these. Our minds, on the other hand, represent the software. The brain can be mindlessly programmed by the world, because the brain receives data from the external world through the five senses of the body. The mind, however, is the compiler and chooses to interpret the data by whatever means it has been programmed. Until we come to Christ, it has been programmed by external sources and internal choices made without the knowledge of God and the benefit of His presence.

Change the Software

The tendency of our Western world is to assume that mental problems are primarily caused by faulty hardware. Clearly, organic brain syndrome, Alzheimer's disease, or lesser organic problems such as chemical imbalances can impede our abilities to function. The best program will not work if the computer is turned off or in disrepair. However, our primary problem is not the hardware, it is the software. We can do little to fix the hardware, but we can change the software. Now that we are in Christ, we internally have the mind of Christ.

The brain and the spinal cord make up the central nervous system. It splits off into a peripheral nervous system. The peripheral nervous system has two channels: the autonomic and the somatic nervous systems. The somatic nervous system regulates our muscular and skeletal movements such as speech, gestures, etc. In other words, that which we can volitionally control. It obviously correlates with our wills.

Our autonomic nervous system regulates our glands. We have no volitional control over our glands. We don't say to our hearts, "beat, beat, beat"; nor to our adrenal glands, "adren, adren, adren"; nor to our thyroids, "thy, thy, thy." They function "automatically."

Different Ways to Handle Stress

Let's apply this to the problem of stress. When external pressures put demands on our physical systems, our adrenal glands respond by secreting cortisone-like hormones into our physical bodies. Our bodies automatically respond to external pressures. If the pressures persist for too long, our adrenal glands cannot keep up, so stress becomes distress. The result can be physical illness, or we may become irritated with things that were not previously irritating to us.

Why can two people respond differently to the same stressful situation? Some actually seize the opportunity and thrive under the pressure while others fall apart. What is the difference between the two? Does one have superior adrenal glands? I don't think so. Although we differ considerably in our hardware, the major difference exists in the software. The degree of stress we experience is determined by more than external factors. We all face the pressures of deadlines, schedules, trauma and temptations. The major difference is in how we mentally interpret the external world and process the data our brains receive.

The mind can either choose to respond by trusting God with the assurance of victory, or choose to see itself as the helpless victim of circumstances. The Israelites saw Goliath in reference to themselves and stressed out. David saw the same giant in reference to God and triumphed. The same situation that left others in defeat brought victory to David. Faith in God greatly affects how we interpret and respond to the pressures of this world. "We know that in all things God works for the good of those who love him, who have been called according to his purpose" (Rom. 8:28, *NIV*).

We Control What We Think

Sex glands are part of the autonomic nervous system. For example, a woman has no volitional control over her menstrual cycle. A man can wake up in the middle of the night with an erection, and it may have nothing to do with lust. It is just part of a rhythmic cycle all men go through about every 90 minutes. That is the way God created us. If we have no control over our sex glands, then how can God expect us to have any sexual self-control?

The good news is we don't need to have any volitional control over our sex glands to have self-control. We have control over what we think. Our sex glands are not the cause of sexual immorality. They will "naturally" function in their God-given way to ensure our sexuality. However, if we load our brains with pornography, we will drive our autonomic nervous systems beyond the stops. We may not have any control over what comes out, but we do have control over what we put in. Just like a computer, garbage in—garbage out!

We also have control over the movies we see and the magazines we read. But we can't totally isolate ourselves from the filth in this world. Christian men often have to work in atmospheres saturated with pin-ups and other sexually explicit material. Businessmen who are on the wagon still need to attend luncheon appointments where alcohol is served. What we see in the world comes through the eye gate. We can stop it by closing our eyes, but even then our imaginations can run wild. If we look at objects of temptation, the signals will be recorded in our brains. At that moment, we have a choice. If we choose to let our minds dwell on these unwholesome images, we can expect an almost instantaneous physiological response, because the peripheral nervous system is fed by the central nervous system.

Have you ever wondered why it is so difficult to remember some things and forget others? I have. I would study Greek all night when I was in seminary, then pray that the register didn't clear before I took the exam. But if I saw one pornographic image, it seemed to stay in my mind for years. Why? When we are visually stimulated, a signal is sent to our adrenal glands. A hormone called *epinephrine* is secreted into the bloodstream when we become emotionally excited. Epinephrine goes to the brain and locks in the visual or audio stimulus present at the time of the emotional excitement. It causes us to involuntarily remember traumatic as well as emotionally positive events. Too bad I couldn't get that emotionally excited about Greek!

We can become emotionally excited and sexually stimulated by simply entertaining thoughts of sexual activity. That is why men and women will have an emotional rush before any sexual contact ever takes place. The man going to the store where pornography is sold will be sexually stimulated long before he sees the magazines. It began in his thoughts that triggered his nervous system that responded by secreting epinephrine into the bloodstream.

Alcoholics have the same problem. They can have an adrenaline rush before they take their first drink. If they let their minds go down that path, alcoholics will have all kinds of physiological and emotional responses within minutes or seconds. Just thinking about it can cause their mouths to water and their palms to sweat. Because of the "involuntary" body reactions, some prefer to think of alcoholism as a disease. But they are not involuntary. Their bodies are just responding to the program installed in the central computer.

Our autonomic nervous systems obviously correlate to the

emotional parts of our inner man. Just as we can't control our glands, we can't control our emotions. If you think you can, give it a try! Try liking someone right now that you previously couldn't stand. We can't order our emotions to feel—no instruction in Scripture suggests that we do that. We must, however, acknowledge our emotions, because we can't be right with God and not be real. What we do have control over is what we think, so Scripture tells us to take responsibility for our thoughts. "Brothers, stop thinking like children. In regard to evil be infants, but in your thinking be adults" (1 Cor. 14:20, *NIV*).

Adults Only

That is why I am so disgusted with the public concept of "adults only"! It implies that the standard of morality for adults is different from the standard of morality for children. If it is wrong for children to drink alcohol, why is it right for adults? At what age does it become right? Adults should have a greater degree of self-control, but how do they develop it? The fruit of the Spirit is self-control (see Gal. 5:23). How much mastery over themselves have adults manifested without Christ? Mature adults should know when to say enough and refuse to allow their minds to be programmed with filth. The law requires television programmers to say, "The content of the following movie is suitable for 'mature' audiences only. Viewer discretion is advised!" It isn't suitable for anyone, and mature people should be the first to know that. We have already been advised by God, "Don't watch!" Once we have programmed it into our minds, it will always be there.

We have no control over how we feel, therefore, I encourage you to eliminate the following line from your vocabulary in reference to yourself and others: "You shouldn't feel that way." It is a subtle form of rejection, and no addict needs any more of that. What can people do about how they feel? Nothing! The real issue is what we think, or how we perceive ourselves and the events around us. Perhaps we haven't fully understood the whole situation, maybe we have wrongly judged someone or maybe we just need to trust God.

Our feelings are primarily products of our thought lives. Our tendency is to believe something or somebody made us feel a certain way, but that isn't true. All external data is processed through our minds, and we have control over them. It logically follows that our feelings can be distorted by what we choose to think or believe. If what we choose to believe does not reflect truth, then what we feel will not reflect reality. If what we see or mentally visualize is morally wrong, then our emotions will be violated.

Mixed Messages and Mixed Emotions

This world is fraught with all kinds of mixed messages. Consequently, mixed emotions also abound. There are Christians who don't feel saved, don't feel like God loves them and don't feel they are worth anything. The message they have received is not true, but they believe it anyway. Scripture teaches that not all messages we receive are necessarily from the visible world. Paul wrote, "The Spirit clearly says that in later times some will abandon the faith and follow deceiving spirits and things taught by demons" (1 Tim. 4:1, *NIV*).

I have counseled hundreds of people who said they were "hearing voices." Every one of these cases have revealed a spiritual battle for their minds. No wonder Paul exhorts us, "Finally, brothers, whatever is true, whatever is noble, whatever is right, whatever is pure, whatever is lovely, whatever is admirable—if anything is excellent or praiseworthy—think about such things" (Phil. 4:8, *NIV*).

If Satan can get us to believe a lie, he can destroy us emotionally and control our lives. His primary intention is to distort the perception we have of ourselves and God. I often have seminary students who correctly answer all the theological questions about God. They intellectually know God is omnipresent, omnipotent, omniscient, kind and loving in all His ways. But when I ask them how they feel towards God, many will respond, "I'm not sure He loves me!" Their feelings have lied to them because thoughts have been raised up against the knowledge of God. Satan can't do anything about our position in Christ. Therefore, if he can get us to believe it isn't true, we will live as though it's not true, even though it is.

Our problems don't just stem from what we have believed

in the past. Paul said we are to presently and continually take every *"thought* captive to the obedience of Christ" (2 Cor. 10:5, emphasis mine). The word "thought" is the Greek word *noema*. Notice how Paul used this word in the

....

I believe the greatest access Satan has to the Church is our unwillingness to forgive those who have offended us.

....

same epistle. "I have forgiven in the sight of Christ for your sake, in order that Satan might not outwit us. For we are not unaware of his schemes [noema]" (2:10,11, *NIV*). I believe the greatest access Satan has to the Church is our unwillingness to forgive those who have offended us. It certainly has been true with the thousands we have worked with at Freedom in Christ.

The Battle for Our Minds
Look at another passage. "The god of this age has blinded the minds [noema] of unbelievers, so that they cannot see the light of the gospel of the glory of Christ" (4:4, *NIV*). Think of the implications this has for world evangelization. Look at one more. "I am afraid that just as Eve was deceived by the serpent's cunning, your minds (noema) may somehow be led astray from your sincere and pure devotion to Christ" (11:3, *NIV*). I'm concerned too.

Attend almost any AA meeting, and they will tell you not to pay attention to that "committee" in your head. What do you think that committee is? "Stinking thinking" is the norm for those struggling with alcohol. Solomon said in reference to those who drink too much, "Your eyes will see strange things, and your mind will utter perverse things" (Prov. 23:33).

If there is a spiritual battle going on for our minds, why don't we know this? For one reason, I can't read your mind, and you can't read my mind. We don't have any idea what is going on in the minds of other people unless they have the courage to share with us. In many cases they won't, because our society wrongly assumes they are mentally ill when they do. They will tell us about their abuses or past experiences, but they will only risk sharing what is going on inside with the right person. Are these people mentally ill or is there a battle going on for their minds?

The lack of any balanced biblical contribution to mental health professionals has left them with only one conclusion: Any problem in the mind must either be psychological or neurological. That is another reason some refer to this bondage as the "disease" of alcoholism.

Strange Voices and Sights

A common medical explanation for those who hear voices, have panic attacks, suffer from severe depression or see things in their rooms is, "You have a chemical imbalance." Usually a prescription for medication is given with the hope of curing the problems or eliminating the symptoms. Others take their own forms of medication, such as alcohol or drugs.

I believe our body chemistries can get out of balance and cause discomfort, and that hormonal problems can throw our systems off. But I also believe other legitimate questions need to be asked, such as, "How can a chemical produce a personal thought?" and "How can our neurotransmitters involuntarily and randomly fire creating thoughts we are opposed to thinking?" Is there a natural explanation for this? I am willing to hear any legitimate explanations, because I sincerely care for people. I want to see their problems resolved by the grace of God, but I don't think that will happen unless we consider the reality of the spiritual world.

When people say they are hearing voices, what are they actually hearing? The only way we can physically hear with our ears is to have a sound source that compresses air molecules. Sound waves move through the physical medium of air and strike our ear drums sending a signal to our brains. That is how we physically hear. But the "voices" people hear, or the "thoughts" they struggle with do not come from that kind of source.

Similarly, when people say they see things (that others don't), what are they actually seeing? The only way we can naturally see something is to have a light source that reflects from a material object back to our eyes sending a signal to our brain.

Satan and his demons are spiritual beings. They do not have material substance, so we cannot see spiritual beings with our natural eyes, nor can we hear them with our ears. "For our struggle is not against flesh and blood, but against the rulers, against the authorities, against the powers of this dark world and against the spiritual forces of evil in the heavenly realms" (Eph. 6:12, *NIV*). Losing control of our minds is a major problem with the effects of alcohol and drugs. This loss of control allows our minds to access any file in the computer. If people have watched a lot of horror movies and looked at a lot of pornography, we can pretty well predict where their minds will go when drugs and alcohol have had their maximum effect. Hallucinations cause the spiritual battle to intensify.

Creating a Stronghold or Habit

Satan knows how to tempt us. We consciously make a choice when we surrender to temptation. When we continue to act upon our wrong choices, we establish a habit within approximately six weeks. If the habit persists, a stronghold develops in our minds. Strongholds are mental habit patterns of thought that have been burned into our minds over time, or by deep traumatic experiences. My friend Ed Silvoso says, "A stronghold is a mind-set, impregnated with hopelessness, that causes one to accept as unchangeable, something known to be contrary to the will of God." Let's examine some common strongholds.

Inferiority is a major stronghold most Christians struggle with to some degree. They did not develop an inferiority complex overnight, it was burned in over time. They were probably raised on a performance basis. No matter how hard they tried, their efforts were never good enough. They continue to search for that elusive acceptance that never comes because they can never measure up. If they were raised in a legalistic church, the problem is compounded. They experience God as a consuming fire, just waiting for them to do one thing wrong, so He can come down and bop them. They can't understand love or acceptance of God. The grace of God is foreign to these driven people.

Stronghold of an Alcoholic Home

Look at the strongholds that come from living in an alcoholic home. Three boys were raised by a father who slowly became an alcoholic after years of drinking. The older boy was strong enough to stand up to Dad. No way was he going to take anything from this drunk. The middle boy didn't think he could stand up to Dad so he accommodated him. The youngest boy was terrorized. When Dad came home, he headed for the closet, or hid under the bed.

Twenty years later, the father is gone. These three boys are now adults. When they are confronted with a hostile situation, how do you think each of them will respond? The older one will fight, the middle one will accommodate and the younger one will run and hide. These are mental strongholds—mental habit patterns of thought that have developed over time.

Stronghold of Homosexuality

Homosexuality is a major stronghold, probably one of the most resistant to normal treatment. Those who are caught in the web of this stronghold were not born that way. Homosexuality is a lie, and another false identity we have used to label others. There is no such thing as a homosexual from birth. God created us male and female. Homosexuality is a behavior, and the Lord condemns it. Condemnation upon those who struggle with this behavior, however, will prove counterproductive. They don't need any more condemnation. They already suffer from an incredible identity crisis. Overbearing authoritarianism is what initially drives many to this lifestyle.

Most of those who struggle with homosexual tendencies or

behaviors have had poor developmental upbringing. Various factors contribute to the mental and emotional development of homosexuality: sexual abuse, dysfunctional families where the roles of mom and dad are often reversed, exposure to homosexual literature before they have had an opportunity to fully develop their own sexual identities, playground teasing and poor relationships with the opposite sex. Mixed messages lead to mixed emotions.

Suppose a decent young boy with a nice family has a tempting thought towards another boy. It is just a tempting

....
Mixed messages lead to mixed emotions.
....

thought, and he will probably dismiss it the first time. But what if this thought continues and he doesn't have any knowledge about the battle going on for his mind, nor any understanding about the necessity to take every thought captive to the obedience of Christ? He wonders, *If I am thinking like this I must be one of them.* If he continues to entertain those thoughts, his emotions will be affected. That is how God made us. Now he is attracted to the same sex, which is not what God intended. Then one day he acts upon those impulses and enters into a sexual relationship using his body as an instrument of unrighteousness. Sin is now reigning in his mortal body. He is in bondage.

Casting Out Demons
Please don't try to cast out a demon of homosexuality. I don't believe there is a demon of homosexuality or a demon of lust or a demon of alcoholism. That kind of simplistic thinking has damaged the credibility of the Church and left the addict without an adequate answer.

I have seen Christianity mocked on prime time television by a parade of "homosexuals" and "lesbians" who have left the Church because well-meaning Christians have tried to cast demons of this or that out of them. Don't get me wrong. Unquestionably Satan is part of the problem, and his demons will tempt, accuse and deceive. They will take advantage of any ground given to them.

The simplistic solution of just casting a demon out of someone doesn't take into consideration all the other factors, and I personally don't think this method of resolving spiritual conflicts is best. People have addictive problems because of the responses they have chosen in their early developmental training and the pressures of life. They have turned to alcohol and drugs as a means of coping. They have all made choices for which they must assume personal responsibility. In the process, they have listened to a pack of lies. They have either not known how to or chosen not to resolve their personal and spiritual conflicts leading to their freedom in Christ.

Our Protection from Satan
Paul admonishes us to put on the armor of God (see Eph. 6:10-18). The belt of truth defends us against the father of lies. The breastplate of righteousness is our protection against the accuser of the brethren. Then Paul summarized by saying, "In addition to all, taking up the shield of faith with which you will be able to extinguish all the flaming missiles of the evil one" (Eph. 6:16). The "flaming missiles" are just the tempting, accusing and deceptive thoughts everybody has to deal with daily. Healthy Christians don't pay attention to them. They know the truth and choose to believe it. What happens when we don't take every thought captive to the obedience of Christ? If we entertain such thoughts, we will develop strongholds in our minds and emotional attachments that will be difficult to break.

Choose to Think the Truth
Don't assume all disturbing thoughts are from Satan. Where the thoughts came from—the television set, our memory banks, the pit or our own creative reservoirs—doesn't matter

as much as understanding that the answer is always the same. Choose to think the truth. We can analyze the origin of every thought, but that won't resolve it. We will only get caught up in our own subjective mazes. Too much of the recovery movement is locked in the paralysis of analysis. People can give

....

The battle is in the mind; therefore, it is truth that sets the captives free.

....

brilliant analyses of why they chose to drink, but that won't solve their drinking problems. We can find a million ways to go wrong, but the path back to God is not that complex.

Each Person—Responsible
People must assume personal responsibility for their actions to find their freedom in Christ. We can't forgive for them or renounce for them or think for them. Every individual must become responsible "to submit therefore to God [and] resist the devil" (Jas. 4:7). The role of the pastor or counselor is defined by Timothy: "The Lord's servant must not quarrel; instead, he must be kind to everyone, able to teach, not resentful. Those who oppose him he must gently instruct, in the hope that God will grant them repentance leading them to a knowledge of the truth, and that they will come to their senses and escape from the trap of the devil, who has taken them captive to do his will" (2 Tim. 2:24-26, *NIV*). This is not a power model; it is a kind, patient and able to teach model. It clearly shows that the Lord is the one who grants repentance and sets people free. It also reveals that the battle is in the mind; therefore, it is truth that sets the captives free.

In my book *Helping Others Find Freedom In Christ* (Regal Books), I show how this is done. People throughout the world are using the "Steps to Freedom" to help others resolve their personal and spiritual conflicts. Please understand that the "Steps to Freedom" don't set us free. Christ sets us free. We are set free by our responses to Him in repentance and faith.

A missionary I had the privilege of helping to find her freedom in Christ wrote, "I'm firmly convinced of the significant benefits of finding our freedom in Christ. I was making some progress in therapy, but there is *no comparison* with the steps I am able to make now. My ability to "process" things has increased manyfold. Not only is my spirit more serene, but my head is actually clearer! It's easier to make connections now. It seems like everything is easier to understand now."

When people don't know how to responsibly deal with their pain or resolve their conflicts, they choose other ways. Eventually they will dig some pretty deep grooves in their minds. Some call these strongholds "flesh patterns." After a habit is established, they will "automatically" choose those flesh patterns.

Flesh patterns or strongholds can be likened to a truck that has driven on the same road for so long it has developed some deep ruts. The driver doesn't even have to steer anymore. The truck will just stay in those ruts. After awhile, any attempt to steer out of the ruts will cause the wheel to jerk in the hands of the driver. Some finally conclude it is easier to stay in the ruts and continue on down the same old path. Others break free from the ruts and commit themselves to getting on the right road to recovery. We have prepared an "Overcomers Covenant in Christ" to help you stay on the right road. You will find it in appendix B. The "Steps to Freedom in Christ" can be found in appendix A. Instructions for establishing a "Freedom Ministry" in your church are provided in appendix C.

Break the Strongholds
Can we break the strongholds? Yes we can. If we have been incorrectly trained, can we be retrained? If our minds have been incorrectly programmed, can they be reprogrammed? If we have incorrectly learned something, can we re-learn it? If we have believed a lie, can we now choose to believe the truth? Of course we can.

Will it take time? Absolutely. It will take the rest of our lives to renew our minds and develop our characters. We will never be perfect in our understanding, nor will our characters be as completely perfect as Christ's. We must, however, continue to look to Him as we pursue the reflection of His perfection in our lives. This cannot fully take place unless we are free in Christ. People who are not free in Christ go from book to book, program to program, pastor to pastor and counselor to counselor without success. How can they grow if they are chained to their pasts?

We do not just battle the world—the system in which we were raised. And we do not just battle the flesh—those pre-programmed habit patterns of thought that have been burned into our minds over time or by the intensity of traumatic experiences. We battle the world, the flesh and the devil. We cannot have a complete answer if the third element of the equation is missing.

The world system remained after the Cross. Television, for example, will never be totally cleaned up. Some of you will have to work where pornography is displayed, all the employees drink and people use the Lord's name in vain. As Paul identified himself more with Christ and less with the world, he was able to say, "May I never boast except in the cross of our Lord Jesus Christ, through which the world has been crucified to me, and I to the world" (Gal. 6:14, *NIV*).

The flesh also remains with the Christian after salvation, but as we bond to Christ we must crucify the flesh. "Those who belong to Christ Jesus have crucified the sinful nature [flesh] with its passions and desires. Since we live by the Spirit, let us keep in step with the Spirit" (5:24,25, *NIV*). We can "resist the devil and He will flee" from [us] (Jas. 4:7). Spiritual conflicts are the easiest to resolve, but the least understood.

"It is for freedom that Christ has set us free. Stand firm, then, and do not let yourselves be burdened again by a yoke of slavery. You, my brothers, were called to be free. But do not use your freedom to indulge the sinful nature [flesh]" (Gal. 5:1,13, *NIV*). Obviously the freedom Christ purchased for us on the cross can be lost to the bondages of legalism and license. These strongholds can be broken when we find our freedom in Christ. As we discussed in the last chapter, it requires complete repentance.

Clean Up Your Mind

As a young Christian, I decided to clean up my mind. Do you think the battle became easier or more difficult after I made that decision? Of course it became more difficult. Temptation is not much of a battle if we easily surrender to it. It is fierce when we decide to stand against it. Even though I had gone to church all my life, I did not become a Christian until I was in my 20s. Fortunately, I had a very clean upbringing; but after four years in the Navy, my mind had been exposed to a lot of junk. I did not drink for the first two years, but eventually I began to join my friends. I didn't drink long enough or often enough to establish a major habit, but I had seen enough pornography to develop a problem. Images would dance in my mind for months and years after one look. I hated it. I struggled every time I went anywhere pornography was available. Let me share how I found victory.

Think of your mind as a coffee pot. You desire the water inside to be pure, but unfortunately, you have put in some coffee grounds. There is no way to filter out the grounds. So the water inside is dark and polluted. Sitting beside the coffee pot is a huge bowl of crystal clear ice representing the Word of God. Because you are only able to place one or two cubes a day in the polluted water, it may seem a little futile at first. But over time the water begins to look clearer, and you can barely taste or smell the presence of coffee. The process works provided you stop putting in more coffee grounds.

For most people winning the battle for their minds will initially be a two-steps-forward and one-step-backward process. Slowly it becomes three steps forward and one step backward; then four and five steps forward, as we learn to take every thought captive in obedience to Christ. We may despair with all the backward steps, but God is not going to give up on us. Remember, our sins are already forgiven. We need only fight for our own personal victories over sin. The war is winnable, because we are alive in Christ and dead to sin.

The bigger battle has already been won by Christ. Freedom

to be all God has called us to be is the greatest blessing we can have in this present life. This freedom is worth fighting for. As we learn more about who we are as children of God and the nature of the battle going on for our minds, the process gets easier. Eventually it will become 20 steps forward and 1 step backward, until finally the steps are all forward with only an occasional slip in the battle for the mind.

Fill Our Minds with God's Word

Paul wrote, "Let the peace of Christ rule in your hearts, since as members of one body you were called to peace. And be thankful" (Col. 3:15, *NIV*). He explained how we can do that in the next verse. "Let the word of Christ dwell in you richly" (v. 16, *NIV*). We have to fill our minds with the crystal clear Word of God. God has no alternative plan. Merely trying to stop thinking bad thoughts won't work. Should we rebuke all those tempting, accusing and deceiving thoughts? No. If attempted to win the war for our minds that way, we would be doing nothing but rebuking thoughts every waking moment for the rest of our lives.

It would be like telling a man in the middle of a lake to keep 12 corks submerged with a small hammer in his hand. His entire life would be nothing more than treading water and bopping down corks. What should he do? He should ignore the stupid corks and swim to shore. We are not called to dispel the darkness, we are called to turn on the light. We overcome the father of lies by choosing the truth!

The psalmist said it well. "How can a young man keep his way pure? By living according to your word. I seek you with all my heart; do not let me stray from your commands. I have hidden your word in my heart that I might not sin against you" (Ps. 119:9-11, *NIV*). There is a peace of God, which surpasses all comprehension, that will guard your hearts and your minds in Christ Jesus (see Phil. 4:7). "For the law of the Spirit of life in Christ Jesus has set you free from the law of sin and of death" (Rom. 8:2). Jesus Christ is the bondage breaker, and through Him we can have victory over addiction.

Appendix A

....

Steps to Freedom in Christ

It is my deep conviction that the finished work of Jesus Christ and the presence of God in our lives are the only means by which we can resolve our personal and spiritual conflicts. Christ in us is our only hope (see Col. 1:27), and He alone can meet our deepest needs of life, acceptance, identity, security and significance. The discipleship counseling process upon which these steps are based should not be understood as just another counseling technique that we learn. It is an encounter with God. He is the Wonderful Counselor. He is the One who grants repentance that leads to a knowledge of the truth which sets us free (see 2 Tim. 2:24-26).

The "Steps to Freedom in Christ" do not set you free. *Who* sets you free is Christ, and *what* sets you free is your response to Him in repentance and faith. These steps are just a tool to help you submit to God and resist the devil (see Jas. 4:7). Then you can start living a fruitful life by abiding in Christ and becoming the person He created you to be. Many Christians will be able to work through these steps on their own and discover the wonderful freedom that Christ purchased for them on the cross. Then they will experience the peace of God which surpasses all comprehension, and it shall guard their hearts and their minds (see Phil. 4:7).

Before You Begin
The chances of that happening and the possibility of **maintaining that freedom will be greatly enhanced if you read** *Victory Over the Darkness* **and** *The Bondage Breaker* **first.** Many Christians in our western world need to understand the reality of the spiritual world and our relationship to it. Some can't read these books or even the Bible with comprehension

because of the battle that is going on for their minds. They will need the assistance of others who have been trained. The theology and practical process of discipleship counseling is given in my book, *Helping Others Find Freedom in Christ*, and the Study Guide that accompanies it. The book attempts to biblically integrate the reality of the spiritual and the natural world so we can have a whole answer for a whole person. In doing so, we cannot polarize into psychotherapeutic ministries that ignore the reality of the spiritual world or attempt some kind of deliverance ministry that ignores developmental issues and human responsibility.

You May Need Help

Ideally, it would be best if everyone had a trusted friend, pastor or counselor who would help them go through this process because it is just applying the wisdom of James 5:16: "Therefore, confess your sins to one another, and pray for one another, so that you may be healed. The effective prayer of a righteous man can accomplish much." Another person can prayerfully support you by providing objective counsel. I have had the privilege to help many Christian leaders who could not process this on their own. Many Christian groups all over the world are using this approach in many languages with incredible results because the Lord desires for all to come to repentance (see 2 Pet. 3:9), and to know the truth that sets us free in Christ (see John 8:32).

Appropriating and Maintaining Freedom

Christ has set us free through His victory over sin and death on the cross. However, appropriating our freedom in Christ through repentance and faith and maintaining our life of freedom in Christ are two different issues. It was for freedom that Christ set us free, but we have been warned not to return to a yoke of slavery which is legalism in this context (see Gal. 5:1) or to turn our freedom into an opportunity for the flesh (see Gal. 5:13). Establishing people as free in Christ makes it possible for them to walk by faith according to what God says is true and live by the power of the Holy Spirit and not carry out the desires of the flesh (see Gal. 5:16). The true

Christian life avoids both legalism and license.

If you are not experiencing freedom, it may be because you have not stood firm in the faith or actively taken your place in Christ. It is every Christian's responsibility to do whatever is necessary to maintain a right relationship with God and mankind. Your eternal destiny is not at stake. God will never leave you nor forsake you (see Heb. 13:5), but your daily victory is at stake if you fail to claim and maintain your position in Christ.

Your Position in Christ
You are not a helpless victim caught between two nearly equal but opposite heavenly super-powers. Satan is a deceiver. Only God is omnipotent, omnipresent and omniscient. Sometimes the reality of sin and the presence of evil may seem more real than the presence of God, but that's part of Satan's deception. Satan is a defeated foe and we are **in Christ.** A true knowledge of God and knowing our identity and position in Christ are the greatest determinants of our "mental health." A false concept of God, a distorted understanding of who we are as children of God and the misplaced deification of Satan are the greatest contributors to "mental illness."

Many of our illnesses are psychosomatic. When these issues are resolved in Christ our physical bodies will function better, and we will experience greater health. Other problems are clearly physical, and we need the services of the medical profession. Please consult your physician for medical advice and the prescribing of medication. We are both spiritual and physical beings who need the services of both the church and the hospital.

Winning the Battle for Your Mind
The battle is for the mind, which is the control center of all that we think and do. The opposing thoughts you may experience as you go through these steps can control you only if you believe them. **If you are working through these steps alone, don't be deceived by any lying, intimidating thoughts in your mind. If a trusted pastor or counselor is**

helping you find your freedom in Christ, he or she must have your cooperation. You must share any thoughts you are having in opposition to what you are attempting to do. As soon as you expose the lie, the power of Satan is broken. The only way that you can lose control in this process is if you pay attention to a deceiving spirit and believe a lie.

You Must Choose
The following procedure is a means of resolving personal and spiritual conflicts which have kept you from experiencing the freedom and victory Christ purchased for you on the cross. Your freedom will be the result of what you choose to believe, confess, forgive, renounce and forsake. No one can do that for you. The battle for your mind can only be won as you personally choose truth. As you go through this process, understand that Satan is under no obligation to obey your thoughts. Only God has complete knowledge of your mind because He is omniscient (all-knowing). So we can submit to God inwardly, but we need to resist the devil by reading aloud each prayer and by verbally renouncing, forgiving, confessing, etc.

This process of reestablishing our freedom in Christ is nothing more than a fierce moral inventory and a rock-solid commitment to truth. It is the first step in the continuing process of discipleship. There is no such thing as instant maturity. It will take you the rest of your life to renew your mind and conform to the image of God. If your problems stem from a source other than those covered in these steps, you may need to seek professional help.

May the Lord grace you with His presence as you seek His face and help others experience the joy of their salvation.

Neil T. Anderson

Prayer

Dear Heavenly Father,

We acknowledge Your presence in this room and in our lives. You are the only omniscient (all-knowing), omnipotent (all-powerful) and omnipresent (always present) God. We are dependent upon You, for apart from You we can do nothing. We stand in the truth that all authority in heaven and on earth has been given to the resurrected Christ, and because we are in Christ, we share that authority in order to make disciples and set captives free. We ask You to fill us with Your Holy Spirit and lead us into all truth. We pray for Your complete protection and ask for Your guidance. In Jesus' name. Amen.

Declaration

In the name and authority of the Lord Jesus Christ, we command Satan and all evil spirits to release (name) in order that (name) can be free to know and choose to do the will of God. As children of God seated with Christ in the heavenlies, we agree that every enemy of the Lord Jesus Christ be bound to silence. We say to Satan and all your evil workers that you cannot inflict any pain or in any way prevent God's will from being accomplished in (name's) life.

Preparation

Before going through the *Steps to Freedom,* review the events of your life to discern specific areas that might need to be addressed.

Family History

_____ Religious history of parents and grandparents

_____ Home life from childhood through high school

_____ History of physical or emotional illness in the family
_____ Adoption, foster care, guardians

Personal History
_____ Eating habits (bulimia, bingeing and purging, anorexia, compulsive eating)
_____ Addictions (drugs, alcohol)
_____ Prescription medications (what for?)
_____ Sleeping patterns and nightmares
_____ Rape or any sexual, physical, emotional abuse
_____ Thought life (obsessive, blasphemous, condemning, distracting thoughts, poor concentration, fantasy)
_____ Mental interference in church, prayer or Bible study
_____ Emotional life (anger, anxiety, depression, bitterness, fears)
_____ Spiritual journey (salvation: when, how and assurance)

Now you are ready to begin. The following are seven specific steps to process in order to experience freedom from your past. You will address the areas where Satan most commonly takes advantage of us and where strongholds have been built. Christ purchased your victory when He shed His blood for you on the cross. Realizing your freedom will be the result of what you choose to believe, confess, forgive, renounce and forsake. No one can do that for you. The battle for your mind can only be won as you personally choose truth.

As you go through these *Steps to Freedom*, remember that Satan will only be defeated if you confront him verbally. He cannot read your mind and is under no obligation to obey your thoughts. Only God has complete knowledge of your mind. As you process each step, it is important that you submit to God inwardly and resist the devil by reading aloud each prayer—verbally renouncing, forgiving, confessing, etc.

You are taking a fierce moral inventory and making a rock-solid commitment to truth. If your problems stem from a source other than those covered in these steps, you have nothing to lose by going through them. If you are sincere, the only thing that can happen is that you will get very right with God!

Step 1

....

Counterfeit vs. Real

The first step to freedom in Christ is to renounce your previous or current involvement with satanically-inspired occult practices and false religions. You need to renounce any activity and group which denies Jesus Christ, offers guidance through any source other than the absolute authority of the written Word of God or requires secret initiations, ceremonies or covenants.

In order to help you assess your spiritual experiences, begin this step by asking God to reveal false guidance and counterfeit religious experiences.

> **Dear Heavenly Father,**
> **I ask You to guard my heart and my mind and reveal to me any and all involvement I have had either knowingly or unknowingly with cultic or occult practices, false religions or false teachers. In Jesus' name, I pray. Amen.**

Using the "Non-Christian Spiritual Experience Inventory" on the following page, carefully check anything in which you were involved. This list is not exhaustive, but it will guide you in identifying non-Christian experiences. Add any additional involvement you have had. Even if you "innocently" participated in something or observed it, you should write it on your list to renounce, just in case you unknowingly gave Satan a foothold.

Non-Christian Spiritual Experience Inventory
(Please check those that apply.)

☐ Astral-projection
☐ Ouija board
☐ Table or body lifting
☐ Dungeons and Dragons
☐ Speaking in trance
☐ Automatic writing
☐ Magic eight ball
☐ Telepathy
☐ Using spells or curses
☐ Seance
☐ Materialization
☐ Clairvoyance
☐ Spirit guides
☐ Fortune telling
☐ Tarot cards
☐ Palm reading
☐ Astrology/horo-scopes
☐ Rod & pendulum (dowsing)
☐ Self-hypnosis
☐ Mental manipula-tions or attempts to swap minds
☐ Black and white magic
☐ New Age medicine
☐ Blood pacts or cutting yourself in a destructive way
☐ Fetishism (objects of worship, crystals, good luck charms)
☐ Incubi and succubi (sexual spirits)
☐ Other
———————

☐ Christian Science
☐ Unity
☐ The Way International
☐ Unification Church
☐ Mormonism
☐ Church of the Living Word
☐ Jehovah's Witnesses
☐ Children of God (Love)
☐ Swedenborgianism
☐ Unitarianism
☐ Masons
☐ New Age
☐ The Forum (EST)
☐ Spirit worship
☐ Other
———————

☐ Buddhism
☐ Hare Krishna
☐ Bahaism
☐ Rosicrucian
☐ Science of the Mind
☐ Science of Creative Intelligence
☐ Transcendental Meditation
☐ Hinduism
☐ Yoga
☐ Echkankar
☐ Roy Masters
☐ Silva Mind Control
☐ Father Divine
☐ Theosophical Society
☐ Islam
☐ Black Muslim
☐ Religion of Martial Arts
☐ Other
———————

1. Have you ever been hypnotized, attended a New Age or parapsychology seminar, consulted a medium, Spiritist, or channeler? Explain.

   _____

2. Do you or have you ever had an imaginary friend or spirit guide offering you guidance or companionship? Explain.

   _____

3. Have you ever heard voices in your mind or had repeating and nagging thoughts condemning you or that were foreign to what you believe or feel, like there was a dialogue going on in your head? Explain.

   _____

4. What other spiritual experiences have you had that would be considered out of the ordinary?

   _____

5. Have you ever made a vow, covenant, or pact with any individual or group other than God?

   _____

6. Have you been involved in satanic ritual or satanic worship in any form? Explain.

   _____

When you are confident that your list is complete, confess and renounce each involvement, whether active or passive, by praying aloud the following prayer, repeating it separately for each item on your list:

> **Lord,**
> **I confess that I have participated in** _____
> _____ *,*
> **and I renounce** _____ .
> **Thank You that in Christ I am forgiven.**

If there has been any involvement in satanic ritual or heavy occult activity, you need to state aloud the following special renunciations which apply. Read across the page, renouncing the first item in the column on the Kingdom of Darkness and then affirming the first truth in the column on the Kingdom of Light. Continue down the page in this manner.

All satanic rituals, covenants, and assignments must be specifically renounced as the Lord allows you to recall them. Some who have been subjected to satanic ritual abuse may have developed multiple personalities in order to survive. Nevertheless, continue through the *Steps to Freedom* in order to resolve all that you consciously can. It is important that you resolve the demonic strongholds first. Every personality must resolve his/her issues and agree to come together in Christ. You may need someone who understands spiritual conflict to help you maintain control and not be deceived into false memories. Only Jesus can bind up the broken-hearted, set captives free and make us whole.

Special Renunciations for Satanic Ritual Involvement

Kingdom of Darkness	Kingdom of Light
I renounce ever signing my name over to Satan or having had my name signed over to Satan.	I announce that my name is now written in the Lamb's Book of Life.
I renounce any ceremony where I may have been wed to Satan.	I announce that I am the bride of Christ.
I renounce any and all covenants that I made with Satan.	I announce that I am a partaker of the New Covenant with Christ.
I renounce all satanic assignments for my life, including duties, marriage and children.	I announce and commit myself to know and do only the will of God and accept only His guidance.
I renounce all spirit guides assigned to me.	I announce and accept only the leading of the Holy Spirit.
I renounce ever giving of my blood in the service of Satan.	I trust only in the shed blood of my Lord Jesus Christ.
I renounce ever eating of flesh or drinking of blood for satanic worship.	By faith I eat only the flesh and drink only the blood of Jesus in Holy Communion.
I renounce any and all guardians and Satanist parents who were assigned to me.	I announce that God is my Father and the Holy Spirit is my Guardian by which I am sealed.

Kingdom of Darkness
I renounce any baptism in blood or urine whereby I am identified with Satan.

I renounce any and all sacrifices that were made on my behalf by which Satan may claim ownership of me.

Kingdom of Light
I announce that I have been baptized into Christ Jesus and my identity is now in Christ.

I announce that only the sacrifice of Christ has any hold on me. I belong to Him. I have been purchased by the blood of the Lamb.

Step 2

....

Deception vs. Truth

Truth is the revelation of God's Word, but we need to acknowledge the truth in the inner self (see Ps. 51:6). When David lived a lie, he suffered greatly. When he finally found freedom by acknowledging the truth, he wrote: "How blessed is the man...in whose spirit there is no deceit" (Ps. 32:2). We are to lay aside falsehood and speak the truth in love (see Eph. 4:15, 25). A mentally healthy person is one who is in touch with reality and relatively free of anxiety. Both qualities should characterize the Christian who renounces deception and embraces the truth.

Begin this critical step by expressing aloud the following prayer. Don't let the enemy accuse you with thoughts such as: "This isn't going to work" or "I wish I could believe this but I can't" or any other lies in opposition to what you are proclaiming. Even if you have difficulty doing so, you need to pray the prayer and read the Doctrinal Affirmation.

Dear Heavenly Father,
I know that You desire truth in the inner self and that facing this truth is the way of liberation (John 8:32). I acknowledge that I have been deceived by the father of lies (John 8:44) and that I have deceived myself (1 John 1:8). I pray in the name of the Lord Jesus Christ that You, Heavenly Father,

will rebuke all deceiving spirits by virtue of the shed blood and resurrection of the Lord Jesus Christ. By faith I have received You into my life and I am now seated with Christ in the heavenlies (Eph. 2:6). I acknowledge that I have the responsibility and authority to resist the devil, and when I do, he will flee from me. I now ask the Holy Spirit to guide me into all truth (John 16:13). I ask You to "Search me, O God, and know my heart; try me and know my anxious thoughts; and see if there be any hurtful way in me, and lead me in the everlasting way" (Ps. 139:23-24). In Jesus' name, I pray. Amen.

You may want to pause at this point to consider some of Satan's deceptive schemes. In addition to false teachers, false prophets and deceiving spirits, you can deceive yourself. Now that you are alive in Christ and forgiven, you never have to live a lie or defend yourself. Christ is your defense. How have you deceived or attempted to defend yourself according to the following?

Self-deception

_____ Hearing God's Word but not doing it (see Jas. 1:22; 4:17)

_____ Saying we have no sin (see 1 John 1:8)

_____ Thinking we are something when we aren't (see Gal. 6:3)

_____ Thinking we are wise in our own eyes (see 1 Cor. 3:18-19)

_____ Thinking we will not reap what we sow (see Gal. 6:7)

_____ Thinking the unrighteous will inherit the Kingdom (see 1 Cor. 6:9)

_____ Thinking we can associate with bad company and not be corrupted (see 1 Cor. 15:33)

Self-defense
(defending ourselves instead of trusting in Christ)

_____ Denial (conscious or subconscious refusal to face the truth)

_____ Fantasy (escaping from the real world)
_____ Emotional insulation (withdrawing to avoid rejection)
_____ Regression (reverting back to a less threatening time)
_____ Displacement (taking out frustrations on others)
_____ Projection (blaming others)
_____ Rationalization (making excuses for poor behavior)
For those things that have been true in your life, pray aloud:

> **Lord,**
> **I agree that I have been deceived in the area of**
> **_____ . Thank You for**
> **forgiving me. I commit myself to know and follow Your truth. Amen.**

Choosing the truth may be difficult if you have been living a lie (been deceived) for many years. You may need to seek professional help to weed out the defense mechanisms you have depended upon to survive. The Christian needs only one defense—Jesus. Knowing that you are forgiven and accepted as God's child is what sets you free to face reality and declare your dependence on Him.

Faith is the biblical response to the truth, and believing the truth is a choice. When someone says, "I want to believe God, but I just can't," they are being deceived. Of course you can believe God. Faith is something you decide to do, not something you feel like doing. Believing the truth doesn't make it true. It's true; therefore, we believe it. The New Age movement is distorting the truth by saying we create reality through what we believe. We can't create reality with our minds; we face reality. It is what, or who you believe in that counts. Everybody believes in something, and everybody walks by faith according to what he or she believes. But if what you believe isn't true, then how you live (walk by faith) won't be right.

Historically, the church has found great value in publicly declaring its beliefs. The Apostles' Creed and the Nicene Creed have been recited for centuries. Read aloud the following affirmation of faith, and do so again as often as necessary to renew your mind. Experiencing difficulty in reading this affirmation may indicate where you are being deceived and under attack. Boldly affirm your commitment to biblical truth.

Doctrinal Affirmation

I recognize that there is only one true and living God (Ex. 20:2-3) who exists as the Father, Son and Holy Spirit and that He is worthy of all honor, praise and glory as the Creator, Sustainer and Beginning and End of all things (Rev. 4:11; 5:9-10; Is. 43:1, 7, 21).

I recognize Jesus Christ as the Messiah, the Word who became flesh and dwelt among us (John 1:1, 14). I believe that He came to destroy the works of Satan (1 John 3:8), that He disarmed the rulers and authorities and made a public display of them, having triumphed over them (Col. 2:15).

I believe that God has proven His love for me because when I was still a sinner, Christ died for me (Rom. 5:8). I believe that He delivered me from the domain of darkness and transferred me to His kingdom, and in Him I have redemption, the forgiveness of sins (Col. 1:13-14).

I believe that I am now a child of God (1 John 3:1-3) and that I am seated with Christ in the heavenlies (Eph. 2:6). I believe that I was saved by the grace of God through faith, that it was a gift, and not the result of any works on my part (Eph. 2:8-9).

I choose to be strong in the Lord and in the strength of His might (Eph. 6:10). I put no confidence in the flesh (Phil. 3:3) for the weapons of warfare are not of the flesh (2 Cor. 10:4). I put on the whole armor of God (Eph. 6:10-20), and I resolve to stand firm in my faith and resist the evil one.

I believe that apart from Christ I can do nothing (John 15:5), so I declare myself dependent on Him. I choose to abide in Christ in order to bear much fruit and glorify the

Lord (John 15:8). I announce to Satan that Jesus is my Lord (1 Cor. 12:3), and I reject any counterfeit gifts or works of Satan in my life.

I believe that the truth will set me free (John 8:32) and that walking in the light is the only path of fellowship (1 John 1:7). Therefore, I stand against Satan's deception by taking every thought captive in obedience to Christ (2 Cor. 10:5). I declare that the Bible is the only authoritative standard (2 Tim. 3:15-16). I choose to speak the truth in love (Eph. 4:15).

I choose to present my body as an instrument of righteousness, a living and holy sacrifice, and I renew my mind by the living Word of God in order that I may prove that the will of God is good, acceptable and perfect (Rom. 6:13; 12:1-2). I put off the old self with its evil practices and put on the new self (Col. 3:9-10), and I declare myself to be a new creature in Christ (2 Cor. 5:17).

I trust my Heavenly Father to fill me with His Holy Spirit (Eph. 5:18), to lead me into all truth (John 16:13) and to empower my life that I may live above sin and not carry out the desires of the flesh (Gal. 5:16). I crucify the flesh (Gal. 5:24) and choose to walk by the Spirit.

I renounce all selfish goals and choose the ultimate goal of love (1 Tim. 1:5). I choose to obey the two greatest commandments: to love the Lord my God with all my heart, soul and mind, and to love my neighbor as myself (Matt. 22:37-39).

I believe that Jesus has all authority in heaven and on earth (Matt. 28:18) and that He is the head over all rule and authority (Col. 2:10). I believe that Satan and his demons are subject to me in Christ since I am a member of Christ's body (Eph. 1:19-23). Therefore, I obey the command to submit to God and to resist the devil (Jas. 4:7), and I command Satan in the name of Christ to leave my presence.

Step 3

Bitterness vs. Forgiveness

We need to forgive others in order to be free from our pasts and to prevent Satan from taking advantage of us (see 2 Cor. 2:10-11). We are to be merciful just as our Heavenly Father is merciful (see Luke 6:36). We are to forgive as we have been forgiven (see Eph. 4:31-32). Ask God to bring to mind the names of those people you need to forgive by expressing the following prayer aloud:

> **Dear Heavenly Father,**
> **I thank You for the riches of Your kindness, forbearance, and patience, knowing that Your kindness has led me to repentance (Rom. 2:4). I confess that I have not extended that same patience and kindness toward others who have offended me, but instead I have harbored bitterness and resentment. I pray that during this time of self-examination You would bring to my mind those people that I need to forgive in order that I may do so (Matt. 18:35). I ask this in the precious name of Jesus. Amen.**

As names come to mind, make a list of only the names. At the end of your list, write "myself." Forgiving yourself is accepting God's cleansing and forgiveness. Also, write "thoughts against God." Thoughts raised up against the knowledge of God will usually result in angry feelings toward Him. Technically, we can't forgive God because He cannot commit any sin of commission or omission. But we need to specifically renounce false expectations and thoughts about God and agree to release any anger we have toward Him.

Before you pray to forgive these people, stop and consider what forgiveness is, what it is not, what decision you will be making, and what the consequences will be. In the following explanation, the main points are in bold print:

Forgiveness is not forgetting. People who try to forget find they cannot. God says He will remember our sins "no more" (see Heb. 10:17), but God, being omniscient, cannot forget. Remember our sins "no more" means that God will never use the past against us (see Ps. 103:12). Forgetting may be the result of forgiveness, but it is never the means of forgiveness. When we bring up the past against others, we are saying we haven't forgiven them.

Forgiveness is a choice, a crisis of the will. Since God requires us to forgive, it is something we can do. However, forgiveness is difficult for us because it pulls against our concept of justice. We want revenge for offenses suffered. However, we are told never to take our own revenge (see Rom. 12:19). You say, "Why should I let them off the hook?" That is precisely the problem. You are still hooked to them, still bound by your past. **You will let them off your hook, but they are never off God's.** He will deal with them fairly, something we cannot do.

You say, "You don't understand how much this person hurt me!" But don't you see, they are still hurting you! How do you stop the pain? **You don't forgive someone for their sake; you do it for your own sake so you can be free. Your need to forgive isn't an issue between you and the offender; it's between you and God.**

Forgiveness is agreeing to live with the consequences of another person's sin. Forgiveness is costly. You pay the price of the evil you forgive. You're going to live with those consequences whether you want to or not; your only choice is whether you will do so in the bitterness of unforgiveness or the freedom of forgiveness. Jesus took the consequences of your sin upon Himself. All true forgiveness is substitutionary, because no one really forgives without bearing the consequences of the other person's sin. God the Father "made Him who knew no sin to be sin on our behalf, that we might become the righteousness of God in Him" (2 Cor. 5:21). Where is the justice? It's the cross that makes forgiveness legally and morally right: "For the death that He died, He died to sin, once for all" (Rom. 6:10).

Decide that you will bear the burdens of their offenses by

not using that information against them in the future. This doesn't mean that you tolerate sin. You must set up scriptural boundaries to prevent future abuse. Some may be required to testify for the sake of justice but not for the purpose of seeking revenge from a bitter heart.

How do you forgive from your heart? You acknowledge the hurt and the hate. If your forgiveness doesn't visit the emotional core of your life, it will be incomplete. Many feel the pain of interpersonal offenses, but they won't or don't know how to acknowledge it. Let God bring the pain to the surface so He can deal with it. This is where the healing takes place.

Don't wait to forgive until you feel like forgiving; you will never get there. Feelings take time to heal after the choice to forgive is made and Satan has lost his place (see Eph. 4:26-27). **Freedom is what will be gained, not a feeling.**

As you pray, God may bring to mind offending people and experiences you have totally forgotten. Let Him do it even if it is painful. Remember, you are doing this for your sake. God wants you to be free. Don't rationalize or explain the offender's behavior. Forgiveness is dealing with your pain and leaving the other person to God. Positive feelings will follow in time; freeing yourself from the past is the critical issue right now.

Don't say, "Lord, please help me to forgive," because He is already helping you. Don't say, "Lord, I want to forgive," because you are bypassing the hard-core choice to forgive which is your responsibility. Stay with each individual until you are sure you have dealt with all the remembered pain—what they did, how they hurt you, how they made you feel (rejected, unloved, unworthy, dirty, etc.).

You are now ready to forgive the people on your list so you can be free in Christ, with those people no longer having any control over you. For each person on your list, pray aloud:

> **Lord,**
> **I forgive (name the person) for (verbally share every hurt and pain the Lord brings to your mind and how it made you feel).**

After you have forgiven every person for every painful memory, then finish this step by praying:

Lord,
I release all these people to You, and my right to seek revenge. I choose not to hold on to my bitterness and anger, and I ask You to heal my damaged emotions. In Jesus' name, I pray. Amen.

Step 4

....

Rebellion vs. Submission

We live in rebellious times. Many believe it is their right to sit in judgment of those in authority over them. Rebelling against God and His authority gives Satan an opportunity to attack. As our commanding general, the Lord says, "Get into ranks and follow Me. I will not lead you into temptation, but I will deliver you from evil" (see Matt. 6:13).

We have two biblical responsibilities regarding authority figures: Pray for them and submit to them. The only time God permits us to disobey earthly leaders is when they require us to do something morally wrong before God or attempt to rule outside the realm of their authority. Pray the following prayer:

Dear Heavenly Father,
You have said that rebellion is as the sin of witchcraft and insubordination is as iniquity and idolatry (1 Sam. 15:23). I know that in action and attitude I have sinned against You with a rebellious heart. Thank you for forgiving my rebellion, and I pray that by the shed blood of the Lord Jesus Christ all ground gained by evil spirits because of my rebelliousness will be canceled. I pray that You will shed light on all my ways that I may

know the full extent of my rebelliousness. I now
choose to adopt a submissive spirit and a servant's
heart. In the name of Christ Jesus, my Lord.
Amen.

Being under authority is an act of faith. You are trusting
God to work through His established lines of authority. There
are times when employers, parents and husbands are violating the laws of civil government which are ordained by God
to protect innocent people against abuse. In these cases, you
need to appeal to the state for your protection. In many states,
the law requires such abuse to be reported.

In difficult cases, such as continuing abuse at home, further
counseling help may be needed. And, in some cases, when
earthly authorities have abused their position and are requiring disobedience to God or a compromise in your commitment to Him, you need to obey God, not man.

We are all admonished to submit to one another as equals
in Christ (see Eph. 5:21). However, there are specific lines of
authority in Scripture for the purpose of accomplishing common goals:

Civil Government (see Rom. 13:1-7; 1 Tim. 2:1-4;
    1 Pet. 2:13-17)
Parents (see Eph. 6:1-3)
Husband (see 1 Pet. 3:1-4) or Wife (see Eph. 5:21;
    1 Pet. 3:7)
Employer (see 1 Pet. 2:18-23)
Church Leaders (see Heb. 13:17)
God (see Dan. 9:5, 9)

Examine each area and ask God to forgive you for those
times you have not been submissive, and pray:

Lord,
    I agree I have been rebellious toward_____
_____.
I choose to be submissive and obedient to your
Word. In Jesus' name, Amen.

Step 5

Pride vs. Humility

Pride is a killer. Pride says, "I can do it! I can get myself out of this mess without God or anyone else's help." Oh no, we can't! We absolutely need God, and we desperately need each other. Paul wrote: "We worship in the Spirit of God and glory in Christ Jesus and put no confidence in the flesh" (Phil. 3:3). Humility is confidence properly placed. We are to be "strong in the Lord and in the strength of His might" (Eph. 6:10). James 4:6-10 and 1 Peter 5:1-10 reveal that spiritual conflict follows pride. Use the following prayer to express your commitment to live humbly before God:

Dear Heavenly Father,
You have said that pride goes before destruction and an arrogant spirit before stumbling (Prov. 16:18). I confess that I have lived independently and have not denied myself, picked up my cross daily and followed You (Matt. 16:24). In so doing, I have given ground to the enemy in my life. I have believed that I could be successful and live victoriously by my own strength and resources. I now confess that I have sinned against You by placing my will before Yours and by centering my life around myself instead of You. I now renounce the self-life and by so doing cancel all the ground that has been gained in my members by the enemies of the Lord Jesus Christ. I pray that You will guide me so that I will do nothing from selfishness or empty conceit, but with humility of mind I will regard others as more important than myself (Phil. 2:3). Enable me through love to serve others and in honor prefer others (Rom. 12:10). I ask this in the name of Christ Jesus, my Lord. Amen.

Having made that commitment, now allow God to show you any specific areas of your life where you have been prideful, such as:

_____ Having a stronger desire to do my will than God's will;

_____ Being more dependent upon my strengths and resources than God's;

_____ Too often believe that my ideas and opinions are better than others;

_____ Being more concerned about controlling others than developing self-control;

_____ Sometimes consider myself more important than others;

_____ Having a tendency to think that I have no needs;

_____ Finding it difficult to admit that I was wrong;

_____ Having a tendency to be more of a people-pleaser than a God-pleaser;

_____ Being overly concerned about getting the credit I deserve;

_____ Being driven to obtain the recognition that comes from degrees, titles and positions;

_____ Often thinking I am more humble than others;

_____ These other ways: _____ .

For each of these that has been true in your life, pray aloud:

Lord,
   I agree I have been prideful by:_____
_____ .
I choose to humble myself and place all my confidence in You. Amen.

Step 6

Bondage vs. Freedom

The next step to freedom deals with habitual sin. People who have been caught in the trap of sin-confess-sin-confess may need to follow the instructions of James 5:16, "Confess your sins to one another, and pray for one another, so that you may be healed. The effective prayer of a righteous man can accomplish much." Seek out a righteous person who will hold you up in prayer and to whom you can be accountable. Others may only need the assurance of 1 John 1:9: "If we confess our sins, He is faithful and righteous to forgive us our sins and to cleanse us from all unrighteousness." Confession is not saying "I'm sorry"; it's saying "I did it." Whether you need the help of others or just the accountability to God, pray the following prayer:

> **Dear Heavenly Father,**
> **You have told us to put on the Lord Jesus Christ and make no provision for the flesh in regard to its lust (Rom. 13:14). I acknowledge that I have given in to fleshly lusts which wage war against my soul (1 Pet. 2:11). I thank You that in Christ my sins are forgiven, but I have transgressed Your holy law and given the enemy an opportunity to wage war in my physical body (Rom. 6:12-13; Eph. 4:27; Jas. 4:1; 1 Pet. 5:8). I come before Your presence to acknowledge these sins and to seek Your cleansing (1 John 1:9) that I may be freed from the bondage of sin. I now ask You to reveal to my mind the ways that I have transgressed Your moral law and grieved the Holy Spirit. In Jesus' precious name, I pray. Amen.**

The deeds of the flesh are numerous. Many of the following issues are from Galatians 5:19-21. Check those that apply to you and any others you have struggled with that the Lord has brought to your mind. Then confess each one with the concluding prayer. Note: sexual sins, eating disorders, substance abuse, abortion, suicidal tendencies, perfectionism and fear will be dealt with later.

____ stealing	____ cheating
____ lying	____ gossiping
____ fighting	____ controlling
____ jealousy	____ procrastinating
____ envying	____ swearing
____ outbursts of anger	____ greediness
____ complaining	____ laziness
____ criticizing	____ divisiveness
____ lusting	____ other_____

> **Dear Heavenly Father,**
> **I thank You that my sins are forgiven in Christ, but I have walked by the flesh and therefore sinned by _____. Thank You for cleansing me of all unrighteousness. I ask that You would enable me to walk by the Spirit and not carry out the desires of the flesh. In Jesus' name, I pray. Amen.**

It is our responsibility not to allow sin to reign in our mortal bodies by not using our bodies as instruments of unrighteousness (see Rom. 6:12,13). If you are or have struggled with sexual sins (pornography, masturbation, sexual promiscuity, etc.) or are experiencing sexual difficulty in your marriage, pray as follows:

> **Lord,**
> **I ask You to reveal to my mind every sexual use of my body as an instrument of unrighteousness. In Jesus' precious name, I pray. Amen.**

As the Lord brings to your mind every sexual misuse of

your body, whether it was done to you (rape, incest or other sexual abuse) or willingly by you, renounce every occasion:

Lord,
     I renounce (name the specific misuse of your body) with (name the person) and ask You to break that bond.

Now commit your body to the Lord by praying:

Lord,
     I renounce all these uses of my body as an instrument of unrighteousness and by so doing ask You to break all bondages Satan has brought into my life through that involvement. I confess my participation. I now present my body to You as a living sacrifice, holy and acceptable unto You, and I reserve the sexual use of my body only for marriage. I renounce the lie of Satan that my body is not clean, that it is dirty or in any way unacceptable as a result of my past sexual experiences. Lord, I thank You that You have totally cleansed and forgiven me, that You love and accept me unconditionally. Therefore, I can accept myself. And I choose to do so, to accept myself and my body as cleansed. In Jesus' name. Amen.

Special Prayers for Specific Problems

Homosexuality

Lord,
     I renounce the lie that You have created me or anyone else to be homosexual, and I affirm that You clearly forbid homosexual behavior. I accept myself as a child of God and declare that You created me a man (woman). I renounce any bondages

of Satan that have perverted my relationships with others. I announce that I am free to relate to the opposite sex in the way that You intended. In Jesus' name. Amen.

Abortion

Lord,

I confess that I did not assume stewardship of the life You entrusted to me. I choose to accept your forgiveness, and I now commit that child to You for Your care in eternity. In Jesus' name. Amen.

Suicidal Tendencies

Lord,

I renounce suicidal thoughts and any attempts I have made to take my own life or in any way injure myself. I renounce the lie that life is hopeless and that I can find peace and freedom by taking my own life. Satan is a thief, and he comes to steal, kill, and destroy. I choose to be a good steward of the physical life that You have entrusted to me. In Jesus' name, I pray. Amen.

Eating Disorders or Self-Mutilation

Lord,

I renounce the lie that my value as a person is dependent upon my physical beauty, my weight or size. I renounce cutting myself, vomiting, using laxatives or starving myself as a means of cleansing myself of evil or altering my appearance. I announce that only the blood of the Lord Jesus Christ cleanses me from sin. I accept the reality that there may be sin present in me due to the lies I have believed and the wrongful use of my body, but I renounce the lie that I am evil or that any part of my body is evil. My body is the temple of the Holy Spirit and I belong to You, Lord. I receive Your love and acceptance of me. In Jesus' name. Amen.

Substance Abuse

Lord,

I confess that I have misused substances (alcohol, tobacco, food, prescription or street drugs) for the purpose of pleasure, to escape reality or to cope with difficult situations—resulting in the abuse of my body, the harmful programming of my mind and the quenching of the Holy Spirit. I ask Your forgiveness. I renounce any satanic connection or influence in my life through my misuse of chemicals or food. I cast my anxiety onto Christ Who loves me, and I commit myself to no longer yield to substance abuse, but to the Holy Spirit. I ask You, Heavenly Father, to fill me with Your Holy Spirit. In Jesus' name. Amen.

Drivenness and Perfectionism

Lord,

I renounce the lie that my self-worth is dependent upon my ability to perform. I announce the truth that my identity and sense of worth are found in who I am as Your child. I renounce seeking the approval and acceptance of other people, and I choose to believe that I am already approved and accepted in Christ because of His death and resurrection for me. I choose to believe the truth that I have been saved, not by deeds done in righteousness, but according to Your mercy. I choose to believe that I am no longer under the curse of the law because Christ became a curse for me. I receive the free gift of life in Christ and choose to abide in Him. I renounce striving for perfection by living under the law. By Your grace, Heavenly

Father, I choose from this day forward to walk by faith according to what You have said is true by the power of Your Holy Spirit. In Jesus name. Amen.

Plaguing Fears

Dear Heavenly Father,

I acknowledge You as the only legitimate fear object in my life. You are the only omnipresent (always present) and omniscient (all-knowing) God and the only means by which all other fears can be expelled. You are my sanctuary. You have not given me a spirit of timidity, but of power and love and discipline. I confess that I have allowed the fear of man and the fear of death to exercise control over my life, instead of trusting in You. I now renounce all other fear objects and worship You only. I pray that You would fill me with Your Holy Spirit that I may live my life and speak Your Word with boldness. In Jesus' name, I pray. Amen.

After you have confessed all known sin, pray:

Dear Heavenly Father,

I now confess these sins to You and claim my forgiveness and cleansing through the blood of the Lord Jesus Christ. I cancel all ground that evil spirits have gained through my willful involvement in sin. I ask this in the wonderful name of my Lord and Savior, Jesus Christ. Amen.

Step 7

Acquiescence vs. Renunciation

Acquiescence is passively giving in or agreeing without consent. The last step to freedom is to renounce the sins of your ancestors and any curses which may have been placed on you. In giving the Ten Commandments, God said: "You shall not make for yourself an idol, or any likeness of what is in heaven above or on the earth beneath or in the water under the earth. You shall not worship them or serve them; for I, the Lord your God, am a jealous God, visiting the iniquity of the fathers on the children, on the third and fourth generations of those who hate Me" (Ex. 20:4,5).

Familiar spirits can be passed on from one generation to the next if not renounced and if your new spiritual heritage in Christ is not proclaimed. You are not guilty for the sin of any ancestor, but because of their sin, Satan may have gained access to your family. This is not to deny that many problems are transmitted genetically or acquired from an immoral atmosphere. All three conditions can predispose an individual to a particular sin. In addition, deceived people may try to curse you, or satanic groups may try to target you. You have all the authority and protection you need in Christ to stand against such curses and assignments. Ask the Lord to reveal to your mind the sins and iniquities of your ancestors by praying the following prayer:

Dear Heavenly Father,
I thank You that I am a new creation in Christ. I desire to obey Your command to honor my mother and my father, but I also acknowledge that my heritage has not been perfect. I ask you to reveal to my mind the sins and iniquities of my ancestors in order to confess, renounce and forsake them. In Jesus' name, I pray. Amen.

Now claim your position and protection in Christ by making the following declaration verbally, and then by humbling yourself before God in prayer.

Declaration

I here and now reject and disown all the sins and iniquities of my ancestors, including (<u>name them</u>). As one who has been delivered from the power of darkness and translated into the kingdom of God's dear Son, I cancel out all demonic working that has been passed on to me from my ancestors. As one who has been crucified and raised with Jesus Christ and who sits with Him in heavenly places, I renounce all satanic assignments that are directed toward me and my ministry, and I cancel every curse that Satan and his workers have put on me. I announce to Satan and all his forces that Christ became a curse for me (Gal. 3:13) when He died for my sins on the cross. I reject any and every way in which Satan may claim ownership of me. I belong to the Lord Jesus Christ who purchased me with His own blood. I reject all other blood sacrifices whereby Satan may claim ownership of me. I declare myself to be eternally and completely signed over and committed to the Lord Jesus Christ. By the authority I have in Jesus Christ, I now command every familiar spirit and every enemy of the Lord Jesus Christ to leave my presence. I commit myself to my Heavenly Father to do His will from this day forward.

Prayer

Dear Heavenly Father,
I come to You as Your child purchased by the blood of the Lord Jesus Christ. You are the Lord of the universe and the Lord of my life. I submit my

body to You as an instrument of righteousness, a living sacrifice, that I may glorify You in my body. I now ask You to fill me with Your Holy Spirit. I commit myself to the renewing of my mind in order to prove that Your will is good, perfect and acceptable for me. All this I do in the name and authority of the Lord Jesus Christ. Amen.

Once you have secured your freedom by going through these seven steps, you may find demonic influences attempting reentry, days or even months later. One person shared that she heard a spirit say to her mind "I'm back" two days after she had been set free. "No, you're not!" she proclaimed aloud. The attack ceased immediately. One victory does not constitute winning the war. Freedom must be maintained. After completing these steps, one jubilant lady asked, "Will I always be like this?" I told her that she would stay free as long as she remained in right relationship with God. "Even if you slip and fall," I encouraged, "you know how to get right with God again."

One victim of incredible atrocities shared this illustration: "It's like being forced to play a game with an ugly stranger in my own home. I kept losing and wanted to quit, but the ugly stranger wouldn't let me. Finally I called the police (a higher authority), and they came and escorted the stranger out. He knocked on the door trying to regain entry, but this time **I recognized his voice and didn't let him in.**" What a beautiful illustration of gaining freedom in Christ. We call upon Jesus, the ultimate authority, and He escorts the enemy out of our lives. Know the truth, stand firm and resist the evil one. Seek out good Christian fellowship, and commit yourself to regular times of Bible study and prayer. God loves you and will never leave or forsake you.

After Care

Freedom must be maintained. You have won a very important battle in an ongoing war. Freedom is yours as long as you keep choosing truth and standing firm in the strength of the Lord. If new memories should surface or if you become aware of "lies" that you have believed or other non-Christian experiences you have had, renounce them and choose the truth. Some have found it helpful to go through the steps again. As you do, read the instructions carefully.

For your encouragement and further study, read *Victory Over the Darkness* (or youth version *Stomping Out the Darkness*), *The Bondage Breaker* (adult or youth version), and *Released from Bondage*. If you are a parent, read *The Seduction of Our Children*. *Walking in the Light* (formerly *Walking Through the Darkness*) was written to help people understand God's guidance and discern counterfeit guidance. Also, to maintain your freedom, we suggest the following:

1. Seek legitimate Christian fellowship where you can walk in the light and speak the truth in love.
2. Study your Bible daily. Memorize key verses.
3. Take every thought captive to the obedience of Christ. Assume responsibility for your thought life, reject the lie, choose the truth and stand firm in your position in Christ.
4. Don't drift away! It is very easy to get lazy in your thoughts and revert back to old habit patterns of thinking. Share your struggles openly with a trusted friend. You need at least one friend who will stand with you.
5. Don't expect another person to fight your battle for you. Others can help, but they can't think, pray, read the Bible or choose the truth for you.
6. Continue to seek your identity and sense of worth in Christ. Read *Living Free in Christ* and the devo-

tional, *Daily in Christ.* Renew your mind with the truth that your acceptance, security and significance is in Christ by saturating your mind with the following truths. Read the entire list of who you are "in Christ" and the Doctrinal Affirmation (in Step 2) aloud morning and evening over the next several weeks (and look up the verses referenced).

7. Commit yourself to daily prayer. You can pray these suggested prayers often and with confidence:

Daily Prayer

Dear Heavenly Father,

I honor You as my sovereign Lord. I acknowledge that You are always present with me. You are the only all-powerful and wise God. You are kind and loving in all Your ways. I love You and thank You that I am united with Christ and spiritually alive in Him. I choose not to love the world, and I crucify the flesh and all its passions.

I thank You for the life that I now have in Christ, and I ask You to fill me with Your Holy Spirit that I may live my life free from sin. I declare my dependence upon You, and I take my stand against Satan and all his lying ways. I choose to believe the truth, and I refuse to be discouraged. You are the God of all hope, and I am confident that You will meet my needs as I seek to live according to Your Word. I express with confidence that I can live a responsible life through Christ who strengthens me.

I now take my stand against Satan and command him and all his evil spirits to depart from me. I put on the whole armor of God. I submit my body as a living sacrifice and renew my mind by the living Word of God in order that I may prove that the will of God is good, acceptable, and perfect. I ask these things in the precious name of my Lord and Savior, Jesus Christ. Amen.

Bedtime Prayer

> Thank You, Lord, that You have brought me into
> Your family and have blessed me with every spiri-
> tual blessing in the heavenly realms in Christ.
> Thank You for providing this time of renewal
> through sleep. I accept it as part of Your perfect plan
> for Your children, and I trust You to guard my mind
> and my body during my sleep. As I have meditated
> on You and Your truth during this day, I choose to
> let these thoughts continue in my mind while I am
> asleep. I commit myself to You for Your protection
> from every attempt of Satan or his emissaries to
> attack me during sleep. I commit myself to You as
> my Rock, my Fortress and my Resting Place. I pray
> in the strong name of the Lord Jesus Christ. Amen.

Cleansing Home/Apartment
After removing all articles of false worship from home/apart-
ment, pray aloud in every room, if necessary:

> Heavenly Father, we acknowledge that You are
> Lord of heaven and earth. In Your sovereign
> power and love, You have given us all things rich-
> ly to enjoy. Thank You for this place to live. We
> claim this home for our family as a place of spiri-
> tual safety and protection from all the attacks of
> the enemy. As children of God seated with Christ
> in the heavenly realm, we command every evil
> spirit claiming ground in the structures and fur-
> nishings of this place, based on the activities of
> previous occupants, to leave and never return. We
> renounce all curses and spells utilized against this
> place. We ask You, Heavenly Father, to post
> guardian angels around this home (apartment,
> condo, room, etc.) to guard it from attempts of the
> enemy to enter and disturb Your purposes for us.
> We thank You, Lord, for doing this, and pray in
> the name of the Lord Jesus Christ. Amen.

Living in a Non-Christian Environment
After removing all articles of false worship from your room, pray aloud in the space allotted to you:

> **Thank You, Heavenly Father, for my place to live and be renewed by sleep. I ask You to set aside my room (portion of my room) as a place of spiritual safety for me. I renounce any allegiance given to false gods or spirits by other occupants, and I renounce any claim to this room (space) by Satan based on activities of past occupants or me. On the basis of my position as a child of God and a joint-heir with Christ who has all authority in heaven and on earth, I command all evil spirits to leave this place and never to return. I ask You, Heavenly Father, to appoint guardian angels to protect me while I live here. I pray this in the name of the Lord Jesus Christ. Amen.**

Who I Am in Christ

I Am Accepted

John 1:12	I am God's child.
John 15:15	I am Christ's friend.
Rom. 5:1	I have been justified.
1 Cor. 6:17	I am united with the Lord, and I am one spirit with Him.
1 Cor. 6:19,20	I have been bought with a price. I belong to God.
1 Cor. 12:27	I am a member of Christ's body.
Eph. 1:1	I am a saint.
Eph. 1:5	I have been adopted as God's child.
Eph. 2:18	I have direct access to God through the Holy Spirit.
Col. 1:14	I have been redeemed and forgiven of all my sins.
Col. 2:10	I am complete in Christ.

I Am Secure

Rom. 8:1,2	I am free forever from condemnation.
Rom. 8:28	I am assured that all things work together for good.
Rom. 8:31-34	I am free from any condemning charges against me.
Rom. 8:35-39	I cannot be separated from the love of God.
2 Cor. 1:21,22	I have been established, anointed and sealed by God.
Col. 3:3	I am hidden with Christ in God.
Phil. 1:6	I am confident that the good work that God has begun in me will be perfected.
Phil. 3:20	I am a citizen of heaven.
2 Tim. 1:7	I have not been given a spirit of fear but of power, love and a sound mind.

Heb. 4:16   I can find grace and mercy to help in time of need.

1 Jn. 5:18   I am born of God and the evil one cannot touch me.

I Am Significant

Matt. 5:13,14   I am the salt and light of the earth.

John 15:1,5   I am a branch of the true vine, a channel of His life.

John 15:16   I have been chosen and appointed to bear fruit.

Acts 1:8   I am a personal witness of Christ.

1 Cor. 3:16   I am God's temple.

2 Cor. 5:17-21   I am a minister of reconciliation for God.

2 Cor. 6:1   I am God's coworker (1 Cor. 3:9).

Eph. 2:6   I am seated with Christ in the heavenly realm.

Eph. 2:10   I am God's workmanship.

Eph. 3:12   I may approach God with freedom and confidence.

Phil. 4:13   I can do all things through Christ who strengthens me.

Appendix B

The Overcomer's Covenant in Christ

Shortened Edition

1. I place all my trust and confidence in the Lord and I put no confidence in the flesh—I declare myself to be dependent upon God. I know that I cannot save myself, nor set myself free by my own efforts and resources. I know that apart from Christ I can do nothing. I know that all temptation is an attempt to get me to live my life independently from God, but God has provided a way of escape.

2. I consciously and deliberately choose to submit to God and resist the devil by denying myself, picking up my cross daily and following Jesus. I know that my soul was not designed by God to function as master. I know that rebellion is as the sin of witchcraft, and insubordination is as iniquity and idolatry.

3. I choose to humble myself before the mighty hand of God that He may exalt me at the proper time. I know that God is opposed to the proud, but gives grace to the humble.

4. I declare the truth that I am dead to sin, freed from it and alive to God in Christ Jesus, because I have died with Christ and was raised with Him. I know that the law and all my best efforts are unable to impart life, and that Jesus came to give me life.

5. I gladly embrace the truth that I am now a child of God, who is unconditionally loved and accepted. I reject the lie that I have to perform to be accepted, and I reject my fallen and natural identity which was derived from the world. I know that it is not what I do that determines who I am, but who I am that determines what I do.

6. I declare that sin shall no longer be master over me because I am not under the law, but under grace; and there is no more guilt or condemnation because I am spiritually alive in Christ Jesus. I am a servant of a new covenant, not of the letter, but of the Spirit; for the letter kills, but the Spirit gives life.

7. I renounce every unrighteous use of my body, and I commit myself to no longer be conformed to this world, but rather to be transformed by the renewing of my mind. I choose to believe the truth and walk in it, regardless of my feelings or circumstances. I know that before I came to Christ my mind was programmed according to this world and I used my body as an instrument of unrighteousness thereby allowing sin to reign in my mortal body.

8. I commit myself to take every thought captive to the obedience of Christ. I choose to think upon that which is true, honorable, right, pure and lovely. I know that the Holy Spirit explicitly says that in later times some will fall away from the faith, paying attention to deceitful spirits and doctrines of demons.

9. I commit myself to God's great goal for my life to conform to His image. I know that I will face many trials, but God has given me the victory. I am not a victim, but an overcomer in Christ. The grace of God will enable me to triumph over every trial resulting in proven character.

10. I choose to adopt the attitude of Christ, which is to do nothing from selfishness or empty conceit, but with humility of mind I will regard others as more important than myself. I will not merely look out for my own personal interests, but also the interest of others. I know that it is more blessed to give than to receive.

The Overcomer's Covenant in Christ Expanded Edition

1. I place all my trust and confidence in the Lord and I put no confidence in the flesh, and I declare myself to be dependent upon God. I know that I cannot save myself, nor set myself free by my own efforts and resources. I know that apart from Christ I can do nothing (see John 15:5). I know that all temptation is an attempt to get me to live my life independent of God, but God has provided a way of escape (see 1 Cor. 10:13).

    Programs, ministries, and strategies do not save us nor do they set us free. Who saves us and sets us free is Christ, and what saves us and sets us free is our response to Him in repentance and faith. This faith is based in the truth of God's word and the finished work of Christ. The Lord does work through biblically based ministries that are alive in Christ and committed to the truth that sets people free. We wholeheartedly recommend, support, and encourage every overcomer to be a part of a redemptive fellowship under the New Testament Covenant of grace. But working in a program and depending on a group will not save us nor set us free in Christ, even with the best of intentions. Such programs and groups can be very caring, and may result in abstinence from alcohol and drugs, but ultimately salvation and freedom can only come in Christ.

The Lord never created humanity to live independent of Him. Adam's sin was an act of rebellion against God, and the result was a severed relationship with Him. Jesus modeled a life totally dependent upon His heavenly Father. Without Christ we are not handicapped nor less effective. Without Christ we can do nothing. The basis for temptation is legitimate needs which only Christ can meet. Alcohol, sex, and drugs are only the object of our temptation. To believe that we need them to be somebody, succeed or even survive is to believe a lie. We need Christ, because only He can meet all our needs according to His riches in glory.

2. I consciously and deliberately choose to submit to God and resist the devil by denying myself, picking up my cross daily, and following Jesus. I know that my soul was never designed by God to function as master, and I know that rebellion is as the sin of witchcraft, and insubordination is as iniquity and idolatry. (see 1 Sam. 15:23).

The ultimate lie of Satan is to believe that we are God. We are not the master of our fate nor the captain of our soul. We are either serving the true God or the God of this world while being deceived into thinking that we are serving ourselves. It seems to be the great ambition of mankind to be happy as animals instead of being blessed as children of God. Indulging our fleshly appetites does not satisfy them, it only creates a greater dependency upon them. Only those who hunger and thirst for righteousness will be satisfied (see Matt. 5:6).

Jesus said, "For whoever wishes to save his life shall lose it; but whoever loses his life for My sake shall find it" (Matt. 16:25). Those who look for their purpose and meaning in life in the natural order of things will lose it. We cannot take it with us. But those who find their identity, significance, and security in Christ will have it now and for all eternity. Paul said, "discipline yourself for the purpose of godliness; for bodily discipline is only of little profit, but godliness is profitable for all things, since it holds promise for the present life and also for the life to come (1 Tim 4:7,8).

Paul instructed, "Let every person be in subjection to the governing authorities. For there is no authority except from God, and those which exist are established by God. Therefore, he who resists authority has opposed the ordinance of God; and they who have opposed will receive condemnation upon themselves" (Rom. 13:1,2). To win the spiritual battle we must be under God's authority. Only then can you resist the devil. Trying to resist the devil without first submitting to God will be a dog fight. Submitting to God without resisting the devil will keep you in bondage. We must first submit to God and then resist the devil and he will flee from us (see Jas. 4:7).

3. I choose to humble myself before the mighty hand of God in order that He may exalt me at the proper time. I know that God is opposed to the proud but gives grace to the humble (see Jas. 4:6).

Pride says, "I can get out of this by myself. I don't need God or anyone else. When it comes to drinking or using I can stop any time I want." The only way to prove that, of course, is to stop. Pride refuses to acknowledge our need for God and each other. The truth is, we absolutely need God and we necessarily need each other. Our pride will rob us from the grace of God. We must humble ourselves by walking in the light (see 1 John 1:7), and speaking the truth in love for we are members of one another (see Eph. 4:25). Not to do so would give the devil a place (see Eph. 4:27).

You can't help someone who doesn't want to be helped, nor can someone get help unless they are willing to admit that they need it. Even the Lord intends to pass by the self-sufficient (see Mark 6:48). If we want to row our own boat against the storms of life, He will let us. Only those who call upon the name of the Lord will be saved (see 1 Cor. 1:2). Brokenness is the essential prerequisite to victory. As long as the person in bondage can hide their sin, they likely will. Eventually, however, those who lie and cover up their addictions will be exposed. "For nothing is hidden, except to be revealed; nor has anything been secret, but that it should come to light" (Mark 4:22). Secret sin on earth is open scandal in heaven. It is better to "Humble yourselves in the presence of the Lord, and He will exalt you" (Jas. 4:10).

4. I declare the truth that I am dead to sin, freed from it, and alive to God in Christ Jesus, since I have died with Christ and was raised with Him. I know that the law and all my best efforts are unable to impart life, and that Jesus came to give us life.

It will be futile to live up to someone else's standards, much less our own. Even living in a controlled atmosphere with external constraints will eventually prove futile. As soon as the external constraints are removed, the unregenerate man will return to his former state. Jesus didn't come to give us a new law, He came to give us life. He didn't come to change our behavior; He came to change our basic nature. Every child of God is alive in Christ and dead to sin, and we are to consider it so (i.e., continue to believe it so) in order to live free in Christ. The law of life in Christ Jesus has set us free from the law of sin and of death (see Rom.8:2). We have become partakers of the divine nature (see 2 Pet.1:4), because our souls are in union with Him. Human effort cannot accomplish this because we cannot do for ourselves what Christ has already done for us. Lacking this vital truth, most believers are desperately trying to become somebody they already are. "Beloved, now we are children of God" (1 John 3:3).

5. I gladly embrace the truth that I am now a child of God, who is unconditionally loved and accepted. I reject the lie that I have to perform to be accepted, and I reject my fallen and natural identity which was derived from the world. I know that it is not what I do that determines who I am, but who I am that determines what I do.

We are not alcoholics, addicts, or co-dependents. We are children of God who are trusting in Christ to be our life and our freedom. Rehearsing a fallen identity may reinforce the lie that we have to sin. We are children of God who struggle to overcome the temptations of alcohol, sex, drugs, and many other sins that so easily beset us. We are not sinners in the hands of an angry God; we are saints in the hands of a loving God. We can do all things through Christ who strengthens us (see Phil. 4:13).

6. I declare that sin shall no longer be master over me because I am not under the law but under grace, and there is no more guilt or condemnation because I am spiritually alive in Christ Jesus. I am a servant of a new covenant, not of the letter, but of the Spirit; for the letter kills, but the Spirit gives life.

Every child of God has been transferred out of the kingdom of darkness into the kingdom of the Lord Jesus Christ (see Col. 1:18). We are no longer dead in our trespasses and sins (see Eph. 2:1). We are to consider ourselves to be alive to Christ and dead to sin (see Rom. 6:11). We don't make that true by our experience. We choose to believe what God says is true and walk accordingly by faith, and then it works out in our experience. We don't try to live a victorious and fruitful life with the hope that God may someday love and accept us. God already loves and accepts us, that is why we live a fruitful and victorious life by the grace of God.

We no longer attempt to live only on the basis of laws and principles which call for us to respond in obedience. We have died and our life is hidden with Christ in God (see Col. 3:3). We respond to the life of Christ within us by faith according to what God says is true, and walk (live) by the Spirit and not carry out the desire of the flesh (see Gal. 5:16).

Paul says, "Not that we are adequate in ourselves to consider anything as coming from ourselves, but our adequacy is from God, who also made us adequate as servants of a new covenant, not of the letter, but of the Spirit; for the letter kills, but the Spirit gives life" (2 Cor. 3:5,6).

7. I renounce every unrighteous use of my body and I commit myself to no longer be conformed to this

world, but rather be transformed by the renewing of my mind, and I choose to believe the truth and walk in it, regardless of my feelings or circumstances. I know that before I came to Christ my mind was programmed according to this world and I used my body as an instrument of unrighteousness thereby allowing sin to reign in my mortal body (see Rom. 6:12,13).

The two most critical and basic issues that confront every born-again Christian may be summarized as follows: "Do something about the neutral disposition of your physical body and be transformed by the renewing of your mind." Paul writes, "I urge you therefore, brethren, by the mercies of God, to present your bodies a living and holy sacrifice, acceptable to God, which is your spiritual service of worship. And do not be conformed to this world, but be transformed by the renewing of your mind, that you may prove what the will of God is, that which is good and acceptable and perfect" (Rom. 12:1,2).

Scripture assures us that we are alive in Christ, and dead to sin because of the great work of Christ on the cross and in His resurrection (Rom. 6:1-11). We cannot do for ourselves what Christ has already done for us, but Romans 6:12 teaches that it is our responsibility to not allow sin to reign in our mortal bodies that we should obey its lusts. The next verse tells us how: "And do not go on presenting the members of your body to sin as instruments of unrighteousness; but present yourselves to God as those alive from the dead, and your members as instruments of righteousness to God" (Rom. 6:13).

Every time we commit a sexual sin or abuse our bodies with an excessive use of alcohol or drugs we are using our bodies as instruments of unrighteousness. We are allowing sin to reign in our mortal bodies. James 4:1 says, "What is the source of quarrels and conflicts among you? Is not the source your pleasures that wage war in your members?" Complete repentance would require us to renounce every use of our bodies as instruments of unrighteousness, and then present our bodies to God as a living sacrifice, and be transformed by the renewing of our minds.

"Do you not know that your body is a temple of the Holy Spirit who is in you, whom you have from God, and that you are not your own? For you have been bought with a price: therefore glorify God in your body" (1 Cor. 6:19,20). We are violating the temple of God with substance abuse or when we commit sexual sins. In so doing we have allowed sin to reign in our mortal bodies. We have become enslaved to the lusts of our flesh instead of buffeting our body and making it our slave (see 1 Cor. 9.27). "Do not get drunk with wine, for that is dissipation, but be filled with the Spirit" (Eph. 5:18).

We were all born into this world physically alive, but spiritually dead (see Eph. 2:1). During those early formative years of our lives we had neither the presence of God in our lives nor the knowledge of His ways. We all learned to live our lives independent of God. Some of us turned to alcohol, sex, and drugs as a means of coping, escaping the pressures of life, or seeking pleasure. When we were born again, we became new creations in Christ, but everything that was programmed into our minds was still there. We must be transformed by the renewing of our minds. It will never be sufficient enough to try to change our behavior, we must change what we believe. People don't always live what they profess, but they will always live what they believe.

8. I commit myself to take every thought captive to the obedience of Christ, and choose to think upon that which is true, honorable, right, pure, and lovely. I know that the Holy "Spirit explicitly says that in later times some will fall away from the faith, paying attention to deceitful spirits and doctrines (teachings) of demons" (1 Tim. 4:1).

In the High Priestly Prayer, Jesus prays, "I do not ask Thee to take them out of the world, but to keep them from the evil one. They are not of the world, even as I am not of the world. Sanctify them in the truth; Thy word is truth" (John 17:15-17). Paul says, "I am afraid, lest as the serpent deceived Eve by his craftiness, your minds should be led astray from the simplicity and purity of devotion to Christ" (2 Cor. 11:3). There is a battle going on for the minds of all believers, hence the necessity to take "every thought captive to the obedience of Christ" (2 Cor. 10.5).

When we put on the armor of God, we take up the shield of faith which enables us to extinguish the flaming missiles of the evil one (see Eph. 6:16). The way we overcome "the father of lies" (John 8:44) is by choosing the truth of God's Word. Jesus said, "If you abide in My word, then you are truly disciples of Mine, and you shall know the truth, and the truth shall make you free" (John 8:31,32). We are not called to dispel the darkness; we are called to turn on the light. We do this by choosing to believe the truth of God's Word.

"Finally, brethren, whatever is true, whatever is honorable, whatever is right, whatever is pure, whatever is lovely, whatever is of good repute, if there is any excellence and if anything worthy of praise, let your mind dwell on these things, The things you have learned and received and heard and seen in me, practice these things; and the God of peace shall be with you (Phil 4:8,9).

9. I commit myself to God's great goal for my life to conform to His image. I know that I will face many trials, but God has given me the victory and I am not a victim, but an overcomer in Christ. The grace of God will enable me to triumph over every trial resulting in proven character.

Salvation ensures us that we are forgiven and alive in Christ, but God isn't finished with us yet. We have, "Laid aside the old self with its evil practices, and have put on the new self who is being renewed to a true knowledge according to the image of the One who created him" (Col. 3:9,10). God's will for our lives is our sanctification (see 1 Thess. 4:3), i.e., that we conform to His image by growing in Christlike character. Bondages to alcohol, sex and drugs have arrested our growth in character. When life became difficult, we chose the path of sin which we thought was easier or more fun, rather than the path of sanctification.

Paul taught the right path of hope. "We also exult in our tribulations, knowing that tribulation brings about perseverance; and perseverance, proven character; and proven character, hope; and hope does not disappoint, because the love of God has been poured out within our hearts through the Holy Spirit who was given to us" (Rom. 5:3-5). Drowning our sorrows in alcohol, or running away from our problems does not resolve them or cause them to go away. It only makes them worse. Our hope lies in the proven character that comes by facing the hard issues of life and deciding to hang in there and grow up. This is God's goal for our lives, and is made possible by the Holy Spirit who dwells in us.

10. I choose to adopt the attitude of Christ, which was to do nothing from selfishness or empty conceit, but with humility of mind I will regard others as more important than myself; and not merely look out for my own personal interests, but also the interest of others (see Phil. 2:3-5). I know that it is "more blessed to give than to receive" (Acts 20:35).

Excessive use of alcohol and drugs, and having sex for our own pleasure are the ultimate acts of selfishness. We must assume responsibility for our own character, and seek to meet the needs of those around us. We all need acceptance and affirmation, but don't wait until others extend it to you. Commit yourself to love others as Christ has demonstrated His love for you. "We know love by this, that He laid down His life for us; and we ought to lay down our lives for the brethren. But whoever has the world's goods, and beholds his brother in need and closes his heart against him, how does the love of God abide in him? Little children, let us not love with word or with tongue, but in deed and truth" (1 John 3:16-18).

It is one of life's great compensations that we cannot sincerely help another person without helping ourselves in the process. We get out of life what we put into it. If you want a friend, be a friend. If you want someone to love you, love someone. Don't give people what they deserve; give them what they need. Whatever life asks of you, give just a little bit more. You will not only be living a responsible life, you will also enjoy a greater degree of freedom.

"Be merciful, just as your Father is merciful. And do not judge and you will not be judged; and do not condemn, and you will not be condemned; pardon, and you will be pardoned. Give, and it will be given to you; good measure, pressed down, shaken together, running over, they will pour into your lap. For by your standard of measure it will be measured to you in return" (Luke 6:36-38).

Appendix C

Materials and Training for You and Your Church

by Neil T. Anderson

Christ is the answer and truth will set you free. I have never been more convinced of that. Jesus is the bondage breaker, and He is the wonderful counselor. You can go through all the following material for your own benefit, and chances are you will find your freedom in Christ to start becoming the person that God wants you to be. That would be tremendous, but I think the Lord has something far bigger in mind. Let me explain.

One church, Crystal Evangelical Free Church, hosted our "Resolving Personal and Spiritual Conflicts" conference. They immediately began their own "Freedom Ministry" by training encouragers. Within three years they had led over 1,500 hurting and desperate people to freedom in Christ. They also hosted their own conference to show other churches how they could do it. Ninety-five percent of their trained encouragers are lay people. That has to happen, because there are not enough professional pastors or counselors in our country to reach more than five percent of our population. All we have to do is to equip the saints to do the work of ministry.

Suppose your church carefully chose 20 people and trained them as I will outline. Now suppose each person agreed to help just 1 other person every other week. By the end of one year, your church would have helped 520 people, and the ministry growth wouldn't stop there. These people would become witnesses without even trying. Your church would become known in the community as a place that really cares for their people and has an answer for the problems of life. How can a person witness if they are in bondage? But a child of God who is established free in Christ will naturally (supernaturally) be a witness as he or she glorifies God by bearing fruit.

Our society has treated chemical addictions as a problem by itself. We have excluded addicts from the life of the Church or subtly encouraged them to go underground. That has been counterproductive to their recovery, and an embarrassing admission that maybe we don't have an answer for them. I think we do have an answer in Christ, and they need to know what all the rest of us need to know in order to be alive and free in Christ. Some of the chemically addicted will need to go through detoxification to rid their bodies of poisonous chemicals. Then they need to eat the right food, get some rest and exercise to stay physically healthy. Think of the "Steps to Freedom" as a means to detoxify their souls. Once they are free, then they need the same fellowship and the same truth to live by that we all need. That is what the following materials are intended to provide.

The material for training encouragers includes books, study guides and tape series (both video and audio). The tape series all have corresponding syllabi. The best training would take place if the trainees watched the videos, read the books and completed the study guides. The study guides will greatly increase the learning process and help them personalize and internalize the message. Because of the cost, some choose not to use the videos and use only the books and study guides. The basic and advanced material are given as follows in the order they should be taught:

Basic Level Training

First four weeks:

Purpose: To understand who we are in Christ, how to walk by faith and win the battle for our minds, understand our emotions and the means by which we relate to one another.

Video/Audio Series:	"Resolving Personal Conflicts"
Reading:	*Victory Over the Darkness* and *Study Guide*
Youth Edition:	*Stomping Out the Darkness* and *Study Guide*
Supplemental Reading:	*Living Free in Christ*: The purpose of the book is to establish us as complete in Christ and to show how He meets our most critical needs of life: acceptance, security and significance. This is the first book we ask a person to read after they go through the "Steps" or when they have prayed to receive Christ.

Second four weeks:

Purpose:	To understand the natural and spiritual worlds; know the position, authority, protection and vulnerability of the believer; and understand how to set the captives free.
Video/Audio Series:	"Resolving Spiritual Conflicts"
Reading:	*The Bondage Breaker* and *Study Guide*
Youth Edition:	*The Bondage Breaker Youth Addition* and *Study Guide*
Supplemental Reading:	*Released from Bondage*: This book has chapter-length personal testimonies of people who have found freedom in Christ from depression, incest, lust, panic attacks, eating disorders, etc., with explanatory comments by Neil.

Note:
Breaking Through to Spiritual Maturity is the adult curriculum.
Busting Free is the youth curriculum.

Third and fourth four weeks:

Purpose:	To understand the theology and practical means by which we can help others find freedom in Christ with a discipleship/ counseling approach.
Video/Audio Series:	"Spiritual Conflicts and Counseling" and "How to Lead a Person to Freedom in Christ"
Reading:	*Helping Others Find Freedom in Christ* and *Study Guide*: The study guide also details how your church can establish a discipleship/counseling ministry, and it has answers for the most commonly asked questions.
Youth Edition:	*Helping Our Children Find Freedom in Christ*
Supplemental Reading:	*Daily in Christ*: We encourage individuals as well as families to go through this 1-year devotional. Davie Park, Rich Miller and Neil Anderson are completing four 40-day devotionals for youth that will soon be published by Harvest House.

The following are prerequisites to successfully completing the basic training:

1. Complete the "Steps to Freedom" with an encourager.
2. Complete two or more freedom appointments as a prayer partner.
3. Receive a recommendation by the director of the Freedom ministry and meet the qualifications established by your church.

In addition to our basic training, Freedom in Christ has appropriate materials available for advanced training for specific issues. The topics can be covered by offering additional training, special meetings or regularly scheduled encourager meetings. We strongly suggest that your team of encouragers meet regularly for prayer, instruction and feedback. It has been our experience that cases become more difficult as the group matures. On-the-job training is essential for any ministry. None of us have arrived. About the time you think you have heard it all, along comes a case that shatters all stereotypes and doesn't fit into any mold. This keeps us from falling into patterns of complacency and relying on our own cleverness instead of God. The advanced training material should be studied in the order given:

Advanced Level Training

First four weeks:

Purpose:	To discern counterfeit guidance from divine guidance; explain fear and anxiety; and learn how to pray in the Spirit and walk in the Spirit.
Reading:	*Walking in the Light*
Youth Edition:	*Know Light, No Fear*

Second four weeks:

Purpose:	To understand the culture our children are being raised in, what they are thinking, how to parent them according to their needs and how to lead them to freedom in Christ.
Reading and Video Series:	*The Seduction of Our Children*
Supplemental Reading for Youth:	*To My Dear Slimeball* by Rich Miller

Third four weeks:

Purpose:	To understand how people get into sexual bondage and how they can be free in Christ.
Reading:	*A Way of Escape*
Youth Edition:	*Purity Under Pressure*

Fourth four weeks can include the following:

Reading: *Freedom from Addiction*
Subjects include: The nature of substance abuse and how
                            the bondage can be broken in Christ.
Supplemental
Reading: *Freedom from Addiction Study Guide*
                            (in process)
Reading
and Video
Series: *Setting Your Church Free*: This book and
                            video series by Neil Anderson and
                            Charles Mylander is for Christian
                            leaders. It teaches a biblical pattern
                            of leadership. It also shows how churches
                            can resolve their corporate conflicts and
                            establish Christ as the head of their
                            ministries.

Reading: *Setting Your Marriage Free* (in process)
Reading: *Spiritual Warfare* by Dr. Timothy Warner
Video and
Audio Series: "Resolving Spiritual Conflicts and
                            Cross-Cultural Ministry" also by
                            Dr. Timothy Warner.

Schedules for Basic Level Training:

A 16-week format would require meeting one night each week for two to three hours. Viewing two video lessons each night, it will take 12 weeks to view the first three video series. The last 4 weeks, the video series "How to Lead a Person to Freedom in Christ" should be viewed. It has four one-hour-long segments. Showing a one-hour video each evening would allow ample time for discussion. This schedule does not include much time for discussing the books and inductive studies or the content of the video series. Another meeting could be scheduled for that purpose, such as Sunday morning. If necessary, the material could be discussed after the video has been shown. A summary of the schedule is as follows:

Weeks 1-4	Weeks 5-8	Weeks 9-16
Resolving Personal Conflicts	Resolving Spiritual Conflicts	Spiritual Conflicts and Counseling & How to Lead a Person to Freedom in Christ.
Two video lessons each night.	Two video lessons each night, the last tape has the "Steps to Freedom." They can be done as a group or done separately with an encourager.	Two video lessons each night for 4 weeks, then one hour per night for 4 weeks.

Although these meetings can be open to all who will commit the time, it should be clearly understood that attending the seminar does not automatically qualify anyone to participate in the ministry. Another possible schedule would be showing one video series on a Friday night and Saturday format each month. This would require only one facilitator giving one weekend each month. It would be possible to cover all the material in four weekends. Generally the time for discussion of the videos is less with this schedule, but Sunday morning or a week night could be devoted to discussing the books and the inductive studies.

Weekend #1	Weekend #2	Weekend #3
Resolving Personal Conflicts	Resolving Spiritual Conflicts	Spiritual Conflicts and Counseling
Friday night: video Lessons: 1—2 Saturday: 3—8	Friday night: video Lessons: 1—2 Saturday: 3—8	Friday night: video Lessons: 1—2 Saturday: 3—8

"Steps to Freedom"

The fourth weekend could be completed on Saturday only, using the shorter video series "How to Lead a Person to Freedom in Christ." We realize it is a lot of material to cover, but there are no shortcuts. I cover almost all of this material when I conduct a "Resolving Personal and Spiritual Conflicts" conference in a week. These materials can all be purchased from:

Freedom in Christ Ministries
491 E. Lambert Rd.
La Habra, California 90631
(310) 691-9128
(310) 691-4035 FAX

BEST-SELLERS FROM NEIL ANDERSON!

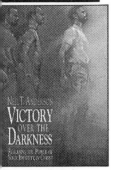
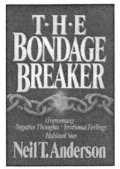
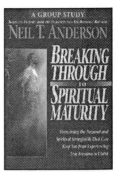
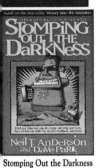

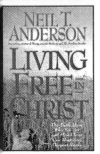

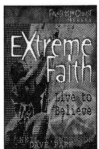

FREEDOM IN CHRIST SPECIAL RESOURCES

VIDEO SEMINARS

Resolving Personal Conflicts PART I
reveals the power of your identity in Christ
in 8 messages covering: The Search for
Identity and Meaning, Faith Renewal,
Walking by Faith, Strongholds, The Battle
for our Minds, Relational Perspectives,
Healing Damaged Emotions, Forgiving
from the Heart.

Workbook 1-884284-02-7

Resolving Spiritual Conflicts PART II
reveals the powerful truth that will break
even the most stubborn habits or private
sins in 8 messages covering: The Position
of the Believer, The Authority of the
Believer, The Protection of the Believer,
The Vulnerability of the Believer,
Temptation, Accusation, Deception, Steps
to Freedom.

Workbook • ISBN 1-884284-07-8

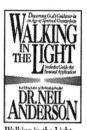

Walking in the Light–
Thomas Nelson Publishing
Neil T. Anderson
Learn to discern God's guidance in an age of
spiritual counterfeits. Dr. Anderson explains
the spiritual dimension of divine guidance and
exposes the nature of counterfeit guidance.

Paperback • ISBN 08407.43866

RESOURCES FOR PEOPLE AT-RISK

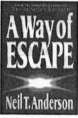

A Way of Escape–Harvest House
Neil T. Anderson
We've all faced sexual struggles. For those
who feel caught by unwanted thoughts,
compulsive habits, or a painful past, A
Way of Escape provides concrete steps to
overcome the bondage of sexual strongholds battling in your mind.

Paperback • ISBN 15650.71700

Purity Under Pressure–Harvest House
Neil T. Anderson and Dave Park
In this book, you'll find out the difference
between being friends, dating and having
a relationship. You'll see how the physical
stuff fits in. And you'll get answers to the
questions you're asking.

Paperback • ISBN 15650.72928

The Seduction of Our Children –
Harvest House
Neil T. Anderson and Steve Russo
A battle is raging for the minds of our
children. It's a battle parents must win! The
book will prepare parents to counter Satan'
assault by understanding his strategies and
warring against them.

Paperback • ISBN 08908.18886
Video • 1-884284-15-9

SPECIAL READING

To My Dear Slimeball–Harvest House
Rich Miller
In the spirit of C.S. Lewis, Rich creates the
secret world of Slimeball and Spitwad–two
demons intent on making life miserable for
15-year-old David. As you gain access to
their private plans, you'll see how to detect
their crafty schemes in your own life.

Paperback • ISBN 15650.71875

Released from Bondage–
Thomas Nelson Publishing
Neil T. Anderson
Released from Bondage contains gripping true stories of freedom from obsessive thoughts, compulsive behavior,
childhood abuse and many more.

Paperback • ISBN 08407.43882

FOR CHURCHES

Setting Your Church Free
Neil T. Anderson and Charles Mylander
Spiritual battles can effect entire churches
as well as individuals. Setting Your Churc
Free shows pastors and church leaders how
they can apply the powerful principles from
Victory Over the Darkness to lead their
churches to freedom.

Hardcover • ISBN 08307.16556

NEW FROM
NEIL ANDERSON

The Christ
Centered Marriage

Neil T. Anderson and Charles Mylander
A step-by-step process to break the
enemy's grip and establish Christ at the
center of your marriage.

Hardcover • ISBN 08307.18494
Available July '96

Helping Young People Find
Freedom in Christ

Neil T. Anderson and Rich Miller
A guide to connecting youth to God through
discipleship counseling.

Paperback • ISBN 08307.18400
Available April '97

Help Others Find Freedom in Christ

The **Helping Others Find Freedom in Christ** resources.

Help people become better connected to God using a process called "discipleship counseling." Neil Anderson gives clear guidelines for leading others through the steps to freedom outlined in his best-selling books, **Victory over the Darkness** and **The Bondage Breaker.**

Helping Others Find
Freedom in Christ
By Neil T. Anderson
ISBN 0-8307-1740-4

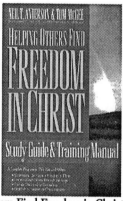

Helping Others Find
Freedom in Christ
Training Manual & Study Guide
A guide to establishing a
freedom ministry in your church.
Includes an inductive study of
Helping Others Find
Freedom in Christ.

Helping Others Find Freedom in Christ
Training Manual & Study Guide
By Neil T. Anderson and Tom McGee, Jr.
ISBN 0-8307-1759-5

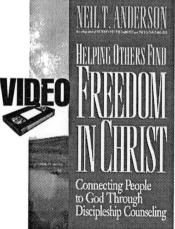

Helping Others Find Freedom in Christ
Video Training Program
A complete program to help you train others to be
part of a freedom in Christ ministry. Includes two
videocassettes, six copies of **The Steps to Freedom in
Christ** guidebook, one copy of **Helping Others Find
Freedom in Christ** and one copy of the Helping
Others Find Freedom in Christ Training Manual &
Study Guide.

Helping Others Find Freedom in Christ
Video Training Program
SPCN 8-5116-0094-9

Also available:
The Steps to Freedom in Christ
A step-by-step guide to use in leading someone through the steps to freedom.
Includes a questionnaire and personal inventory as well as instructions.
8.5"x11" guidebook   ISBN 0-8307-1850-8